Geir Hønneland is Director of the Fridtjof Nansen Institute in Norway. He has published widely on Russian politics and international relations in the Arctic, and his books have been translated into Russian and Chinese. He gained his PhD from the University of Oslo in 2000 and is one of the most respected commentators in the field of Arctic Studies.

'Geir Hønneland is one of the most productive researchers I have known, and his works have been warmly received in China by people from a variety of academic fields. *Russia and the Arctic* is one of my favourites – here we find Geir the scholar, sharing his understanding of Russian Arctic policy. We also find Geir the humourist, telling stories in such a way that I cannot put down the book until finishing the chapter. More often than not, academic works need updating when later editions come – but not this book, which has proven surprisingly timeless.'

Professor Leilei Zhou, Shanghai Ocean University

'Hønneland vividly contextualizes different narratives of suspicion, hope and self-perception with broader frameworks of identity and Russianness. His personal tone, vast empirical data and the strong theoretical underpinning provide *Russia and the Arctic* with an identity itself. Apart from the groundbreaking knowledge that his book holds, it is also incredibly fun to read!'

Nikolas Sellheim, University of Lapland and book review editor of *Polar Record*, University of Cambridge

'Geir Hønneland's book explores the narrative environment in which Russian foreign policy is elaborated, and gives us unique insight on how sensitive Arctic issues are talked about in Russia. He also convincingly demonstrates the gap between narrative and action, and between the different actors in charge of Arctic affairs in Russia. A must-read book for all those wanting to go beyond the usual, confrontational Arctic buzz and comprehend Russia's policy.'

Marlene Laruelle, George Washington University, author of *Russia's Arctic Strategies and the Future of the Far North* (2014)

'Hønneland brings depth to debates on Russia's role in the Arctic. His almost uncanny ability to put us in Russians' shoes is the most remarkable achievement of this oeuvre. As he unravels, page by page, layer by layer, the rich cultural fabric underpinning current Russian narratives of the Arctic, he takes the wind out of the sails of Arctic warmongers and doomsayers.'

Martin Müller, University of Zürich, author of *Making Great Power Identities in Russia* (2010)

'*Russia and the Arctic* is a timely read. For those of us interested in the Arctic region and the role of the world's largest Arctic state, this is more than a reliable guide. It offers an intimate portrait of how Russian newspapers and public culture more generally engage with "their Arctic" and "their interests", and how we need to better understand in the West. Geir Hønneland shows us how Russia's policies and practices towards the Arctic are part of what we might consider a "demanding geopolitics" without demonizing Russia itself. The take-away message for me was that Russia's voice will be heard and Russia's presence will be felt in the contemporary Arctic and beyond.'

Klaus Dodds, Royal Holloway, University of London, co-author of *The Scramble for the Poles: The Geopolitics of the Arctic and Antarctic* (2015)

RUSSIA AND THE ARCTIC

RUSSIA AND THE ARCTIC

Environment, Identity and Foreign Policy

Second Edition

Geir Hønneland

I.B.TAURIS
LONDON • NEW YORK • OXFORD • NEW DELHI • SYDNEY

I.B. TAURIS
Bloomsbury Publishing Plc
50 Bedford Square, London, WC1B 3DP, UK
1385 Broadway, New York, NY 10018, USA

BLOOMSBURY, I.B. TAURIS and the I.B. Tauris logo are trademarks of
Bloomsbury Publishing Plc

First published in Great Britain 2020

Copyright © Geir Hønneland, 2020

Geir Hønneland has asserted his right under the Copyright, Designs and Patents
Act, 1988, to be identified as Author of this work.

Cover design by Adriana Brioso
Cover image: Nuclear powered icebreaker Yamal seen on the Northern Seaway.
(© ITAR-TASS / Lev Fedoseyev / Alamy Stock Photo)

All rights reserved. No part of this publication may be reproduced or
transmitted in any form or by any means, electronic or mechanical, including
photocopying, recording, or any information storage or retrieval system, without
prior permission in writing from the publishers.

Bloomsbury Publishing Plc does not have any control over, or responsibility for,
any third-party websites referred to or in this book. All internet addresses given
in this book were correct at the time of going to press. The author and publisher
regret any inconvenience caused if addresses have changed or sites have ceased to
exist, but can accept no responsibility for any such changes.

A catalogue record for this book is available from the British Library.

A catalog record for this book is available from the Library of Congress.

ISBN: PB: 978-1-8386-0123-2
ePDF: 978-1-8386-0125-6
eBook: 978-1-8386-0124-9

Typeset by RefineCatch Limited, Bungay, Suffolk
Printed and bound in Great Britain

To find out more about our authors and books visit www.bloomsbury.com and
sign up for our newsletters.

For Leah

CONTENTS

List of Maps xi
Foreword xiii
Preface to Second Edition xvii
Preface to First Edition xix

Introduction 1
1. Russian Identity between North and West 23
2. The Rush for the North Pole 43
3. Delimitation of the Barents Sea 71
4. Management of Marine Resources 103
5. Region Building, Identity Formation 127
6. Arctic Talk, Russian Policy 151

Notes 179
Bibliography 193
Index 201

LIST OF MAPS

3.1 Zone configuration in the Barents Sea
Source: Fridtjof Nansen Institute 74

5.1 The Barents Euro-Arctic Region
Source: Fridtjof Nansen Institute 131

FOREWORD

Nikolas Sellheim

We live in such interesting times! On the one hand, atmospheric CO_2 levels have reached unprecedented levels, and the rise of nationalism is shaking up the international order. On the other hand, more and more young people are standing up against injustice and threats to the environment, shaking up long-standing political orders. This is a simplification, of course – an attempt at encapsulating the many far-reaching changes that our world is undergoing today.

And then there is Donald Trump. At first, his rise to global prominence seemed out of the question – but then he was elected US President in November 2016. Now, almost three years later, we are beginning to see how international modes of cooperation, 'gentlemen's agreements' and global communication have been or will be affected by an 'America First' policy.

Inevitably, Arctic cooperation is not exempted from these developments. One particularly clear example is the 11th Ministerial Meeting of the Arctic Council in May 2019 in Rovaniemi, Finland. Rovaniemi lies directly on the Arctic Circle – and has been a town of considerable importance in Arctic cooperation. It was in Rovaniemi in 1992 that the Arctic Environmental Protection Strategy (AEPS), the first pan-Arctic cooperative effort was launched, culminating in the establishment of the Arctic Council in 1996. At that time, it was more in the interest of the 'Western' states to cooperate with Russia and to overcome the divisions of the Cold War. How difficult this cooperation would become – and has remained – is clearly depicted by Geir Hønneland in *Russia and the Arctic*. Mistrust and lack of understanding of the motivations of the other side have long clouded East–West cooperation, leading to long-intractable disputes, for instance on the delimitations of the Barents Sea.

But there is also a silver lining. Despite the often harsh and oversimplified language of news outlets in both the East and the West, there is no such actor as a 'wild card' in Arctic cooperation. From a Western perspective, Russia's behaviour might appear unreasonable and even erratic, but, as is shown in *Russia and the Arctic*, this is far from being the truth. Russia has always acted on the basis of its own views and interests, but never forgetting that Arctic cooperation is advantageous for all. That is not to say that the picture has always been rosy. As in other international arenas, cooperation between countries – or blocs – is often difficult, emotional, tense, or unproductive. But in the Arctic case, there are efforts towards a common goal, a solution, or at least a modus operandi.

Russia and the Arctic shows that, despite differences and problems, Arctic cooperation is driven by the premise of working together towards a common goal. This claim is backed by the theories of IR scholarship that Hønneland applies, especially in light of the East–West dichotomy that has long dominated mutual perceptions. This book offers rich insights into how Arctic cooperation really works. Not in the Arctic Council as such, but in arenas where hard decisions are taken that affect the lives of thousands of people.

The first edition of this book was published in 2016, the year when Donald Trump was elected US President. This second edition is being issued in 2019. Those years have seen significant shifts in geopolitical developments – in directions that cannot yet be foreseen. However, what has become clear is that the traditional blocs in Arctic cooperation have started to dissolve. There is no longer a sharp East–West dichotomy. What the 2019 Arctic Council ministerial meeting has shown is that there is now a 'climate change yes/no'-dichotomy. The failure to adopt a ministerial declaration (merely a joint statement instead) is a first in the history of the Council. Whereas all Arctic Council members pressed for a clear statement regarding climate change and the associated longer-term pathways for the Icelandic chairmanship, it was the United States which refused to support the declaration, on the grounds of the references to climate change in the document.

That was not all. US Secretary of State Mike Pompeo made it clear that the 'America First' policy applies in the Arctic as well. By verbally attacking Russia and China (the latter has had Council Observer Status since 2013), Pompeo broke the collaborative spirit of the Arctic Council. Never before in its history had a member state and an observer been attacked in such a fashion. Even when the Russian Association of Indigenous Peoples of the North (RAIPON), a Permanent Participant of the Council, was temporarily disbanded in 2012 for violating Russian federal law, none of the Arctic Council member states directly criticized the Russian government. Instead, all Senior Arctic Officials (SAOs) issued a statement highlighting the important role of RAIPON and requesting its reinstatement as an active contributor to the Arctic Council. Diplomacy had reigned supreme.

Mike Pompeo's conduct at the 2019 ministerial meeting underlined that, at least concerning Arctic cooperation, Russia can no longer be considered an unpredictable actor, even from a pro-Western perspective. With the current Trump administration, which might achieve a second term in 2020, it is the United States which is roiling the peaceful waters of the Arctic Council and Arctic cooperation.

But also here we find a silver lining. While the United States currently appears to be seeking to reinstate a Cold War – a somewhat ironic term, given the Trump administration's refusal to accept climate-change language – the other Arctic states have agreed that climate change is indeed the most serious threat in the Arctic. Otherwise they would not have insisted on the terms of the draft declaration.

Despite these major recent shifts in Arctic affairs, Geir Hønneland's *Russia and the Arctic* is timeless, as it integrates theory and empirical findings relating to Russia's role in the Arctic and the role of the Arctic in Russia. Practitioners and scholars alike would do well to make use of the wealth of information presented in this volume. In the longer run, and in light of current developments, another book ought to be written by a scholar equally skilled as Hønneland: a book on the United States and the Arctic, and on the Arctic in the United States. Perhaps those of us outside the USA could then get a better understanding of what Arctic diplomacy means for US decision-makers. Hønneland's book(s) can be used as methodological blueprint here, as the insights offered serve an essential purpose: to make politics and diplomacy understandable, transparent and visible.

The year 2019 may well mark the beginning of a paradigm shift in Arctic cooperation, its trajectory as yet unknown. The 'old' factions have shifted, previous alliances are being replaced by new ones. Is this going to be an Arctic Game of Thrones? Regardless, if collaboration in the Arctic implodes, the Arctic will melt as quickly as the Iron Throne – but who will take up the role of the fiery dragon?

Nikolas Sellheim
Helsinki Institute of Sustainability Science (HELSUS),
University of Helsinki /
Scott Polar Research Institute, University of Cambridge
10 June 2019

PREFACE TO SECOND EDITION

Every Arctic nation has its own reasons for 'being Arctic'. Sometimes 'Arctic politics' is smaller than Arctic politics itself, aimed, for instance, at domestic needs of a, strictly speaking, non-Arctic nature. Sometimes 'Arctic politics' is larger than Arctic politics itself, furthering wider, non-Arctic foreign policy aims. Sometimes Arctic politics is the playground for the cultivation of a national idea; sometimes it just happens.

In Russia, all expressions of national identity converge in the Arctic – the Arctic becomes more Russian than Russia itself. The Other is the West, but it changes with the circumstances and evades definition. In the public discourse, narratives can be juggled, oppositions combined. It's not actually so important who the Other is, it just has to be someone. And the West is always there to play with.

This is the essence of the book that you are now holding in your hands and which I am thrilled and deeply honoured to see published in a new edition. The original manuscript evolved over many years, and once out, the book started to live its own life. It was widely reviewed, picked up on reading lists, and quickly sold out – I also received a lot of response from general readers. Most have focused on the book's accessibility to a broader readership than academia – many have also described it as 'fun to read', which fills me with joy to hear. I've heard that the stories told in the book are relevant for our understanding of Russia's policies not only in the

Arctic, but also elsewhere in the world, not least in the aftermath of the Crimean and Ukrainian crises. I also feel, and have been told, that I'm on to something theoretically, but I'm the first to admit that theory is there primarily to provide structure to the empirical discussion. As I have now largely moved away from academia into the world of business and administration, *Russia and the Arctic* might well become my main academic legacy in the field of Russian studies, along with *Borderland Russians*, which appeared a few years earlier. And I'm happy with that – this is what I had to contribute.

Thanks to my publisher Tomasz Hoskins at I.B.Tauris/Bloomsbury for his initiative and support.

The book is still dedicated to my daughter Leah, with endless love and admiration.

Geir Hønneland
Hirtshals, July 2019

PREFACE TO FIRST EDITION

This book has been in preparation for several years. The Norwegian Ministry of Defence gave me financial support to conduct the empirical investigation back in 2010, under its international relations research programme. My master's degree student Torstein Vik Århus conducted the media search for the study the following year, which I have subsequently updated. Having just published the book *Borderland Russians: Identity, Narrative and International Relations* (2010), I was eager to expand both my theoretical and empirical coverage, as far as the relationship between identity and foreign policy was concerned. With MoD money in my pocket – yes, the Russian story-tellers cited throughout the book will have their suspicions confirmed – I planned a book provisionally entitled *Arctic Talk*.

The first few pages of a book are always the most difficult. Although I began writing full of optimism and enthusiasm in early 2011, it didn't take long – one and a half pages to be precise – before I came to an impasse. I made a new attempt in the summer months of 2012. This time, total output numbered four or five pages. But then events in the outside world intervened. In spring 2010, Norway and Russia had unexpectedly agreed on a delimitation line in the Barents Sea, after 40 years of negotiations. The Russians greeted the agreement with considerable scepticism, which I discuss at length in Chapter 3 of this book (the

Norwegians, conversely, were ecstatic). In early 2013, I came across an article in the Russian press called 'What should Putin do to get the Barents Sea back?'. I wrote an op-ed in response and gave it the same title; the article was printed in several Norwegian newspapers before being translated into Russian and posted on various Russian websites. Russian criticism of the Barents Sea delimitation agreement, I argued, was based on inaccurate assumptions about Norway's intentions in the Barents Sea region. A few weeks later, I received a 'Current Affairs and Debate Book' grant from the Norwegian Non-Fiction Writers' Association and the Norwegian Freedom of Expression Foundation to finance the writing of a short book on the topic, to be published within eight to ten months. The Russian media material could finally be put to good use. I wrote the book quickly during the summer of 2013, in the tranquil surroundings of the Department of Languages and Culture at the Royal Danish Defence College in Copenhagen. Bearing the same title as the original Russian article and my response, it was in print by the end of the year. The book was well received by reviewers and readers alike, and a second edition was ready before the summer was over. In the meantime, an English-language version had appeared under Palgrave's Pivot imprint (mid-length publication, longer than a journal article but shorter than a traditional monograph), now titled *Arctic Politics, the Law of the Sea and Russian Identity: The Barents Sea Delimitation Agreement in Russian Public Debate*.

Arctic Politics became a step on the way to the present book. That book was not theoretically framed, and only parts of my empirical material had been used. I still hoped to complete *Arctic Talk*, but had to admit to myself that the masterpiece-in-waiting would have to wait for some time yet. My *deus ex machina* became my eminent colleague and generous friend Leif Christian Jensen. In late winter 2014, he landed a contract with indie publisher I.B.Tauris for his monograph on Norwegian Arctic politics. Friends as we are, his achievement still jangled my competitive nerve, and I was good for a race. Well, he beat me to the finish. I had been writing like a man possessed throughout the spring and hoped to finish before starting on a three and a half month paternity leave that summer. With only

Preface to the First Edition

a chapter and a half to go, I realized it was a long shot, so I decided in May to let the material mature. Again, however, it proved hopelessly difficult to pick up the thread after a long break. A single paragraph in September joined by another in November was the miserable outcome. Spring came and I forced myself to start working the keyboard, a sentence at a time.

The resulting pages, i.e. the present book, did not turn out to be the theory-packed monograph I had originally envisaged. It is informed by theory on narrative and foreign policy, but essentially I tell the story about how the Arctic is talked about in Russia, or rather four short stories: about the 'scramble for the Arctic'; the Barents Sea delimitation line; management of marine resources in the Arctic; and East–West region building in Northern Europe. The Introduction sets the theoretical stage, and while theories on the narrative constitution of the self of individuals and states work below the surface in the case studies, I do not engage explicitly in a theoretical debate, apart perhaps from the concluding chapter where I try to adapt the stories to a theoretically relevant exposition of how public narratives make states 'ready for action' in their foreign policies.

Many people have inspired and influenced on this book – few mentioned, few forgotten. Above all, I extend my gratitude to my longstanding friend and colleague Anne-Kristin Jørgensen, whose translations of and sharp-eyed observations on the media material represent the scaffolding. (While I do speak Russian, I prefer to come to the data with fresh academic eyes, rather than after translating them myself.)

Two of my best mates at work and in life, Jørgen Holten Jørgensen and Lars Rowe, are also two of the best people to sound out ideas about 'who are the Russians?' Chris Saunders has been my English language consultant for one and a half decades now; not only does he correct my mistakes, he lets me keep my own voice – and even improves it at times. My old colleague and copy-editor Maryanne Rygg, now retired, comes into the office when I have a new manuscript in preparation – it's a real pleasure to see her professionalism at work. Finally, I wish to thank my editor at

I.B.Tauris, Tomasz Hoskins, for his unstinting enthusiasm for Leif Christian's and my work on Arctic politics, and his swift but never less than professional turnaround of our manuscripts.

I have opted for an 'easy' reference system for this book. Since it is not a legal treatise, I do not provide references to international agreements, laws and regulations. Nor is it an historical dissertation: events and facts are not substantiated by reference to archive material. I adhere in the main to the (not always particularly lucid) norms of the social sciences on source attribution. When I quote the same source several times in the same section, I note just the one reference, after the first quotation. The source of a non-referenced direct quote can be found in the immediately preceding endnote.

In my transliteration of Russian characters, I generally keep to -y rather than -i for the Russian 'short-i' (except following a vowel at the end of a name, such as Nikolai) and the letters -yo, -yu and -ya, and -e instead of -ye for the Russian -e (which is actually pronounced -ye). Hence, *Vzglyad* rather than *Vzgliad* and *russkie* instead of *russkiye*. I have also omitted the 'short-i' at the end of a word when it follows a regular 'i'. I make exceptions, however, for personal names whose English spelling is more or less standardized. I write Yeltsin instead of Eltsin and Zhirinovsky instead of Zhirinovski (or Zhirinovskiy). For the sake of readability, not least for those without a command of the Russian language, I do not use the Russian soft sign in the English translations of the transcripts. Due to the relatively informal tone of the text, I minimize the use of capital letters for proper nouns; hence 'fishery protection zone around Svalbard' (but 'Grey Zone').

This book is dedicated to my daughter Leah, the apple of her father's eye.

INTRODUCTION

Sometimes we must change the story to accommodate the events, sometimes we change the events, by acting, to accommodate the story. (Carr 1986: 61)

The Arctic is getting warmer, in more than one way. The ice is melting and scientists are uncertain about its impact on the Arctic ecosystems. Will the Polar bear survive without the Polar ice? Will new species migrate to the Arctic once the climate gets warmer? How will Arctic human settlements be affected by climate change? But in addition to biology and meteorology, the political discussion surrounding the Arctic is also getting hotter. Who does the oil and gas in the Arctic continental shelf belong to? How will marine delimitation lines be decided? Who will control the new sea routes? Who actually owns the Arctic?

What is often referred to as 'the scramble for the Arctic' started when Russia planted its flag on the seabed at the North Pole in August 2007.[1] Many presented the event as if Russia had laid claim to the North Pole itself, though governments around the world would doubtless contest the matter. A race for the Arctic was underway, with Russia playing the wild card. Relations among the other Arctic states – Canada, Denmark (Greenland), Norway and the US – are excellent and cemented by a strategic alliance in NATO. Russia, on the other hand, is the successor state of the

Soviet Union, NATO's declared enemy during the Cold War. The country is often shrouded in mystery: Winston Churchill called Russia 'a riddle, wrapped in a mystery inside an enigma' (1948: 449) – it also has an image as a northern country, with Arctic expeditions and endless Siberian forests. What people are worried about is that Russia will do as it pleases in the Arctic, international law and other norms for civilized political behaviour notwithstanding.

Much of what animates the 'Arctic buzz' is about what Russia wants. Russia obviously has aggressive intentions in the Arctic, some say, warning that one never knows what the Russians are up to. But what do they actually want in the Arctic? In this book, I approach this question through a study of Russian media discourse and political declarations. I ask how Russian politicians, journalists and others with access to the media talk about the political challenges in the Arctic. In line with theories that link narrative, identity and foreign policy – concepts that will be further explained in the following – I aim to demonstrate 'the bandwidth of possible outcomes' (Neumann 2008: 62) available to Russian policy makers in their Arctic policies. The assumption is that the way you talk constitutes who you are. Who you consider yourself to be, in turn, defines the range of possible actions – this goes for individuals and for collectives, such as states.

Narrative and identity

Identity has gained prominence as an object of study across the social sciences in recent decades, but the concept is seldom defined. Common everyday understandings are 'self-image' or 'people's perception of who they are'. In their textbook on discourse and identity, Benwell and Stokoe (2006) understand the latter concept 'in its broadest sense, in terms of *who people are to each other*, and how different kinds of identities are produced in spoken interaction and written texts' (p. 6, emphasis in original). Here they depart from the assumption that identity is something strictly internal to the subject: 'It is [often] assumed that although people may present themselves differently in different contexts, underneath that presentation lurks a private, *pre-discursive* and stable identity' (p. 3, emphasis in original). An alternative understanding of identity is as a public phenomenon: 'a performance or construction that is interpreted by other people' (p. 4). Several 'moves' are visible here: from identity as something stable to something mutable, from something private to something social, from something attached to the individual to something created by the individual, and from something ready to be discovered by the observer to something the observer himself or herself actively interprets.

Benwell and Stokoe (2006: 17ff) note how identity was largely conceived of as an internal 'project of the self' until the second half of the twentieth century, when sociologists became more concerned with collective identities, based upon criteria such as age, gender and class. The assumption was still of identity as pre-discursive, unified and essential. For instance, this was the case for the 'social identity theory' developed in the 1980s (see, e.g., Tajfel 1982), which saw identity as 'something that lies dormant [in each individual], ready to be "switched on" in the presence of other people' (Benwell and Stokoe 2006: 26). It was only towards the end of the twentieth century that this view was challenged and identity came to be seen as 'an *unfinished product of discourse*' (p. 30, emphasis in original), that is fluctuating and shaped by language and social practice. After the turn of the millennium, many observers agree that 'rather than being *reflected* in discourse, identity is actively, ongoingly, dynamically *constituted* in discourse' (p. 3, emphasis in original).

This resonates with contemporary theories on the narrative constitution of identity.[2] Narrative can be viewed as a sub-category of discourse. While discourse is often perceived of as wider language (and social) practice,[3] a narrative is a stretch of talk about specific events and the order in which they happened. Czarniawska (2004: 17) defines a narrative as 'a spoken or written text giving an account of an event/action or series of events/actions, chronologically connected'. Stories she views as a sub-category of narrative, distinguished by the existence of a plot, understood as 'the basic means by which specific events, otherwise represented as lists or chronicles, *are brought into one meaningful whole*' (p. 7; emphasis added).[4] Somers (1994) argues convincingly for a reconfiguring of the study of identity formation through the concept of narrative. Leaning on criticism of the traditional conception of narrative as simply a mode of representation, she claims 'it is through narrativity that we come to know, understand, and make sense of the social world, and it is through narratives and narrativity that we constitute our social identities' (p. 606). And further, '[We] come to *be* who we *are* (however ephemeral, multiple, and changing) by being located or locating ourselves (usually unconsciously) in social narratives *rarely of our own making*' (p. 606, emphasis in original). There are two important claims here. First, narratives are not just reflections about the world, but rather constitutive of the self. In that sense, narratives acquire an ontological dimension in addition to their traditional epistemological one. They give expression to the outside world about who people are, but they also take part in *making* people who they are. Along similar lines, Gubrium and Holstein (2009: 8) note, 'If human experience is viewed as narrative, our stories become our selves; narratives structure who we are as meaningful beings in the world.' Second, narratives are 'rarely of our own making'. Gergen (2001: 249), in a similar vein, writes: '[people] do not author their own lives'; instead, 'stories serve as communal resources' that people avail themselves of when they construct their life stories.[5] In order to maintain intelligibility in the culture, the story one tells about oneself must adhere to commonly accepted rules of narrative construction. When we use these narrative conventions, we generate a coherence and direction in our lives: 'Certain forms of narrative are broadly shared within the culture; they are frequently used, easily identified, and highly functional. In a sense, they constitute a syllabary of possible selves' (p. 253).

Somers (1994: 617ff) identifies four dimensions of narrative: ontological, public, conceptual and meta-narratives. Ontological narratives are the stories that individuals use to make sense of their lives; they 'process events into episodes' (p. 618) in their everyday life. Public narratives are the inter-subjective frames, attached to cultural or institutional formations larger than the single individual (typically family, workplace, local community or nation), which sustain and transform narrative over time. The third dimension of narrativity refers to the 'master narratives' in which we are embedded as contemporary actors in history: epic dramas such as Capitalism vs Communism, the Individual vs Society, the Emergence of Western Civilization and the Rise of Nationalism or Islam. Finally, conceptual narratives are the concepts and explanations that we construct as social researchers.

*

Many recent narrative theorists stand in debt to Carr's (1986) exposition about the relationship between time, narrative and history. One of Carr's ambitions is to challenge the prevailing assumption among historians of narrative as primarily a method to give shape to historical events, to craft stories with beginnings and ends out of the continuous flow of happenings in the world. Quite rightly, he argues, historians read into the past a narrative structure that it, strictly speaking, does not really have (since beginnings and ends are more or less randomly set), but so do we as human beings in our efforts to make sense of the world. Narrative is simply our primary way of organizing our experience of time. It is not just a tool for historians (or for the common story-teller), but our *modus operandi* as human beings when we try to come to grips with our here and now, in-between past and future. 'Historical and fictional narratives [are] not distortions of, denials of, or escapes from reality, but *extensions and configurations of its primary features*' (p. 16, my emphasis). The past and the future, according to Carr, are involved in our experience even when we are not explicitly thinking about them. Present and past function together in our perception of time, just like foreground and background or focus and horizon do in our spatial perception (pp. 21ff). Narration is not just a passive recounting of events but is informed and influenced by our knowledge of the past and expectations for the future.[6]

Carr claims that there are three distinguishable points of view of events: those of the story-teller, the audience and the characters (pp. 58ff). When we recount our own actions, social expectations lead us, consciously or subconsciously, to adopt if possible the story-teller's position, rather than just that of a character. When asked what you have been doing, for example, you will often not just chronicle a series of events (with yourself as one of the characters), but add coherence and justification to the account (as the story-teller). You craft a story that hangs together and makes sense, a story that goes to show that your actions are credible and legitimate. Knowing the ways in which stories are normally expected to be composed (and knowing that what you do will subsequently often have to be recounted to others), you sometimes adapt your actions to these conventions. At least, narrative convention is part of the structure that constitutes action. Hence, Carr argues, narrative activity has a *practical function in life* (in addition to its mere social function), structuring human action:

> [Stories] are told in being lived and lived in being told. The actions and sufferings of life can be viewed as a process of telling ourselves stories, listening to those stories, and acting them out or living them through. [. . .] It is not the case [. . .] that we first live and act and then afterward, seated around the fire as it were, tell about what we have done, thereby creating something entirely new thanks to a new perspective. The retrospective view of the narrator, with its capacity for seeing the whole in all its irony, is not in irreconcilable opposition to the agent's view but is an extension and refinement of a viewpoint inherent in actions itself. *To be an agent or subject of experience is to make the constant attempt to surmount time in exactly the way the story-teller does. It is the attempt to dominate the flow of events by gathering them together in the forward-backward grasp of the narrative act.* [. . .] [N]arration constitutes something, creates meaning rather than just reflecting or imitating something that exists independently of it. But narration, intertwined as it is with action, does this

in the course of life itself, not merely after the fact, at the hands of authors, in the pages of books.

(pp. 61–2, emphasis added)

Narrative is not a dress which covers something else but a structure inherent in human experience and action, for both individuals and communities (pp. 122ff). A community exists wherever there is a narrative account of a 'we' which has continuous existence over time. Such a community is 'constantly in the process, just like the individual is, of composing and re-composing its own autobiography. Like the autobiography of an individual, such a story seeks a unifying structure for a sequence of experiences and actions' (p. 163). And just as it does at the individual level, narrative performs a practical function at community level. Narrative is not external to community action and experience, but part of its fabric: 'Discovering or rediscovering the story, picking up the thread, reminding ourselves where we stand, where we have been and where we are going – these are typical narrative-practical modes of discourse which are as prevalent and as important for groups as they are for individuals' (p. 168). To return to Carr's primary quest, narratives are not just tools that historians avail themselves of; they are, or at least they should be, the *object* of historical research. Reality is constituted by narratives, so reality should be *studied* as thus constituted. But historical narratives are also extensions of historical existence itself: 'To tell the story of a community and of the events and actions that make up its history is simply to continue [...] the story-telling process through which the community constitutes itself and its actions' (p. 177). Narrative is our way of being in and dealing with time.

To sum up, identity has increasingly come to be seen as constituted and amended in social relations, rather than as fixed and internal to the subject. Narrative, in turn, is viewed not just as a medium through which the self is projected, but as constitutive of the self – or identity. Narrative convention offers a 'syllabary of possible selves'. But narratives do not only constitute identity, they also constitute action. People are enmeshed in webs of narrative that they cannot disentangle themselves from when they act. Life is, according to Carr, a process of telling ourselves stories, listening to those stories and acting them out. Claiming that we first act and then tell about what we have done, 'seated around the fire as it were', is a simplification at best, as we cannot separate our actions from stories previously told and stories yet untold.

Identity and foreign policy

The IR discipline has seen an upsurge in interest in identity since the end of the Cold War.[7] The maps of Eastern Europe and Central Asia were being redrawn, the European Union was effectively dismantling national borders in Western Europe, and globalization was picking up speed; it was no longer feasible to view identity as a unitary, fixed and given substrate derived from an individual's nationality. Identity came to be viewed as a relation rather than a possession, a quality conditioned by changeable, fluid situations rather than rock solid categories. Identities, wrote Lapid in 1996, had become 'emergent and constructed (rather than fixed and natural), contested and polymorphic (rather than unitary and singular), and interactive and process-like (rather than static and essence-like)' (p. 8). Goff and Dunn (2004b) wanted to test empirically whether identities are in fact constructed (as opposed to given by membership of, e.g., race, ethnic group or political entity), multiple (as opposed to singular), fluid (as opposed to static) and relational (as opposed to autonomously defined). Not unexpectedly, their conclusions are not unequivocal. Identities are fluid, but not constantly changing. Identities are relational, but the effect of the process of othering differs according to the situation. Likewise, the propensity of individuals to move back and forth between multiple identities varies with the context. And finally, 'Even though identity is a social construction, it is not whatever we want it to be. A limited reserve of discursive resources constrains the ways in which identities evolve [...]' (Goff and Dunn 2004c: 244).

K.E. Jørgensen (2010: 173-4) categorizes the study of identity, which he considers a generic term rather than a specific theory, within the post-positivist tradition. Post-positivists have primarily used identity, he notes, to explain where interests come from. Instead of assuming the existence of an externally given or geographically determined national interest (such as realists and geopolitically oriented theorists do), post-positivists search for the *origins* of interest. In this perspective, the question is not whether interests *or* identity determine politics, but how specific identities cause specific interests and, in turn, how these interests translate into policy making. As a prominent example, Wendt (1992) claims that the international system is created and recreated in processes of interaction, where identities are not given (although relatively stable), but continuously developed, sustained and transformed by inter-subjectively grounded practice. The behaviour of states is not reducible to where they stand in the distribution of power in the international system,[8] or to the maximization of their material interest. States have selves that colour their interaction with other states, and are themselves shaped, maintained or modified in this very interaction. There is an ongoing struggle within the state about which of the many stories of the self should be activated at any specific time.

Drawing on Carr (1986), among others, Browning (2008) elaborates a theory of foreign policy analysis in which action is explained as the result of state interest determined by narratively constructed identities. In his view, action only becomes meaningful in the process of narrating a constitutive story of the self: 'By establishing a linear story from whom we were in the past up until the present a narrative framework is created within which experiences become intelligible to ourselves and to others, and future action becomes meaningful (p. 46).' It is only by telling stories about who we are that it becomes possible to say what we want. Interestingly, Browning claims (p. 275), although advocates of the narrative approach have criticized rational, materialist accounts for assuming implicitly that identities as pre-given, this is probably how identities must be presented by state authorities to resonate with the population.

Ringmar (1996) proposes a narrative theory of action which, he argues, under certain circumstances explains states' behaviour towards other states as a defence not of their interests, but of their identity: 'It is through the stories that we tell that we make sense of ourselves and our world, and it is on the basis of these stories that we act' (p. 66). The stories we tell define not only what we want, but also who or what *we are like*. The narratives through which our selves are constituted are always the more fundamental; stories of selves are preconditions for stories told about interests.

> 'Interests' can only be *someone's* interests and the establishing of this 'someone' is of course precisely what the action in question is designed to accomplish. The action does not seek to maximise utility or minimise loss, but instead to establish a standard – a self – by which utilities and losses can be measured. These are consequently not 'rational actions', but instead actions undertaken in order to make rational actions possible. We act, as it were, in 'self defence' in the most basic sense of the word – in defence of the applicability of our descriptions of our selves. (Ringmar 1996: 83)

Ringmar emphasizes the importance of *recognition* for persons' and communities' identity, including that of states. It is through our quest for recognition that our identity is established. Identity is a precondition for interest, and in certain situations identity-driven explanations of foreign policy can substitute for interest-driven explanations altogether. This can happen when a state has experiences a loss of recognition under humiliating circumstances ('lost face'), or at 'formative moments' when new metaphors are launched and individuals tell new stories about themselves, and new sets of rules emerge through which identities are classified – in short, 'when the very definition of the meaningful is up for grabs' (p. 85). Meanings are contested and fought over, through, for instance, propaganda and other forms of rhetoric. Old identities can prevail, be defeated or revised. 'Formative moments, we could say, are characteristically periods of symbolic hyper-inflation – times when new emblems, flags, dress codes, songs, *fêtes* and rituals are continuously invented' (ibid.). At these moments, there is an urgent need to have one's constitutive stories recognized. In his own study, Ringmar explains Sweden's entry into the Thirty Years War in the 1630s by the country's need to have other states to accept the story Sweden told about itself, rather than by material interest.

In a later work, Ringmar (2002) shows how Soviet policy towards the West was a constant quest for recognition, first of Soviet Russia as a legitimate state, then as a great power, subsequently as a superpower and finally under Gorbachev as a legitimate inhabitant of the 'Common European Home/House'.[9] Studying Soviet foreign policy as the outcome of given material interests would equal the assumption that 'world politics is a game played by players without faces'; the fact that Russia is *Russia* and not any other state 'makes all the difference in the world' (p. 131). The self-inscription of Soviet leaders needed to be *recognized* before it could be securely established.

> This explains why the early Bolshevik regime oscillated between confrontation and conformism to diplomatic rules; why Stalin struck the deal with Hitler which was to bring about the Second World War; why the nuclear arms race went on far beyond the levels needed for physical security; and why the Communist system eventually collapsed. None of these events can be properly explained with the help of rationalistic theories. (Ibid.)

Campbell (1998) examines the ways in which US identity has been written and re-written through foreign policies, which, he argues, help produce and reproduce state identity through the inscription of threat and foreignness. States do not possess pre-discursive, stable identities, they are never finished as entities, they are 'always in a process of becoming' (p. 12). Campbell distinguishes between 'Foreign Policy' and 'foreign policy', the former being the state's actual policy towards other states, the latter the pool of narrative resources that is drawn upon in producing this policy. 'Foreign Policy' is the boundary-producing performance through which state identity is produced and reproduced. Danger, in turn, is not an objective condition, but the effect of interpretation, which implies 'the inscription of boundaries that serve to demarcate an inside from an outside, a self from an other, a domestic from a foreign' (p. 9), and 'the ability to represent things as alien, subversive, dirty, or sick' (p. 3). For this to happen, no external action is required:

> The mere existence of an alternative mode of being, the presence of which exemplifies that different identities are possible and thus denaturalizes the claim of a particular identity to be the true identity, is sometimes enough to produce the understanding of a threat. (p. 3)

Most IR studies of identity presuppose some form of othering, either externally (towards other states), internally (within the state) or historically (in relation to previous and future selves). Campbell is a good case in point by highlighting external and historical othering in US foreign policy. While the role of external othering clearly dominates the IR debate on identity, ontological security theory (Delehanty and Steele 2009) focuses instead on internal othering through the construction of autobiographical narratives that draw on national histories and experience in order to create continuity to a state's identity. Wæver (1998) likewise argues that the other may also be a former incarnation of the self – he mentions the EU as an example, the primary ambition of which has been the 'never again' of European wars. And the other need not, according to Berenskoetter (2007), be the 'foreigner', an 'enemy'; recognition can also be sought from 'friends'. Othering in its more malign form, like dehumanization, is little studied in IR, Medvedev and Neumann (2012) tell us, but all the more in adjacent disciplines, such as history, philosophy and psychology. 'Soviet communism is a key modern case in point. These cases are characterized by substantial use of

INTRODUCTION

dehumanizing metaphors: humans are not humans but dogs, rats, insects (roaches seem to be particularly popular), etc.' (p. 19).

As we saw above, narratives may be distinguished by the presence of a plot, the means by which events are brought together into a meaningful whole. Indeed, as Nishimura (2011: 05) notes, in IR, '[p]lotting is political action *sui generis*'. Only after being plotted in a meaningful order, can experience make sense to the state's self (and make the state ready for action). Ringmar (2006) contributes a particularly refreshing addition to his earlier work through his study of conflicting stories of the Iraq war, using literary theory to categorize decision makers into different types of story-tellers. *Romances* usually involve a hero whose task is to save the world. They are recounted by people who 'believe that evil can be defeated, that the world can be made into a better place, and usually also that they are the very instruments chosen by God, Providence or History to carry out this task' (p. 405). *Tragedy* provides a completely different plot structure. Here the hero rebels against the established order but is himself destroyed in the process. He follows his own mind, 'proud, passionate or obsessed with some fanciful idea' (ibid.). The *comedy* is 'an account of oppositions and misunderstandings which in the course of the narrative are resolved thanks to some fortuitous intervention' (p. 406). The comic element lies in the twists and turns taken by the plot as the narrative gradually comes to a happy end. Finally, there is *satire*, which assumes an ironic distance to the world. It is 'parasitic on other narrative forms' (ibid.), as its strategy is to 'turn other plot structures inside-out, upside-down, or to deconstruct and reassemble them in unrecognizable patterns' (ibid.).

So here we are: identity has come to be seen as constructed, multiple, fluid and relational – in IR theory as in the social sciences more widely. Foreign policy is viewed as the result of state interest determined by narratively constructed identities, national power in conjunction with state identity and interest, or by the protection of identity alone, for instance in the face of a perceived threat. Action only becomes meaningful when we know what we want, and we get to know what we want by telling stories about who we are. We act in defence of our descriptions of ourselves. States are always 'in the process of becoming', subject to the constant negotiation and re-negotiation of identities. In moments of great societal change – 'periods of symbolic hyper-inflation' – new interpretations of meaning are 'up for grabs', old and emerging identities are fought over. Identities – and action – are determined by storied threat, foreignness, 'the alien, subversive, dirty, or sick'. The fact that other identities exist, the realization that one's own identity is not the only possible self-image, is sometimes enough to spur inscriptions of foreignness and danger.

From 'the Age of the Arctic' to 'the Scramble for the Arctic'

'Quietly, and almost unbeknownst to the general public, the Arctic has emerged during the 1980s as a strategic arena of vital importance to both of the superpowers.' This is how Oran R. Young, generally considered to be the leading international expert on Arctic politics, opened his 1985 article 'The Age of the Arctic' (p. 160). He was indeed right in his predictions about the world's growing interest in the Arctic, even though the most ground-breaking event in this process – the dismantling of the Cold War – was yet to happen. In autumn 1989, the Communist regimes in Eastern and Central Europe fell, and just over two years later the Soviet Union itself ceased to exist. The Cold War was over, and European governments were keen to draw the young Russian Federation into new forms of transnational institutional arrangements aimed at reducing the potential for future East–West conflict. In the European North, the Barents Euro-Arctic Region (BEAR) was established on Norwegian initiative in 1993. The EU Northern Dimension was launched in 1998, on Finnish initiative. These regional collaborative arrangements spanned several functional fields, with infrastructure, business cooperation and environmental protection at the core. At the circumpolar level, the Arctic Environmental Protection Strategy (AEPS) was created in 1990 by the 'Arctic eight' (Canada,

Denmark, Finland, Iceland, Norway, Sweden, the Soviet Union and the US). Canada soon proposed the establishment of an Arctic Council, to embrace policies on indigenous peoples in addition to the environmental focus of AEPS. The US initially opposed this, but then agreed, on condition that the new council would be established through a non-binding agreement, that the states would not commit to financial contributions, and that secretarial functions would be reduced to a minimum. The Arctic Council was established in 1996, with the AEPS programmes subsumed under the new structure. Indigenous peoples' associations representing several indigenous groups within one Arctic state or one indigenous people in several Arctic states were included in the Council as 'permanent participants'.

Three years into the Arctic Council's existence, Scrivener (1999: 57) concluded that creating the Council seemed 'to have done nothing to increase the momentum of circumpolar cooperation on pollution and conservation issues and to assist the AEPS's progression beyond monitoring and assessment into the realm of policy action'. By and large, Arctic cooperation – whether circumpolar or regional – was long considered to be 'a thing of the early 1990s': an immediate post-Cold War initiative that failed to spark sustainable high-level political interest. The Arctic Council remained a forum for coordinating Arctic environmental monitoring and science, with strong participation from the region's indigenous peoples, while the regional BEAR collaboration and the EU Northern Dimension were struggling to meet the initial expectations of thriving East–West cooperation on trade and industry.[10]

Much changed with the planting of a Russian flag on the seabed at the North Pole in August 2007. That action was performed by a Russian scientific expedition involved in collecting data for Russia's submission to the Continental Shelf Commission – in accordance with the Law of the Sea – but was widely perceived as a Russian demonstration of power in the Arctic. The incident happened at the same time as the summer ice melting in the Arctic Ocean reached ominous proportions, and there was growing interest in the prospects of petroleum development in the Arctic. Borgerson (2008) famously captured the atmosphere in his seminal article 'Arctic Meltdown': 'The Arctic Ocean is melting, and it is melting fast. [...] It is no longer a matter of if, but when, the Arctic Ocean will open to regular marine transportation and exploration of its lucrative natural-resource deposits (p. 63).' Further: 'The situation is especially dangerous because there are currently no overarching political or legal structures that can provide for the orderly development of the region or mediate political disagreements over Arctic resources or sea-lanes' (p. 71); and '[T]he Arctic countries are likely to unilaterally grab as much territory as possible and exert sovereign control over opening sea-lanes wherever they can. In this legal no man's land, Arctic states are pursuing their narrowly defined national interests by laying down sonar nets and arming icebreakers to guard their claims' (pp. 73–4).

Russia's flag-planting and Borgerson's article spurred a new wave of high-level political interest in the Arctic, even though the former had not been intended as a Russian 'claim' to the North Pole. There emerged a global media buzz about a 'scramble for the Arctic', and a marked surge in political interest could be observed. In the Arctic Council, high-level participation from the member states gradually increased, and the 2011 biannual ministerial meeting in Nuuk was the first to which all eight countries sent their foreign affairs ministers. It was also the first Arctic Council meeting attended by the US Secretary of State; and here the first binding treaty negotiated under the Arctic Council – on search and rescue in the Arctic – was signed. The interest of non-Arctic states in Arctic affairs was also heightened, especially among Asian nations. In 2013, China, Japan, Singapore and South Korea, among others, were given status as permanent observers in the Arctic Council.

*

The IR literature on the politics of the Arctic has been mainly empirical in orientation. Contributions from the late 1980s and early 1990s are largely descriptive, partly speculative: The 'age of the Arctic' is coming, but what kind of international cooperation in the Arctic can possibly be expected? Authors tend to focus on the prospects for cooperation in areas such as science and environmental protection.[11] During the 1990s and the first part of the initial decade of the twenty-first century, descriptions and preliminary assessments of the emerging circumpolar collaboration followed,[12] along with substantive evaluations of the (more tangible) regional cooperative arrangements in the European Arctic.[13] Despite this largely empirical orientation, we can catch glimpses of all the three major theory traditions within the study of IR: realism, institutionalism and constructivism. Few contributions take their explicit point of departure in matters of theory,[14] but many seem implicitly situated in the institutionalist camp by their preoccupation with international regimes.[15] The focus is on the potential for cooperation and not conflict among the Arctic states. Many of the early contributions (and some of the later ones) discuss the possible links between emerging circumpolar arrangements and existing global and regional regimes, for instance under international environmental agreements.[16] Later contributions focus more on the potential of boosting the political and institutional clout of the Arctic Council,[17] and of the role of the Law on the Sea in mitigating potential conflicts among Arctic states.[18] A realist stance is apparent in Borgerson's (2008) article and, to a lesser extent, in several ensuing contributions on energy and geopolitics in the Arctic.[19] A constructivist approach is applied in studies of the emergence of the Arctic as a region[20] and, not least, in discussions of identity, region building and geopolitics in the regional collaboration arrangement in the European Arctic.[21] With a few exceptions, the literature on the politics of the Arctic has not contributed to the development of theory. Young (see, e.g., 1994, 1999) has contributed to the development of institutionalist theory in IR with empirical material from the Arctic, and Neumann's (1994) theory-oriented article on region building in Northern Europe gave rise to a lively debate about region building in the European Arctic.[22] Hence, IR theory has to some extent, implicitly or explicitly, structured the empirical presentation of Arctic politics and spurred debate between (implicitly or explicitly defined) camps, but it has not informed analysis to any significant degree, with the constructivist approach as a possible exception.

Substantive empirical debate emerged primarily with the publication of Borgerson's (2008) article on the political implications for the Arctic of global warming. The topic of debate was whether a scramble for the Arctic was underway or not. Most participants concluded that Borgerson's premises were erroneous.[23] Yes, there are prospects for considerable new petroleum findings in the Arctic, but most of these will probably lie in areas where national jurisdiction is undisputed (and those located in what might remain of disputed areas are the least interesting commercially). Yes, jurisdiction of the Arctic continental shelf is not yet finally established, but there is an ongoing process under the UN of settling the outer limits of the continental shelf, to which all Arctic nations adhere (and to which potentially strong non-Arctic actors, such as China, have declared that they will also adhere). Above all, there have been hardly any signs of political conflict in the Arctic, and good reasons to assume that states see cooperation as their primary choice also in the future.

Another substantive debate, also following the 'scramble for the Arctic' buzz, has concerned the possible need for an overarching Arctic treaty to supplement the existing Law of the Sea (with the 1982 Law of the Sea Convention at its core, supplemented by a range of other global, regional and bilateral agreements in specific functional fields). In 2008, the European Parliament issued a resolution advocating such a treaty, but since then all relevant actors (including the European Parliament) have agreed that the existing Law of the Sea is sufficient as a foundation for elaborating more specific requirements to protect the Arctic environment against possible effects of increased human activity in the Arctic, especially related to marine transport and petroleum extraction. In the literature, some authors promote the idea of an Arctic treaty, e.g. on the model of the Antarctic Treaty;[24] others dismiss it, in line with the political arguments of the Arctic states themselves.[25] Finally, at the political level there has been some debate about who should be the legitimate actors in international politics in the Arctic: the 'Arctic five' (the states bordering the Arctic Ocean), the 'Arctic eight' (the 'Arctic five' plus Finland, Iceland and Sweden) or a larger group of states. The 'Arctic five' gathered in Ilulissat in Greenland in 2008 to state that the Law of the Sea serves as the foundation for settling final jurisdiction in the Arctic Ocean (so there is no need for a new Arctic treaty) – which caused some concern among the rest of the 'Arctic eight', and among indigenous peoples' associations, that the Arctic Council would be supplanted by the 'Arctic five' as the central stage for discussions about circumpolar politics. This most recent debate is described in the literature,[26] but has not spilled over into the scientific literature as a topic for discussion.

Russian talk, Arctic policy

A key player in Arctic politics, Russia has the longest Arctic coastline, the largest oil and gas deposits and the best prospects of acquiring more than a fair share of the Arctic continental shelf when it is divided among the five Arctic states. Russia participates actively in the global, regional and bilateral arenas facilitating Arctic cooperation set up after the end of the Cold War, but is the only non-NATO member of the 'Arctic five'. President Putin's foreign policy was long considered emphatically pragmatic, aimed above all at convincing the world of Russia's credentials as a 'civilized' nation, one that observes international law and other norms prescribing what counts as good behaviour in international politics.[27] After Russia's annexation of Crimea, spring 2014, and the ensuing chilling of East–West relations, there is widespread fear in the West that pragmatism has come to an end.

This book maps the narrative fabric within which Russian Arctic politics evolve. I trace major trends in this part of Russian foreign policy during the first decade of the twenty-first century, but I do not aim to explain exactly how it came about, as the result of, say, international or national power constellations in which group and state interests compete for hegemony. In line with the theories mentioned above, narratively constructed state identities are assumed in some way or other to influence foreign policies. It is only by telling stories about who we are that it becomes possible to say what we want. It may well be that, under certain circumstances, identities are the primary foundation of the chosen policies, as in Ringmar's (1996) 'formative moments' – possibly even more so in the Russian case, and on a more regular basis than in connection with exceptional circumstances, as argued by Rigmar (2002).[28] The fact that Russia was *Russia* 'made all the difference in the world', he argues in his explanation of Soviet foreign policy. And I also claim the possibility, like Nau (2002), that power and identity-based explanations can supplement each other in foreign policy analysis. More than anything, I embrace the mainstream assumption of contemporary studies of identity and foreign policy that state *interest* cannot be understood in isolation from state *identity*.

Like other IR theories, narrative analysis and identity theory do not claim to explain it all. Structural theorists such as neorealists, K.E. Jørgensen (2010: 84) suggests in his 'new introduction to international relations', are content to explain a few important things and happy to leave 'what they regard as the nitty-gritty analysis of other issues in international politics' to others. Theories of identity and discourse analysis, which Jørgensen sees as distinct *theories* in the post-positivist *tradition* – and we could add narrative analysis as a sub-domain of discourse analysis, closely related also to theories of identity – are in the same manner not intended to take over the whole field, just to enrich it, fill in the nooks and crannies overlooked by the 'grand theories' – and perhaps occasionally modify the conclusions of scholars working within other research traditions. More than anything, however, adherents of these theories want to contribute to the discussion of how political actors are constituted. As noted by Browning (2008: 35), '[w]hilst brute material forces do place physical limits on the policies and actions of states, what they do not tell us is why any state would want to attack another in the first place'.

In the following chapters, I recount some of the stories Russians tell about Russia and the Arctic in official documents and national and regional media in north-west Russia.[29] Who are the storytellers, who are the characters, who is the audience? Which events are selected for public comment? Does othering take place – if so, is it directed outwards through a determination of foreignness, of threats or dangers (or 'friends' for that matter); inwards against internal 'enemies' or 'outcasts'; or across history, by determining 'who we were' or 'who we want to be'? Is the othering benign or malign? Which narrative structures are in place; what are the plots of stories about Russia's relations with the other Arctic states? Who are the villains, who are the heroes? Are the Russians the fearless, clever and optimistic heroes of the story, determined to save the Arctic from insecurity and degradation ('romance')? Or are they heroes who sacrifice themselves for the common good, their benign intentions as always misinterpreted by the rest of the world ('tragedy')? Are they represented as the innocent players in 'comedies' where misunderstandings are eventually resolved by some unexpected intervention? Or do they figure in 'satires' that measure an ironic distance to the world, where familiar plots are turned upside-down, inside-out, deconstructed and reassembled in unrecognizable patterns?

*

Chapter 1 provides an overview of the existing literature on Russian identity and foreign policy. It takes us through representations of Russian culturedness, morality and sensitivity ('our wide souls'), and absurdity ('our fairy-tale lives'); the Russian myth of the North as 'the land of the future'; the unfalteringly ambivalent attitude towards the West – should we breathe in the fresh air billowing in from the West or turn our backs on the rotten corpse which is Europe?; and the changing attitudes to the West in the post-Soviet period, from the enthusiasm of the early 1990s, via disappointment towards the end of the decade, to pragmatic reorientation under Putin.

Chapter 2 maps the stories told by Russian authorities, journalists and others with access to the media about the delimitation of the Arctic continental shelf. Russia is expected to lay claim to an area that includes the North Pole, but so is Canada (and Denmark already did, in 2014). The story of the delimitation of the shelf is framed as 'the global fight against Canada in the Arctic', and Russia's traditional image of itself as *the* Arctic nation puts Putinian pragmatism to the test. A first indication of Russia's stance on Arctic delimitation politics came with the 2010 signing of the agreement with Norway to divide the long-disputed area in the Barents Sea into two equal parts, which is discussed in Chapter 3. The agreement was hailed in the international community as a sign of Russian willingness to compromise in Arctic politics. Segments of the Russian public, however, saw it as a veritable act of treason and it barely scraped through the ratification process in the State Duma. Russian stories about the country's double-faced neighbour in the northwest are presented in Chapter 4, which deals with management of marine resources in the European part of the Arctic, and in Chapter 5 on regimes aimed at creating a common northern identity across the old East–West border. As Russia's closest collaborator, and at the same time the only NATO member in the region, Norway figures prominently in debates in Russia. But opinions vary, not just from person to person, but from context to context. One moment, Norwegian neighbours are soul-mates who 'breathe in sync' with the Russians; the next, they are cunning Vikings, the errand boys of the CIA and NATO, who take advantage of the naive Russian *muzhik* (country bumpkin) who doesn't know his own best. In the concluding chapter, I try to disentangle the identity-constituting narratives from the chronicles of events presented in earlier chapters. Which specific types of narratives can be grouped together, and what do they tell us about the conditions for Russian policies in the Arctic?

CHAPTER 1

RUSSIAN IDENTITY BETWEEN NORTH AND WEST

Just as books about identity declare 'Identity is back!', books about Russian identity (or politics, for that matter) ask questions like 'What is Russia? What is "Russianness"? Who are Russians?' (Franklin and Widdis 2004: xi).[1] They might quote famous figures on the 'strangeness' of Russia, like Winston Churchill to whom 'Russia is a riddle wrapped in a mystery inside an enigma' (see Introduction) or perhaps the nineteenth-century poet Fyodor Tyuchev: 'Russia is a thing of which / the intellect cannot conceive. / Hers is no common yardstick. / You measure her uniquely: / in Russia you [can only] believe!' (Brunstad et al. 2004: 6). Or how about this one: 'Russia is big. Very big indeed' (Smith 1999: 7)? And one for which I am partly responsible myself: 'Ask any non-Russian what he or she associates with "Russia". The answer is likely to include reference to snow, long winters, and the seemingly endless Siberian forests' (Blakkisrud and Hønneland 2006a: 1). Keywords are 'strangeness' (difficult to comprehend for outsiders, like foreign politicians, and insiders, like the Russian poet), 'otherness' (something different from the Western world), space ('very big indeed') and 'northernness' (snow, long winters, Siberia). Each will be investigated in turn in the following.

Breathe in, hold your nose

Relations with Europe have been a source of unending worry and concern throughout Russian history. Should Russia open up to the West and take from it what it can, or should it close in on itself and cultivate 'Russianness', its own distinctive qualities? The story of how Kievan Rus – the largest of the Slavic-speaking 'city-states' – obtained its first emperor in the 800s is an early example of openness. Lawlessness and conflict kindled a desire among the local tribes for law and order. They therefore dispatched an envoy to the Vikings (Varangians) in the north-west: 'Our country is big and powerful and very abundant, but we have no order – will you govern us?' On the other hand, Russia's Christianization in 988 exemplifies openness to the east. On that occasion, emissaries were sent eastwards, westwards and southwards, that is to the Eastern Orthodox Church in Byzantium (today's Istanbul);[2] to the Western Catholic Church in Rome; and to the Tatar Muslims. The Orthodox Church was chosen because it embodied the beauty and spirituality that best suited the Russian mentality. When, in 1453, Muslim Turks captured Byzantium, the seat of the Eastern Church was transferred to Moscow. Indeed, belief in Russia's special mission in the world as defender of the true faith, of spirituality and goodness, is intimately bound up with the idea of Moscow as the Third Rome (after Rome and Byzantium). By the time Byzantium fell, the eastern parts of the Slavic-speaking world had been ruled for more than two centuries by Genghis Khan's descendants, and after Mongols razed Kiev to the ground in 1224, Moscow emerged as the region's capital, reportedly because it had been more willing to accommodate the invaders than the other Slavic-speaking city-states. Indeed, some see in the Russian autocracy and ruthless government of such rulers as Ivan the Terrible in the 1500s a distinct legacy of the Mongol system of government. Russians still appear to be conscious of their Mongolian heritage. 'Behind every Russian lurks a Mongol' they say, using their fingers to draw their eyes downwards.

These snippets of Russian history underscore the 'differentness' or 'otherness' of Russia as seen from the West. But as seen from

Russia itself, *Europe* was the defining 'constituting other' of Russian identity in the early nineteenth century.[3] Identification with the West had been evident in the efforts of Peter the Great (1682–1725), and to some extent Catherine the Great (1762–96), to Westernize Russia. Napoleon's failed assault on Russia in 1812 added grist to the mill. The Decembrist Uprising of 1825, sparked by Nicholas I's assumption of the throne, and led by army officers dismayed by the treatment of serfs during war and disaffected by the *ancien régime*, sprang also in part from differences over the country's relationship to Europe. It is at this point Neumann (1996) takes up his account of 'Russia and the idea of Europe'. He identifies three positions on Europe in early nineteenth-century Russia. The first is the state's 'conservative nationalist' approach, its aim to preserve the old regime and maintain distance to Europe, far from enlightened despotism. The second was the Romantic nationalist position; influenced by German Romanticism, it was anti-modern and protective of ancient Russian culture, including the organic tie between tsar and people, the hallmark of Russianness. Finally, there was the constitutionalist position. Adherents wanted Russia to adopt European ways of doing politics and running the economy, while adapting them to Russian conditions (p. 13).

Some commentators blamed the constitutionalist uprising on proponents of Europeanism. They were obviously guilty of leading some of Russia's best and brightest astray. The country clearly needed to do something about its subservient attitude to Europe. What presented itself was a new form of Messianism, a recycling of the old idea of Russia as the embodiment of high moral values with a special mission in the world (p. 20). Another group, those who still held Europe to be superior to Russia, was concerned the two were drifting even further apart. A third group engineered the construction of the doctrine of 'official nationality'. To them the Decembrists were 'a fifth column'. Official Russia, they proclaimed, should be defined by the three pillars of autocracy, Orthodoxy and 'nation-mindedness' (*narodnost*). By the 1840s, the various groups were becoming increasingly polarized. There were

Romantic nationalists who rallied under the banner of 'Slavophilism', while others looked to Europe for political and economic guidance. They came to be known as 'Westernizers'. Slavophilism was a radicalization of the Romantic nationalist position. Europe was decadent, even rotten: 'Some saw redemption for Europe if it could only go to school with Russia; others held that Russia should turn its back and hold its nose while the cadaver that was Europe slowly putrefied' (p. 38). The aborted 1848 revolutions in Europe were further confirmation that Westernization was a mistake, and the Russian state offered a conciliatory hand to the Romantic nationalists by embracing, for instance, the idea of 'Holy Russia'. With Russia's defeat in the Crimean War (1853–6), however, the state grew increasingly preoccupied with economic and military capabilities and made several moves that could be interpreted as Westernist (p. 40). Tsar Alexander II abolished serfdom in 1861 and introduced new local government entities, the *zemstva*, in 1864. Slavophilism, which had promoted introspectiveness and detachment from Europe, gave way to pan-Slavism, which wanted expanded relations with the West. The Westernizers, for their part, dismayed by the half-hearted reforms, adopted a more radical stance. Reflecting the situation in many European countries, liberals and socialists were divided in Russia as well. Further divisions emerged between adherents of a specifically Russian form of socialism (one of their offshoots was a populist movement), and internationalists. The reform-minded tsar was assassinated in 1881 by populists. His successors took increasingly harsh steps to stifle public debate – before war and revolution spelled the end of the old rule.

The 1917 October Revolution gave Russia a Western ideology and attendant atheism. The division between Westernizers and those of if not exactly a Slavophile persuasion, at least in favour of isolation or a more Eastern outlook, continued in the Soviet era. After the years of political and cultural experimentation in the 1920s, there followed two and a half decades of Stalinist brutality and isolation from Europe. Nikita Khrushchev attempted to 'thaw' relations with the West in the late 1950s and early 1960s, and the

Western window did indeed open slightly. That was before his own experiments saw him off, and initiated a further two decades of 'stagnation' under Leonid Brezhnev (and his short-lived successors Yuri Andropov and Konstantin Chernenko).

In 1985, a relatively young and very dynamic Mikhail Gorbachev was elected General Secretary of the Soviet Communist Party – the rest is history. 'Gorbie' was a man the West could 'do business with', as Margaret Thatcher remarked after meeting Gorbachev for the first time.[4] He formulated and espoused the idea of 'a common European home/house', urging reconciliation between East and West. He was awarded the Nobel Peace Prize in 1990 for his part in ending the Cold War, but he was never popular among his peers. Even in the heady atmosphere of *perestroika* (reconstruction) and *glasnost* (openness) of the late 1980s, he was disliked. What Russian in his right mind would ration vodka, as Gorbachev had done? In the ensuring years he was positively hated for his central role in dismantling the Soviet Union. The Russian Federation's first president, Boris Yeltsin, cranked up Westernization to full strength, but was liked by the people to a greater extent – he was, after all, a corpulent 'yokel', just like a Russian *muzhik* is supposed to be – at least until alcoholism and volatility took their toll in the late 1990s. One of the most despised political figures in the early Yeltsin years was his first foreign minister, the Western-oriented diplomat Andrei Kozyrev, who led efforts to establish BEAR together with Norwegian Foreign Minister Thorvald Stoltenberg in 1993 (more on this in Chapter 5).

Ebullience, cold peace and pragmatism

The main difference between the pro-Western and Slavophile camps has also informed analyses of Russian politics past and present. Various terms have been used to designate and flesh out the differences. In the early 1990s, for example, Atlanticist was a favoured subcategory of Westernizer: people who were not only attracted by Europe, but continents further afield, on the other side of the Atlantic. They did not last long in Russian politics. A category with deeper historical roots as well as greater staying power is the Eurasianist. Eurasianists highlight Russia's intermediate position between East and West and its responsibility to maintain stability on the Eurasian continent in particular and between the global superpowers in general.

In his analysis of Russian foreign policy, Tsygankov (2013) proposes three categories: Westernism, Civilizationism and Statism. As we have seen, Westernizers believe Russia must learn from the West. The modern version of Westernism flourished towards the end of the Soviet period and especially during the first years of the Russian Federation. Gorbachev's reform policies embraced an attitude of openness and cooperation with the West, without descending into complete submission. In Yeltsin's first years, the ideology of Westernism gained significant ground. He put young Westernized economists in charge of privatizing Soviet wealth, and it became politically acceptable to say capitalism had won the Cold War. They wanted to build a democratic system and create a market economy along Western lines. Privatization spawned a new upper class in Russia, with the so-called oligarchs at the top while the masses languished in poverty at the bottom. However, people soon grew suspicious of the West's enthusiasm for reconciliation between the two former blocs, not least when former Soviet satellite states were invited to join NATO, but not Russia. All the same, Russia sided with the West in the Bosnian War of the mid-1990s.

In January 1996, Yevgeni Primakov replaced Andrei Kozyrev as Russia's foreign minister. Primakov, like his predecessor, was a professional diplomat, but while Kozyrev looked to the west and north (both as a diplomat and a politician), Primakov's expertise and experience were from regions to the east and south: Asia. Kozyrev, in addition to looking westwards, gave Russia's northwestern corner particular attention. He was Norwegian Foreign Minister Thorvald Stoltenberg's partner-in-chief in the 1993 creation of BEAR, and was elected to the State Duma from Murmansk oblast. Primakov's expertise was unquestionable, but as

I said, it lay elsewhere. While he was a pronounced Eurasianist, he was not exactly anti-Western. As said, Eurasianists seek above all to maintain balance in the international community, primarily between East and West. Russia's initial support of the West in the former Yugoslavia grew muted and attitudes towards the West more reserved. Primakov sought instead to strengthen ties eastwards, with India and China. Whereas Russia viewed the former Soviet republics, especially in the south and east, immediately after the Union's collapse as something of a burden, Primakov worked to strengthen relations with them as much as possible.

There are several points of contact between Tsygankov's Civilizationism and a wider Slavophile worldview in which Russian civilization is surrounded by 'competing' civilizations. Civilizationists on Tsygankov's account did not play a particularly prominent role in Russian politics, before or after the collapse of the Soviet Union, though their worldview is clearly shared by certain figures of the post-Soviet opposition. Take the great Russian writer Aleksandr Solzhenitsyn (1918–2008), for example, who spent 20 years in exile for speaking out against the brutality of the secular Soviet state – his most famous work is about life in the Soviet Gulag prison camps. Solzhenitsyn espoused a blend of Orthodox Christianity and humanist philosophy in which Russia stood as a moral beacon to the rest of the world. He was not greeted as a hero on his return to the motherland in 1994, and was marginalized by the new Russian establishment before long.

A cruder form of Civilizationism emerged, with the founding in 1990 of Russia's Liberal Democratic Party (LDPR). Its leader, Vladimir Zhirinovsky, gave expression to the frustration felt by many Russians with the dissolution of the Soviet Union, the loss of territory and economic hardship. He flirted unashamedly with strands of Russian nationalism and was notorious in the West for saying the day would come when Russian soldiers would wash their boots in the Indian Ocean. He was a self-proclaimed anti-Semite, despite the fact, as he later admitted, that his father, Volf Isaakovich, was of Jewish extraction and had changed the family name from Eidelshtein to Zhirinovsky. Before this information became public, he famously fended off questions about his national credentials by saying: 'My mother was Russian, and my father was a lawyer.'[5]

In the elections to the State Duma in 1993, the LDPR was returned as the largest party, with 23 per cent of the vote. In comparison, the president's party, Russia's Choice, achieved only 15 per cent, and the Communists 12 per cent. The Communists were not what they once were, either in terms of domestic or foreign policy or, indeed, ideologically. Instead of Lenin's internationalism, the party espoused an unadulterated strain of nationalism. In terms of practical politics, the party branded itself as the defender of ordinary Russians and their livelihoods. Above all, however, it has condemned all traces of Western influence while campaigning for the re-introduction of Soviet-style forms of governance. Both the LDPR and the Communists seemed to capture the mood of the moment around the mid-1990s, however. There would be no more fraternizing with the West, whose offer of help many now suspected of having an ulterior motive, that is to continue the Cold War by more subtle means. Hadn't the Cold War actually turned into a Cold Peace?[6] According to some commentators, the West had fooled Russia into embracing a market economy and democracy well knowing they wouldn't work in the country. Why? To weaken their old adversary.

Since the millennium, Russian foreign policy in Putin's hands has veered towards what Tsygankov calls Statism, a relatively de-ideologized but all the more pragmatic approach to the outside world. In a way it is a continuation of Primakov's Eurasianist project given the importance of maintaining balance in international politics, although with less emphasis on the East–West axis on the Eurasian continent. Putin's Statism is essentially geared to defending Russian interests by means of an active trade policy and compliance with internationally accepted standards of behaviour. In spite of anti-Western rhetoric and heavy-handed domestic policies – in respect of NGOs and other projects funded from abroad, for example – Putin obviously wanted Russia to be seen as a civilized partner in international politics because it is in Russia's best interests. In his intermezzo as president, Medvedev continued the pragmatic approach of Putin's two terms in presidential office, and was arguably the more pro-Western of the two, with his frequent references to Western democratic ideals. At the same time, Eurasianist ideas retained a strong hold on the Russian bureaucracy, not least in the power structures,[7] while a Civilizationist opposition has survived in the State Duma. Few foreign observers have immediate access to what goes on behind closed doors when Russian foreign policy is made, although there is widely believed to be constant infighting between the president's staff, the government and economic interests, representing different points along the ideological axis between Statism (with an occasional trace of Westernism) and Eurasianism. Russia's annexation of Crimea in spring 2014 clearly implied a sharp Eurasianist turn, with its reference to the re-establishment of the old Russian Empire. As Putin stated in his speech to the Federal Assembly, the Russian parliament's upper house, the evening before the Assembly's ratification of the annexation: 'Everything that has happened with Crimea [in the last few days] and everything that happens right now, at this moment, in this assembly hall, was predestined.' And about the 'Bolsheviks' who gave away Crimea to Ukraine: 'Let God be their judge.'[8]

Our North, our future

After the Siberian Khanate as one of the last remaining fragments of the Golden Horde was conquered by the Cossack Ermak Timofeevich in the sixteenth century, it became both a symbol of freedom for fugitive peasants, slaves, Old Believers[9] and other settlers, and a place for political prisoners forced into exile. 'Siberia set forth a popular (and populist) patriotic self-image of Russia as an epitome of unlimited freedom, a treasury of possible riches, an El Dorado for the self-made man, the adventurer, the entrepreneur, the explorer, the "virgin-lander"' (Hellberg-Hirn 1999: 54). As Gibson (1993: 68ff) argues, while the upper classes often regarded the untamed wilderness of Siberia with horror, the lower classes 'viewed it positively as a kind of Belovod'e, the mythical Promised Land of abundance and freedom' (pp. 68–9). At the same time, it was a 'territory of terror' for those sent there against their will – it was 'heaven and hell' (Diment and Slezkine 1993).

Boele (1996) provides an intriguing account of the North as a symbol of national identity in Russian Romantic literature. He takes as his point of departure the historical prominence of the opposition between East and West in the Russian worldview, where East has embodied 'own', 'clean' and even 'holy', and West came across as something 'alien', 'unclean' and 'heretical' (p. 251). In the beginning of the eighteenth century, however, the importance of the East as a symbol of national identity diminished. In the worldview of the ever more Westernized upper classes, the North took precedence over the East as Russia's spatial-ideological point of reference.

> As a symbol of Russia's new European identity, the North initially articulated people's belief that the Russians have caught up with the West, or even surpassed it. In eighteenth century panegyric poetry, this miraculous leap forward is often visualised as a paradisiac garden, a 'northern Eden', which has replaced the chaos of 'old' Russia. Northern 'imagery' (snow, ice, barren swamps) almost exclusively represents that state of non-existence from which the 'new' Russia is believed to have emerged. (p. 251)[10]

Reacting to what they considered slavish imitation by the Russian aristocracy, writers of Russian eighteenth-century Romantic literature employed the North increasingly as a symbol of a distinctly autochthonous sense of Russianness. French culture was ridiculed for its affectations, artificiality and effeminacy, diametrically opposed to the Russian winter and the simple folk of the Russian countryside. 'Once turned into a vehicle for expressing a supposedly manly and northern national character, winter comes to be increasingly regarded as the most

"Russian" time of the year' (p. 252). These sentiments grew in intensity, naturally enough, when Napoleon's forces succumbed to the Russian winter in 1812. To Russians, he was the Antichrist, and the providential part played by the Russian winter in the outcome of the war acquired a truly apocalyptic dimension. Winter and northernness were increasingly internalized as symbols of Russianness.

> However, whereas East and West were considered antithetical in the days before Peter the Great, Russia still identifies itself with the North, as opposed to the West or even the South (both referring to Europe). Thus the ideological significance of the North as the 'national point of the compass' has been completely reversed: in the middle of the eighteenth century it signified Russia's European character, now it embodies its cultural and religious 'otherness'. The spirit of this 'Northern' Messianism is captured by Maksim Nevzorov in the line: 'From the North comes God himself.' (p. 252).

But interest in the North was not limited to the pre-Revolutionary Romantic Russian writers and intellectuals. During the Soviet era, the North became important politically and economically. Boele (p. 256) distinguishes in this period between an official Soviet version of the North (site of exploration and resource extraction), unofficial accounts of camp life in the North, and a semi-official 'countryside literature' where the North is portrayed as the iconic and 'authentic' image of indigenous Russia. In his attempt to explain Soviet Arctic politics on the basis of cultural variables, Griffiths (1990) notes the connection between the North and famous representatives of the two latter groups: '[Aleksandr] Solzhenitsyn's idea of North is one of salvation. In the Northeast he sees an undefiled space in which a Russia purged of Soviet error can once again be herself and pursue her own unique course.' It is in this northern landscape that Russia can 'regain her culture – reknitting her ties with the past, giving true spiritual meaning to the present and greeting the future'. The north-east represents 'an opportunity to reconstitute the old ways of European Russia in a new setting with new means. It is a place to be moved to, opened up, even "conquered", albeit with benign technology and sustainable economic practices' (pp. 51–2). And speaking of the 'countryside writer' Valentin Rasputin, Griffiths notes,

> To him, Siberia is as much a notion as a place. He likens it to a bell, sounded long ago, whose echoing peal gives rise to conceptions of 'something vaguely mighty and impending', of 'trust and hope', of the 'anxious step of man on the far land', of 'relief', 'renewal' and indeed 'salvation'. (p. 53)[11]

From 1920 onwards, the Soviet authorities sought increasingly to explore and develop the industrial and economic potentials of the Arctic, the impact of which is still felt today. These efforts peaked during the 1930s, when the Soviet Union launched the most systematic and comprehensive series of Arctic expeditions in the history of polar exploration accompanied by a project to cultivate a particular idea of the Arctic through propaganda and popular culture, what McCannon (1998) refers to as the 'Arctic myth':

> The Arctic myth was a product of social realism, the hegemonic cultural framework of the Stalin period. "Social realism" in this sense refers not merely to the literary formula of that name, but to the overarching aesthetic that held sway over fact and fiction, fantasy and reality, official doctrine and public mindset from the beginning of the 1930s. Social realism's principal motifs are well known: the cults of Lenin and Stalin, a keen sense of patriotism, emphasis on technological and industrial prowess, and, above all, heroism. The Arctic culture of the high-Stalinist period embraced all these themes in combination with two other symbols of great potency: the North Pole, whose enigmatic mystique was age old, and aviation, perhaps the twentieth century's most triumphant expression of modernity. It was an extraordinarily successful blend, and the Arctic became one of

the most visible and appealing elements of a cultural environment already saturated with attempts to make every deed seem heroic and epic. (p. 9)

The Soviet policy of 'conquering the North' (*osvoenie severa*) fundamentally changed patterns of settlement and industry in the Russian North (see, e.g., Blakkisrud and Hønneland 2006a: 11ff). The population of the 16 federal subjects which make up what the Russians conceive of as the North, numbered less than 2 million in the late 1920s. By the end of the Soviet period, it had grown to nearly 10 million. The new post-Soviet Russian rulers were unwilling to pay for the maintenance of the North's now extensive infrastructure. Their reluctance sparked a debate in which 'Romantic' (or social realist?) views of the North were frequently voiced. The Russian North is 'at a dangerous crossroads', a leading Russian specialist of the High North warned in 1998 (Agranat 1998). He speaks of the 'destructive breakdown of the old North' (p. 268) and cites a former governor of Alaska who likened his own state to a child requiring long years of 'highly subsidized' care, but which, in the end, will 'yield a return', if not to his 'parents', then at least to society (p. 270). In his experience, he says, other Arctic states usually support their northern regions. Investing in the Arctic regions could, moreover, be highly profitable for society as a whole. The reason Finns own so many personal computers and mobile telephones is because the country has embraced its 'northernness', Agranat suggests. 'Is this phenomenon not confirmed by the principle, long ago established by Soviet specialists, that the most progressive, latest technology, will go to the North, or, at least, should go there?' (p. 274).

Laruelle (2014: 39ff) maintains that there are three 'geographical meta-narratives' in post-Soviet Russia, each advancing territorial size and location in space as main components of Russian identity. 'Russia's territory is *larger* than other countries in the world and forms a specific continent (Eurasianism); Russia is going *higher* in the universe (Cosmism); and Russia is going *farther* north (Arctic mythology)' (p. 39). The latter can take either a geopolitical, a domestic political or a spiritual form. The Arctic is the possible battleground for a World War III, where Russia has to prove its heroism in the face of aggressive Western powers. It is also a 'rightful compensation for the hegemony lost with the disappearance of the Soviet Union' (p. 40). Domestically, the North is both 'forgotten' and 'future', neglected in post-Soviet Russia but the country's most important 'reserve of space' (pp. 49– 50). The Arctic meta-narrative 'reinforces a spatial representation of Russia in which the "south" is the region from where all dangers arise, while the "north" is the place where the Russian nation will be able to take refuge and preserve itself' (p. 42). It cultivates 'the national imagery of regeneration of great Russian power through a kind of Arctic rebirth' (p. 43). The Arctic is referred to as 'a new political and spiritual continent', 'the last "empire of paradise"', Russia's 'last chance [...] to take revenge on history', Russia's 'cosmic destiny' (p. 40).

Wide souls and fairy-tale lives

But 'space' is more than just northernness, more than mere geography in Russia's self-perception. Widdis (2004: 33) explores the different ways in which space acts as a metaphor for and expression of Russianness. '[The concept of] neob"iatnyi prostor (boundless territory) offers a powerful symbol of Russian national identity', she suggests. There is a tendency in eighteenth- and nineteenth-century texts and Soviet films, she notes, to depict Russia in terms of limitless open space, 'a land with no end and no edge [...], a flatness which seems to curve *around* the horizon, which seems to deny the very existence of an edge to the space – of the horizon' (p. 39). Russia escapes definition – or its definition lies precisely in its emptiness. 'Thus the lack of definition becomes a form of definition in itself. Like the space, Russia itself is characterised by open-ness, which becomes a symbol of freedom, bravery and open-ness of heart' (p. 41).

Along the same lines, Hellberg-Hirn (1999: 56) notes, 'Russian self-stereotypes promote an idealized image of the national soul as being wide-open: *shirokaja dusha* ["wide soul"], full of passionate feelings, generosity, open-mindedness, hospitality, unlimited kindness, and recklessness verging on anarchy in the constant need for a break-out.' In her comprehensive discussion of 'the symbolic world of Russianness' (Hellberg-Hirn 1998: 168), she speaks of 'Russian pride in the sensitivity of the Russian soul and in the unfathomable depth of Russian feelings' and the conception that 'every Russian is moulded into a romantic shape where the Soil and the Soul of Russia harmoniously merge into their nature'. Medvedev (1999: 32), for his part, speaks of the 'inherent Russian desire to move along the plain' and, at state level, of 'inclinations of spread and settlement' (p. 33). 'Siberia as the metaphor for untamed nature offered the ultimate test on the way toward timelessness', writes Slezkine (1993: 5).

Is the question of Russian identity, then, only approachable in terms of time and space, based on history books, archival material, poems and cultural artefacts? True enough, visits to Orthodoxy, Slavophilism/Westernism and Siberia seem to be obligatory exercises for any student of Russian identity. The concept of identity has also been frequently used in analyses of nationalism in the former Soviet republics and of relations between them. But some studies have a more contemporary focus and smaller units of analysis than Russia itself, and make use of a more diverse pool of empirical data than old texts. To take just a sample, Petersson (2001) discusses national self-images on the basis of in-depth interviews with regional politicians in St Petersburg, Volgograd, Khabarovsk and Perm, as well as parliamentarians in Moscow. One of his findings is that the Russian national self-image rests mainly on past events (particularly the Great Patriotic War[12] and the accomplishments of Peter the Great). Arutiunova (2008) makes the same point in her study of national identity among college students in Moscow: the country's history constitutes a key element of Russian identity. In her survey, around half of the respondents refer to 'our past, our history' when asked to say what first comes to mind when they think of the Russian people. It was along these same lines that the students expressed themselves: 'There is a great deal in the sciences and in cultural achievements that were accomplished by our people', 'a nation that won the Great War for the Fatherland. It is not even just a matter of military achievements but rather the fact that we were able to end it [...] The nation did something special in this regard' (p. 63).

In Petersson's (2001) study, othering largely takes place *within* Russia. It is, in particular, Moscow that is being othered: 'It is the centre that is scapegoated and blamed for all ills that have befallen the country and the regions, and it is the centre that is seen as continuously scheming to worsen the situation even more' (p. 187). White (2004), for her part, studies identities and livelihood strategies in three small towns in Central Russia based on interviews with members of the local intelligentsias. One of her main findings is that in the Russian *glubinka*, that is the country's provincial depths, people became increasingly parochial during the 1990s. As opposed to the 'new Russians', mainly found in Moscow and other large cities, the lower classes had experienced a decline in social and geographical mobility, and lost interest in and respect for Moscow. Their consciousness of being Russian was enriched and partly overshadowed by local patriotism.

Based on ethnographic fieldwork at Moscow State Institute of International Relations (MGIMO), Müller (2008) focuses particularly on the distinction between 'Westernness' and Europeanness made by MGIMO students. Many students at the institute, he argues, explicitly address their lifestyle as *European*, not Western. While a Western lifestyle in general is understood rather pejoratively, the European signifier signals a more open, two-way relationship between Europeanness and Russianness. Identifying with Europe in this way does not mean imitating Europe or wanting to leave Russia for Europe, but to engage selectively with European attributes. 'Here the European signifier is rather used as a marker of positive distinction from "ordinary" Russianness' (p. 17).

Less empirical, but all the more fascinating, is Kelly's (2004) discussion of identity and everyday life in Russia.[13] She takes the untranslatable Russian word *byt* as her point of departure to reflect upon Russian disdain of plain, everyday life. ('Everyday life' is the common lexical translation of *byt*, but there are strong connotations with a sense of dullness.) A preoccupation with the *big* questions in life – art, philosophy, religion – is what it means to be Russian; *byt* is just a troublesome by-product of existence. '"Life without daily life" would sound absurd in English; *zhizn' bez byta* makes perfect sense' (p. 167). On a similar note, Waage (1990) argues that the inwardness and mysticism of the Orthodox Church, its refutation of trivial everyday life, and its contention that contemplation may give us a glimpse of heavenly glory even in this life, are constitutive of Russian identity. The religious mentality of Russians is reflected, for example, in the Soviet version of Marxism. When Khrushchev in 1961 located the Communist paradise 'just below the horizon' – and predicted its arrival in the early 1980s – he was echoing ancient Orthodox prophecies. It helps us understand the paradox between the Soviet Union's ability to conquer outer space and inability to make television sets that worked. Grandiose projects like space programmes and changing the course of Siberian rivers were the stuff of dreams, as were achievements in sports and arts, all of which contributed to 'life without daily life'. Boym (1994, p. 2) states that, 'in Russian intellectual tradition as well as in Soviet official ideology, a preoccupation with everyday life for its own sake was considered unpatriotic, subversive, un-Russian, or even anti-Soviet'. Another key component of Russian self-perception, according to Boym, is the liberal attitude to compliance with the law. Again, the distinction between what is considered patriotic and unpatriotic behaviour is drawn into the equation: 'In Russia driving through the red light when the police is not watching is an acceptable practice; there, public opinion would be more critical of eating ice cream on the subway, a practice classified as foreign or "uncultured" behaviour' (p. 289).[14]

Finally, there is Ries's (1997) acclaimed study of Russian talk. '[S]pontaneous conversational discourses are a primary mechanism by which ideologies and cultural stances are shaped and maintained', she suggests (p. 3). The stories she heard 'implicitly or explicitly addressed the structures and practices of power in Russian (Soviet) society' (p. 5).[15] Her main theoretical contribution is arguably on the identity-constituting role of litanies in Russian talk:

> Litanies were those passages in conversation where a speaker would enunciate a series of complaints, grievances, or worries about problems, troubles, afflictions, tribulations, or losses, and then often comment on these enumerations with a poignant rhetorical question ('Why is everything so bad with us?'), a sweeping, fatalistic lament about the hopelessness of the situation, or an expressive Russian sigh of disappointment and resignation. (p. 84)

A specific form of litany is what Ries (pp. 42ff) calls 'the Russia tale'. This is the story of Russia as a mythical land where everything is built to go wrong: a gigantic theme park of inconvenience, disintegration and chaos. 'You know what this country is, Nancy?', one of her interviewees asks her, 'this country is *Anti-Disneyland!*' (p. 42). It was the punch line in a conversation in which people traded examples of social chaos and absurdity in late-Soviet Russia. 'Our fairy-tale life' is another of her respondents' metaphors; it refers to the monstrous political projects of the Soviet state (p. 43). Lamentations over Russian fairly-tale life typically ended with the following sigh of resignation, 'Such a thing is only possible in one country – here, in Russia' (p. 49). However, Ries argues, 'Anti-Disneyland' also carries positive cultural value for Russians. Even when 'Russia tales' had tragic elements, they were appreciated for their fascinating, amusing and astonishing epic. They made people feel personally part of the intense Russian drama (pp. 49–50). While Russians may feel ashamed of their country abroad, as one of her respondents puts it, 'within themselves they are all very proud that they are Russians, that they come from such a country, which has such a strange history' (p. 50). 'The Russia tale' is 'an epic absurdist genre', in which participants 'regularly [fashion] personal narratives that embed the self in the larger, ongoing tale', thus 'keeping certain basic types of stories, anecdotes, absurdisms, and laments "in the air"' (p. 51).

*

These stories form the soundboard for my own accounts of Russian Arctic foreign policy narratives in the following chapters. Particularly intriguing is the link between space and soul; between northernness on the one hand and freedom, adventure and timelessness – and ultimately: patriotism and Russianness, on the other. And there is the contrast between the clean and holy East and the dirty, heretical West, between the effeminate and artificial Europe and the manly, authentic Russia. 'Space' spills over onto 'soul': Russia's boundless territory, the flatness that curves around the horizon, denies the existence of an edge – to space, heart and soul. The 'wide soul' with its 'unfathomable depth of Russian feelings', its 'recklessness verging on anarchy in the constant need for a break-out' inevitably explodes, and in the aftermath: the 'gigantic theme park of inconvenience, disintegration and chaos', the fairy-tale life, Anti-Disneyland.

But anything is better than plain everyday life, the intolerable lightness of being, the unbearable, un-Russian *byt*.

CHAPTER 2

THE RUSH FOR THE NORTH POLE

'What priorities? There are none!' This was how the Head of the State Duma's Committee on the Problems of the North responded in 2000 to a question I had asked her about post-Soviet Russian priorities in the country's northern policies.[1] The economic geography inherited by the new Russian government had been established in deliberate defiance of the constraints of both distance and climate. Driven by the urge to secure resource autarchy, and supposedly free from market considerations, Soviet authorities had invested enormous economic and human resources in developing the Russian North. Through the system of central planning, they were able to allocate the means necessary for developing gigantic industrial projects across the vast northern realm. But with the return of market mechanisms, distance and climate suddenly decided to exact their revenge: much of the industrialization of the North that had been hailed as a great victory by Soviet propaganda proved economically non-viable under the conditions of a market economy.

After a number of reorganizations during the 1990s, the federal authority responsible for northern issues, the State Committee for Socio-economic Development of the North, was disbanded in May 2000, shortly after Putin was elected president. Some of its responsibilities were divided among other federal bodies of governance; the rest were abolished. Yeltsin's Russia had disregarded the Arctic, and the new president appeared to be following in his footsteps. This impression would soon change, in large part due to external circumstances: the impending division of the Arctic continental shelf.

All the way to the pole

The 1982 UN Convention on the Law of the Sea (UNCLOS) had introduced economic zones and explained how governments should go about establishing them. Economic zones could only extend 200 nautical miles from the shore line (see Chapter 3). In the case of continental shelves, the rules are different. All states have a right to a continental shelf of 200 miles; the rules governing shelves and water columns follow one another. The principles underlying the determination of the boundaries are also the same: governments shall attempt to find an equitable solution. In certain circumstances, however, states can claim sovereignty over their continental shelf *beyond* the 200 nautical mile line, but only if the extended shelf is a natural prolongation of the area within the 200-mile limit – which is what a shelf *is*, that is the relatively shallow basin between land and the deep ocean floor, the abyssal plain. There is an opportunity under UNCLOS for states to acquire jurisdiction to explore, extract and manage the natural resources on their continental shelf within 350 nautical miles, or 100 nautical miles beyond the 2,500-metre isobath (a line connecting points of equal underwater depth). In contrast to the economic zones and the continental shelf within 200 miles, however, permission is not granted automatically. Governments must file a claim with the international Commission on the Limits of the Continental Shelf in New York, along with scientific evidence that the area beyond 200 miles is, in geological terms, a prolongation of the landmass. The members of the Continental Shelf Commission are scientists and technology experts. They assess the scientific merits of the documentation provided by governments to substantiate their claims. The Commission in that sense is neither a court of law nor a political body. And states have only the one opportunity to get the international community to agree to an extension of their continental shelf beyond the 200-mile limit: governments have to file the claim within ten years of ratifying UNCLOS.[2]

Ratification of the Convention has been slow. The US and other Western governments were wary about signing it in 1982 because they disliked the provision concerning jurisdiction over the seabed outside the shelf, that is, in deep waters. Developing countries had successfully managed to have the resources of the deep ocean classified as the common heritage of mankind. If a company discovers resources in these areas and wants to exploit them, it has to submit plans to a dedicated body, the International Seabed Authority (ISA), based in Kingston, Jamaica. The Authority divides the proceeds from the planned commercial operation equitably, while heeding the interests of the nearest coastal states. These companies are usually from the industrialized north, while the resources are generally located in waters off the coasts of developing countries in the southern hemisphere. The US saw these constraints on the earning capacity of large international corporations as a 'socialist' intervention, and waited until 1994 to sign UNCLOS, which by then had acquired an amended seabed provision as an appendix. The upshot was that many governments did not ratify the Convention until the mid-1990s and later. The deadline for submitting claims to the shelf Commission therefore moved forward; the clock would not start ticking until 1999.

Russia was the first Arctic state to file a claim, as early as 2000. Considered lacking in several respects, it was quickly rejected by the Commission. The Russians had included large areas of the continental shelf between the eastern and western sector lines. Part of the area went all the way to the North Pole. After their submission was rejected − which the Russians accepted without orchestrating a political protest − they intensified their exploration of the Arctic shelf. During a scientific expedition in August 2007, the research team lowered a mini-submarine to the seabed at the precise point of the North Pole, and planted a metal Russian flag into the ground. As we saw in the Introduction, the event attracted the attention of the worldwide media and political circles. Russia, it was said, is laying claim to the North Pole. In the event, it proved the starting shot for the 'race for the Arctic'. The media tended to depict the Arctic as a no man's land, beyond the reach of international law where governments could do as they liked while the world's reserves of oil and gas elsewhere were running dry. According to estimates drawn up by the US Geological Survey (USGS), the Arctic could hold as much as 25 per cent of the world's undiscovered oil and gas deposits. This naturally provided added sustenance to the story of the race to the Arctic. At the political level, Canada, a country with significant designs on the Arctic itself, was particularly annoyed. 'You can't go around the world these days dropping flags somewhere. This isn't the 14th or 15th century', the Canadian foreign minister, Peter MacKay, was reported as saying.[3]

This story of the race to the Arctic ran at the same time as the most exhaustive scientific study of the Arctic seabed to date was under way. The Arctic states had only a few years to spare before they had to submit their evidence and applications to the Shelf Commission. Expeditions were often portrayed in the media as the prelude to unilateral governmental action in the Arctic. 'Denmark lays claim to the North Pole', the Norwegian media told the public repeatedly in 2010–11.[4] Although the Arctic is not a barren wilderness without governance or rule of law, you could be forgiven for thinking it was from its portrayal in the media. In any event, this sort of publicity was unsettling for the five Arctic states – Canada, Denmark (Greenland), Norway, Russia and the US (Alaska) – all of whom had a vested interest in making sure the UNCLOS rules on continental shelves and their delimitation extended to the Arctic as well. That being the case, the Arctic shelf could only be divided among the five; no other state would have a rightful claim. As of writing, no government has said it will not respect the existing Law of the Sea in the Arctic, but specialists in ocean law and NGOs (such as WWF) have nevertheless urged the international community to adopt a dedicated Arctic treaty.[5] The European Parliament likewise floated the idea of a separate treaty, but later changed its mind.[6] The Arctic governments therefore held a summit at Ilulissat on Greenland in May 2008. The Law of the Sea, they declared, applies in the Arctic. Although no one had doubted their position, by issuing a formal declaration they managed to send a clear message to the outside world.

Norway filed its claim with the Shelf Commission in 2006; it was approved in 2009. In addition to agreeing with Norway that the seabed under the Barents Sea and the Norwegian Sea beyond 200 nautical miles from land belongs to the continental shelf (i.e. is not deep sea), the Commission agreed that a small sliver of seabed beyond the 200-mile limit north of Svalbard, the so-called Nansen Basin, also qualified as continental shelf. The Danish claim, which also covers the North Pole, was submitted in December 2014 and will be on the agenda at the Commission's session in September 2015. Canada was due to submit its claims by 2013, but the Commission has not enforced these deadlines strictly. Russia has no definite time limit because its first submission was rejected, but there are apparently plans to make a new claim in 2015. The US has yet to ratify UNCLOS. All presidents in office have wanted the US to go ahead and ratify the Convention, but conservative-minded Congress representatives have obstructed moves in that direction. At present, then, the US is prevented from making use of the Convention's rules on fixing the outer limits of the continental shelf, and how the superpower will react when the Commission starts approving the continental shelf claims of other Arctic states remains something of a moot point.

However the Arctic continental shelf is divided in the end, the biggest winner will be Russia. The question is really how much more the Russians will get than everyone else. Russia has everything to gain from cementing the application of the Law of the Sea in the Arctic.

*

Russia adopted its first Arctic policy document in 2001, back when the Arctic was still not much of an issue in international politics.

The document focused mainly on the region as a potential zone of conflict among great powers. As global interest escalated, the Arctic powers all put together their own Arctic strategies. Russia's Fundamentals of the State Policy of the Russian Federation, published in 2008, was the second to be issued by a member of the 'Arctic Five', a couple of years after Norway had unveiled its High North Strategy in 2006. Canada and the US followed suit in 2009, Denmark in 2011. The main objective of the Russian strategy is to transform the Arctic into the country's most important strategic natural resource base by 2020, and to preserve Russia's role as a leading Arctic power.[7] It calls for the development of the Russian Arctic in a number of fields, most notably resource extraction, transport (primarily the Northern Sea Route) and other forms of infrastructure, but also 'softer' policy areas such as science and environmental safety. It presupposes a new Russian continental shelf claim by 2015, and also the formation of a new Arctic military unit for use in combating terrorism, smuggling and illegal immigration. While the Russian strategy is considered somewhat 'harder' than those of the other Arctic states, with its explicit emphasis on national interests and sovereignty,[8] it downplays the potential for international tension in the Arctic, at least compared to the Russian policy plan of 2001. The need for international collaboration to preserve the Arctic as a zone of peace is among the priorities in the strategy. A follow-up strategy appeared in 2013, covering more or less the same priorities as the 2008 strategy, but as assessed by Zysk (2015), it appears to be somewhat more realistic and dispassionate than its predecessor. Acknowledging that Russia is not capable of effectively exploring the energy resources in the Arctic by itself, the document recognizes Russia's need for domestic and foreign private sector investment and experts to develop the country's northern regions.[9]

The political leadership in Russia have generally emphasized the need to follow the rules of international law in the Arctic, and have usually downplayed threats from other countries in the region. However, senior Russian officials have expressed fear of other states' intensions in the Arctic. FSB director Nikolai Patrushev, for example, is quoted as saying that 'the United States, Norway, Denmark, and Canada, are conducting a united and coordinated policy of barring Russia from the riches of the shelf'.[10] Artur Chilingarov, famous polar explorer and the President's special envoy on Arctic affairs, stated after the episode of the Russian flag planting – he was leader of the expedition and on board the submarine when the flag was planted – that 'we have exercised the maritime right of the first night'.[11] Two years later he added, 'we will not give the Arctic to anyone'.[12] Even President Medvedev, who was usually inclined to emphasize the cooperative aspect of international Arctic politics (see Chapter 3), made similar statements on occasion: 'Regrettably, we have seen attempts to limit Russia's access to the exploration and development of the Arctic mineral resources [...] This is absolutely inadmissible from the legal viewpoint and unfair given our nation's geographical location and history.'[13]

References to Russian history and territory were key features of many of the statements of President Medvedev and Prime Minister Putin around this time. In 2009, Putin was appointed head of the trustees of the Russian Geographical Society and in his address to the Society's congress introduced the topic of the Arctic as follows: 'When we say great, a great country, a great state – certainly, size matters [...] When there is no size, there is no influence, no meaning.'[14] Medvedev, in turn, in his first address as chairman of the national Security Council in 2008, entitled 'Defending Russia's National Interests in the Arctic', made the following remark:

> I want to especially underline that this is our duty, this is simply a direct debt [we owe] to those who have gone before us. We must firmly, and for the long-term future [of our country], secure the national interests of Russia in the Arctic.[15]

'The global fight against Canada in the Arctic'

Laruelle (2014: 7ff) argues that there are two different Russian strategies for the Arctic: the 'security first' and the 'cooperation first'. The former – supported by the Security Council (which produced the Arctic policy document), the military complex and security services – views the Arctic as a territorial arena where Russia can revive its former status as a great power. Security comes first in this strategy, and foreign presence must be curbed. The second approach – reflecting primarily the objectives of the Ministry of Natural Resources – is motivated by economic concerns and is pragmatic in its views of how best to achieve its goals: In order to develop the northern regions, Russia must be open to foreign cooperation through investments and sharing of expertise. Private businesses, both Russian and foreign, must be given greater roles in the development of the Arctic; the Russian state cannot do this alone. In addition to the revival of Russian greatness on the international scene, the 'security-first' variant is viewed as having a more immediate domestic aim: to reassert Russian patriotism in order to secure the legitimacy of the political establishment. Since 2008–9, however, Moscow has also sought external recognition by creating an 'Arctic brand' with Russia portrayed as a responsible and highly cooperative state that takes a leading role in the development of law and policy in the Arctic. When Putin speaks of 'our common Arctic home' (p. 12), he clearly alludes to Gorbachev's 'common European home', the incarnation of modern Russian willingness to work with the West.

The Russian media sometimes frames the Arctic in the context of foreign relations; at other times as a domestic issue. The boundary between them is not impermeable, however. A common theme in the foreign-policy oriented newspaper articles is the perception that the other Arctic states are 'actively flexing their muscles',[16] and that Russia must necessarily respond. The debate mainly centres on Canada's intentions in the Arctic. Canada is largely depicted as the 'aggressor' in the region. Canadian Prime Minister Stephen Harper is said to operate under the slogan 'Conquer [the Arctic] or you'll lose it',[17] and is reported to have said: 'The Arctic is our country, our property and our ocean. The Arctic belongs to Canada.'[18] In brief, Russia's mission is to engage in 'the global fight against Canada in the Arctic'.[19]

The alleged discrepancy between Canada's assurances of no aggressive intensions in the Arctic, and the country's simultaneous aggregation of military forces in the region, is another recurrent theme in the Russian press. Reporting from a meeting between the Canadian and Russian ministers of foreign affairs in September 2010, *Rossiyskaya Gazeta* questions the Canadian assurance that the country only has peaceful intentions in the Arctic.[20] Canada has, according to the article, recently constructed new military bases in the Arctic; it has also launched new ice-going patrol vessels for use in the region. The Canadians also conduct annual Arctic military exercises. 'All this forces Canada's partners in the "Arctic five" to question the sincerity of the Canadian party's statements [about peaceful cooperation].' While Russia is here grouped together with the three remaining 'Arctic five', Russia's position as the only non-Western state among the five is also at issue in the article. 'One of the most burning issues for the "Arctic five"', the article states, is 'NATO's interest in the region'. The Russian prime minister gives vent to a certain irritation: 'I don't think NATO behaves in an appropriate manner when it reserves for itself the right to decide who should make decisions in the Arctic', though he does not say exactly how this inappropriate behaviour takes place. Another feature article on the same meeting asks whether Foreign Minister Cannon will succeed in melting the ice of mistrust that has developed in the country's relations with Russia due to 'the Canadians' ambitious view on the ownership of the Lomonosov Ridge'.[21] Harper had recently been speaking, 'in harsh words', about Canada's ambitious programme 'Steering North' and about preserving 'the true North' strong and free, so it's 'no wonder Ottawa [subsequently] sent the minister of foreign affairs [to Russia] to clarify'. The feature writer notes that despite the 'optimistic tone' of the lecture Cannon gave to Russian politicians, journalists and academics, not everything he said sounded particularly friendly to Russian spectators: '"The Arctic has always been a part of us, it still is and always will be", Cannon said, seemingly forgetting for a moment that no country has exclusive rights in this zone.' Cannon goes on, 'again without even wavering', to state that 'there are territories that belong to us, where the continental shelf must be prolonged, for instance the Lomonosov Ridge, as an extension of our territory'. Thus it was that Cannon managed to '[destroy] the good atmosphere of the meeting'. The reporter was not at all convinced of Canada's peaceful intentions in the Arctic.

The other Arctic states are not only fighting to defend their own rights in the Arctic, they are actively mobilizing to wipe Russia off the board. In an article with the rather peculiar heading, 'Without fighting penguins',[22] – the idea being that the establishment of a new Russian Arctic military unit does not signify the militarization of the region – ample evidence is provided to the effect that 'USA, Norway, Denmark and Canada are pursuing a unified and coordinated policy to prevent Russia access to the riches of the continental shelf', and that the 'USA and its partners in NATO are striving to extend their economic presence in the northern waters, and to achieve internationalization of the Northern Sea Route and, as a result, press Russia out of the region'. As proof of this development, the journalist refers to a document obtained from the Security Council's press service showing that foreign intelligence bureaus are intensifying their activities in the border areas with Russia. Norwegian research vessels are being recruited to carry out intelligence work. International NGOs are also used, especially environmental NGOs. There are foreign scientists in the areas around Novaya Zemlya and the White Sea, where Russian submarines perform military exercises. In Norway, there's talk about changing Svalbard's demilitarized status, and about a new policy of using the national armed forces in the Arctic.[23] An article entitled 'Cold NATO'[24] claims that NATO is 'breaking into the Arctic' and that 'the question about when the Polar bears will see American hangar ships is of more than just rhetorical character' – but Russia's response to the world will be: 'We will not give the Arctic to anyone!' By declaring the Arctic as 'strategically important for the alliance', NATO is meddling in the ongoing diplomatic conversations among the 'Arctic five', adding to them an element of power and thus increasing the risk that diplomacy will give way to military demonstrations. At the same time, the US is criticized for trying to 'internationalize most of the Arctic problems, enabling them to subsequently penetrate the region by means of international law and multilateral forces'.[25] To illustrate this ominous situation, *Rossiyskaya Gazeta* states that the first Russian submission to the Commission on the Continental Shelf was rejected 'not without pressure from the US, Norwegian and Canadian side'.[26] As noted above, the UN Continental Shelf Commission is neither political body nor tribunal; it is a commission of scientists, such as geologists, hydrographers and geophysicists.

There is an abundance of resources in the Arctic, the article 'Hot Arctic'[27] notes, and 'the USA has already counted them'. It also reminds the reader of how the US around 1990 tried to take advantage of Russia's political weakness to acquire more of the Bering Sea. There was even talk of ceding Chukotka to the Americans, the environmental project 'Bering Park' being geared to that aim. The article 'On slippery ice' similarly warns readers that the Canadians are prepared to use all underhand methods to grab what's legally not theirs in the Arctic, including 'fine-looking environmental plans' that extend sailing routes a further 100 nautical miles from the shore.[28] And 'Ice War No. 2' takes the rise in US monitoring of cruise traffic in the 'newly ice-free areas' of the Polar Ocean as yet more proof that the West is planning to start 'a tactical ice war' with Russia.[29] The Secretary of the Security Council, Nikolai Patrushev, concludes: 'If we do not act immediately, time will be lost, and then it will simply be too late – they will have squeezed us out.'[30]

Interspersed with these accounts of Western aggression we find stories depicting Russia as a peace-loving nation, one that is 'categorically against any militarization of [the Arctic]',[31] refuses to be pulled into 'what is referred to as a conflict about access to resources',[32] and insists that 'questions about ownership must be decided exclusively by the mechanisms [provided] under UNCLOS'.[33] Even the Commander in Chief of the Russian parachute forces assures us that while he plans to put parachute troops on the North Pole, they will be 'peaceful paratroopers'.[34]

In an article named 'A slice of a Polar bear fur', the Russian Minister of Foreign Affairs comes across as more peace-loving than his Canadian colleague:

> Most of the journalists are less inclined to abandon the idea of a new world conflict unfolding in the third millennium. They asked whether the war in the Arctic was over, and Canada's representative said it was. Lavrov quickly corrected this remark. There had never been any war in the Arctic. Fellow journalists smiled, while the slightly bemused Canadian nodded his agreement.[35]

Occasionally, the straightforward narrative of 'the world is against us, but we just want peace' is interrupted. The article 'Strike below the pole' from *Kommersant* a couple of weeks after the flag planting episode is an example. It starts in recognizable form with a description of East–West antagonism and Russian heroism, but ends up by questioning Russian greatness – I discuss this further in the concluding section of this chapter. For now, let's just hear the story in its entirety.

> The sensational achievement of the 'Arktika-2007' expedition in planting the Russian flag in the seabed at the North Pole was greeted with joy by the Russian people, while our adversaries in marine matters slunked off in a huff. A completely natural response, says *Vlast* commentator Shamir Idiatullin. It's just the latest expression of the celebrated Russian national idea, known to everybody.
> Last week, the expedition team of the difficult 'Arktika-2007' voyage returned home. The expedition was led by the famous polar explorer, member of United Russia, and member and deputy speaker of the State Duma, Artur Chilingarov. Two bathyscaphes were lowered by the team to a depth of more than four kilometres, where they planted a

Russian flag of titanium on the seabed, and returned with a bucket of sediment and two containers of water. Not only was this the first time anyone had descended all the way down to the seabed at the geographical Pole, the 'Arktika-2007' team explained, but they had also collected material that would help Russia prove that its continental shelf extended as far north as the Pole itself. In other words, Russia owns most of the unbelievable reserves of oil and gas concealed in the eastern parts of the Arctic Sea. The US expressed doubts as to this conclusion, Canada said the North Pole was Canadian, and the world's media blew hot and cold about Moscow's scandalous act of annexation.

In reality, Chilingarov did not remonstrate in the Amundsen Sea (because it is precisely in these waters – a good distance from the Lomonosov ridge and, in consequence, the presumed Russian shelf – through which the earth's axis passes) to support [the idea of] an extension to Russia's Arctic Siberia, but rather to promote his party political, propaganda and entertainment agenda, only lightly camouflaged as economic expediency. We must not, however, believe that the conquest of the polar deep was the brainchild of some amateur Arctic explorers.

The lowering of the bathyscaphes Mir I and Mir II was a move on the part of the Russian elite (and a relatively successful one) at the shrine of the national idea. The doctrine of sovereign democracy – you can bake it with poison – only beguiles particularly disingenuous party officials. You can't get it to a Russian ideal. On the other hand, there is an ideal that's dependable and appreciated, a large, powerful country able to accomplish anything anywhere. This country is not loved, naturally; it is feared. But, first, we're not exactly a jewel in your crown; second, fear equals respect; third, we have already lived in a country like that, when the trees were higher and the water wetter. And it's a complete waste of time to create a new one by installing a proletarian dictatorship, with industrialization and collectivization, root and branch purges and everything else out of which the superpower emerged. The old saying is refuted by reality: if you say the word 'halva' enough times, your mouth fills with a sweet taste, and a small country can look big by putting on the airs of the superpower.

It all began in 1999 or thereabouts, this pretence, when Primakov's plane, flying over the Atlantic, turned back and Russian paratroopers were dropped over Pristina. The logic of empire was directed outwards; the Soviet ideologues believed it was possible to find lasting happiness for the state on Freedom Island, in the black continent, Antarctica – on Mars even. The Soviet Union sat firmly on the coupons and stood ankle-deep in shit – on the other hand, the country was dispatching food aid and construction workers to Asia and Africa. Russia learned a lesson. Last year, when Yakutia was paralyzed by impassable roads, a detachment of military construction workers was sent to repair roads in Lebanon. And this year, firemen were shipped to Greece and Montenegro in response to the fires in the selfsame Yakutia, not to mention Sakhalin, Chita and Chukotka (sure, it wasn't free, but that's not the issue).

The latest advances are blatant copies of Soviet advances – such as the Olympic Games, doomed to be a celebration of Russian sports, friendship among nations, and the eviction of local inhabitants, replaced by people from other places. The achievement of the polar explorers is even more touching, because this, my boys, this is Captain Tatarinov, the *SS Chelyuskin*'s ice floe, Schmidt's beard, Papanin's Mauser and Chkalov's non-stop flight. Mercifully, most of the cost of this propaganda exercise in promoting Russian ambitions would be footed by the Swede and Australian onboard bathyscaphe number two. You may just as well get used to the idea of foreign assistance: if Russia is incapable of developing the Shtokman field itself, you can hardly expect the country in the space of fifty years or so to recover and transport even more distant and much less accessible Arctic riches.

Unless, of course, quantity morphs into quality and the revival of the Soviet exploits in the form of construction troops (mentioned by Prime Minister Fradkov recently), acceleration of the space programme and all manner of changes to GTO [Soviet sports norms/sports badges] and Osoaviakhim [a civil society organization that promotes the interests of the defence industry] transform the country into a great-and-powerful something or other. It's not just general aesthetic considerations one can use as a pretext for speeding up the transformation – the activities of the Arctic rivals, led by the United States, who happily subscribed to the Russian idea of the polar shelf, can as well. Anyone with an inkling of American tendencies and opportunities can assume that Washington will shortly be able to discover its own continental shelf in every ocean accessible to the country – and to scientifically justify not only that the Arctic belongs to USA's natural sphere of interest but Eurasia, Africa and Australia too. After this, the discussion about spheres of interest can return to the level that was typical of the '50s and '60s. To the delight of people who remember those years as a golden epoch in the homeland's history.[36]

To return to the 'security-first' and 'cooperation-first' approaches in Russian Arctic policy, both are reflected in the public debate, more or less simultaneously, supporting rather than contesting each other. The debate, if we can call it a debate at all, is more descriptive than normative. Instead of discussing how Russia should angle its Arctic policies, the newspapers tell their readers 'how the world is'. By and large, it is a world where NATO is surreptitiously preparing for the rush for the Arctic, while Russia insists on international cooperation and open dialogue. Canada is the main villain, with its harsh rhetoric and alleged unilateralism. There might be an underlying normative message here that says cooperation doesn't work when your partners are not reliable and should hence be abandoned as Russia's main strategy, but it is seldom openly expressed in the debate.

'The Arctic is our everything'

As discussed in Chapter 1, the Arctic in post-Soviet Russia is both a 'forgotten' (economically neglected and politically marginalized) and a 'future' (the country's most important reserve, economically and spiritually) region. It is plagued with 'everything from bad roads to the notorious Russian propensity to drink'.[37] It is home to 'mythical and half-mythical resources';[38] to a nuclear icebreaker fleet, 'which exists only in our country'[39] and is a 'convincing testimony to man's success in the duel with the ice masses';[40] to 'the legendary Northern Sea Route', 'the Arctic's longest road', in itself 'the most genuine of ministries',[41] but desperately in need of 'a new life' – not to earn money from international transport (as often assumed in the West, and not quite unlikely), but to 'maintain life and activity in the Russian North'.[42]

Certain exclamations recur in the debate: 'The Arctic is our everything', and 'The Arctic always has been and always will remain Russian'. They often turn up without further elaboration – as in the article 'Northern lights', where the latter formulation is immediately followed by a prosaic statement that 'Russian scientists worked on oil and gas extraction projects before the Norwegians even thought about it'.[43] And there's talk about the 'rebirth' of the Arctic[44] – and countless stories of the heroic 'snow man', Artur Chilingarov, 'Hero of the Soviet Union, Hero of the Russian Federation'.[45] Two hundred journalists and 30 TV channels were waiting at the Vnukovo-3 airport terminal when he stepped onto Russian soil after the North Pole flag planting, 'trembling with excitement', and declaring – yes, you're right: 'the Arctic always has been and always will remain Russian'. Two flags were used to mark the event: the flag of the international Polar Year and the Abkhazian flag. Since Chilingarov was 'an old friend of Abkhazia', the Georgian province became the second nation on the North Pole after Russia (a year ahead of the Georgian war), beating 'far more powerful, reputable and prosperous pretenders to the riches in the Polar continental shelf'.[46] Hence, Russian Arctic policies are linked here to territorial disputes along the country's southern borders.

The notions of 'Arctic boom' (the promising future) and 'Arctic doom' (the dreary present) are combined in an article in *Argumenty i fakty* (*AiF*), from autumn 2008, named 'Once again the Russian flag is waving in the Arctic'.[47] The article tells the story of the journalist's trip with the border patrol vessel *Anadyr* to the Chukchi Sea.

Why sail in the Arctic?

A correspondent from *AiF-Kamchatka* accompanied a coastguard patrol vessel in the eastern sector of the Arctic, and was informed by the commander that they hadn't patrolled the area since 1993: 'It was a successful demonstration of the Russian flag. But the main thing is we showed our flag not just for the USA, but for our citizens living in Chukotka. They were no less surprised than the Americans ...'

Has anything changed in Russian policy on the Arctic? Yes, it has. The Arctic is of enormous economic interest to Russia in the form of the richest natural resources, of which oil and gas on the continental shelf are the most important.

The Russian Arctic has been thinly populated for some time, and for this reason our neighbours have been eyeing the area; envy and lust light up in their greedy eyes. America is dreaming about turning the Chukotka Sea into an open area for economic exploitation. Canada, USA, Norway and Denmark would have liked to split the Arctic four ways and push Russia out, and keep it inside the boundaries of its continental shelf. Even China wouldn't say no to a tiny piece.

But Russia is not surrendering yet and has – thank God – started taking action. The President has given his approval to a programme to utilize and protect the Arctic, and there are many references in this document to border forces as guardians of the state's economic interests. [...]

An astounded Chukotka

{The correspondent describes how the vessel 'not only displayed the Russian flag', but also investigated the area to make the journey easier for the next patrol. Then follows an account of Chukotka itself: In his time as governor, Roman Abramovich organized the building of lightweight modular homes, three to seven TV channels, installation of telephones, etc. But... The problem isn't just the lack of industry; unemployment is rife, especially among the indigenous peoples. The hunting of seals and marine mammals together with reindeer husbandry employ only a few, and every time a ship comes in, people dash to the harbour in case there are tourists who want to buy hides or souvenirs of walrus teeth.}

When they heard a Russian border guard boat had arrived, the good people of Chukotka were amazed at its might and beauty. They couldn't believe Russia had military ice-rated ships capable of navigating the Arctic.

And Chukotka made an impression on the border guards with its primeval and wild beauty. The sea here proved literally to boil with whales. Every day, pod after pod, they swam alongside the boat. When *Anadyr* moved into the ice-covered areas, walrus and seal turned up as well. And precisely on Sailors' Day, a Polar bear came swimming, scenting the aroma of *shashlik* rising from the helipad. It was impossible not to be astonished at the swimmer's dexterity – around us the sweep of the open sea – it was 20 miles to the nearest ice.

They served with honour!

{Short interviews with a couple of the crews are reported here. A seaman from Ussuriysk:}

'We were fortunate on this extended trip', he said sincerely. 'Before this, we were patrolling the Sea of Okhotsk, by the Kuril and Komandor islands, but the Arctic left a special impression. And here, I've finally settled on a career – I'm staying onboard as a contracted border guard.'

{The head of the electro-technical team Ruzvelt { =Roosevelt} Gadzhimuradov also sees the voyage as an extraordinary event:}

Obviously, the natural surroundings made an impression, but the harsh life of the people here made an even deeper one. In my opinion, the state has to take this territory seriously, the people of Chukotka deserve better.

{The correspondent talks about the many high points of the voyage – various exercises and target shooting practice.}

It's been misty and cold, the sea has been calm and it has been rough. The people were tired, but invigorated by their impressions, they threw themselves into it body and soul. It was the first time any of them had been to the Arctic, and they fell in love with it.

{On plans for the future: A new boat will soon replace the Anadyr, and the area will be patrolled on a regular basis.}

And Cape Schmidt – it's absolutely not the last stop in the new patrol area. Go further west along the Arctic Ocean! Much further! Because today the whole of Russia is thinking about the Arctic.

This story inscribes itself firmly into the Russia-against-the-rest narrative. The other Arctic nations are ready to divide the region among themselves (even to the extent of giving China a small piece), so Russia needs to remain vigilant. Surely, 'our neighbours have been eyeing the area; envy and lust light up their greedy eyes'. But more than anything, the article is an ode to the Arctic as a Russian 'homeland', and to Russia as the Arctic's patron and guardian. *Anadyr*'s voyage to these northern waters implies a 'welcome home' both to the chukchis – the motherland does care after all – and to the young sailors who have never set foot on this genuinely Russian soil before. The local population is struck by the 'might and beauty' of the patrol vessel, the sailors by the 'primeval and wild' beauty of Chukotka; they all fell in love with the Arctic. But not only did the natural surroundings make an impression –

the harsh life of the local people made an even deeper one: 'The state has to take this territory seriously, the people of Chukotka deserve better.' The Russian North has been neglected for one and a half decades (even though Abramovich set up TV channels and modular homes there), but it is ripe with natural resources: whales and walruses, oil and gas. So now the whole of Russia is talking about the Arctic: 'Go further west along the Arctic Ocean! Much further!'

Our ocean, our future, our foes

The Russian media debate about the Arctic progresses under headings such as 'Cold NATO', 'Hot Arctic', 'Strike below the pole', 'Ice War No. 2' – and with stories of a Canada hungry for new territories: 'A Polar Bear went out to hunt'[48]. The 'Russia vs the West' question looms large.[49] It is not in itself a question about Westernism vs Slavophilism (whether Russia should learn from or distance itself from the West), nor, as already mentioned, about 'security first' or 'cooperation first' (whether Russia should prepare for conflict in the Arctic or seek international cooperation). The 'debaters' might be advocates of one camp or another, but here they are mostly the journalists themselves, not the interviewees. The frame of the debate is rather based on the ontological premise that states are always at loggerheads, and on the more practical premise that Russia is vulnerable to NATO's efforts in the Arctic. Western conflict-oriented intentions are taken for granted, whose ultimate aim is to get Russia out of the Arctic once and for all. The NATO countries are 'breaking into the Arctic'[50] and 'flexing their muscles', while 'envy and lust light up their greedy eyes'. And, '[f]urther into the future, it will be simply too late, they will drive us away from here'. That no one appears to be urging Russia to strengthen its military presence in the region is striking. Yes, some want to see the FSB playing a bigger role in the Arctic and the Northern Sea Route and other infrastructure in the region upgraded – and there is the underlying message that 'Russia needs to remain vigilant'. But hardly anyone is urging the authorities to increase the military defence of the Russian Arctic in order to respond to Western aggression.[51] It is Russian policy that the division of the Arctic shelf should be decided by means of negotiation in international fora and in accordance with the procedural and material rules of international law. Unlike NATO, Russia is 'categorically against any militarization of the Arctic'.

The debate also features depictions of the Arctic as a specifically Russian 'homeland' or site of a 'national idea': The Arctic belongs to Russia, and Russia belongs in the Arctic – the North Pole flag was planted 'at the shrine of the national idea'. As mentioned in Chapter 1, this narrative can take a geopolitical, a domestic or a mythical nature – and, of course, a combination of the three. The geopolitical variant – which shares an interface with the 'Russia vs the West' narrative – is multifaceted. It speaks of the Arctic as something that, by its very nature, belongs to Russia: 'the Arctic always has been and always will remain Russian'; but also as something that needs to be conquered: 'rightful compensation for the hegemony lost with the disappearance of the Soviet Union'.[52] Note, moreover, the somewhat peculiar link to the disputed republic of Abkhazia – over which Russia a year later would find itself at war with Georgia – cited in the report about Chilingarov's happy return from the North Pole. Russia and Abkhazia were the two first 'nations' on the Pole, creating a link between two regions Russia, in some way or other, is claiming as its own. The domestic narrative, in turn, calls for a reverse of the 'Arctic doom' to the 'Arctic boom' idea: The Russian North has been neglected since the end of the Cold War and desperately needs a new commitment and new investments. Indeed, 'the people of Chukotka deserve better'. The mythical narrative takes 'the primeval and wild beauty' of the Arctic as its base point, while raising it to a metaphysical level when speaking of Arctic 'rebirth', the Arctic as 'a promised land of abundance and freedom',[53] 'a new political and spiritual continent', 'the Arctic's 'mythical and half-mythical resources', and Russia's 'cosmic destiny'.[54] As we remember from Chapter 1: 'From the [Russian] North comes God himself'.[55]

These sub-narratives are often interlinked, explicitly or implicitly: the Arctic needs to remain Russian (or be conquered) because it belongs to (or should belong to) Russia in a legal or political sense (by customary law, for instance), but also because it reflects the true spirit of Russia; it is a place where salvation can be found and the Russian nation can be reborn. The Russian North must be materially restored – both decaying Soviet settlements and 'the legendary Northern Sea Route' – not just because 'the people of Chukotka deserve better', but because North is good and genuine; it is 'the last empire of paradise', 'the northern Eden',[56] the 'bell, sounded long ago'.[57] Indeed, the coherence of this narrative is striking: the way geopolitics, domestic northern policies and mythical aspects are combined into one story about Russia and the Arctic as congenital twins.

Most interesting, however, is how the story is linked to territory and time, and how these, in turn, are connected with the ideas of 'pure Russia'/'holy Russia' and the Russian 'wide soul'. 'When there is no size', Putin says, 'there is no meaning'. Russian territory is *larger* than that of other countries in the world; Russia is going *higher* in the universe and *farther* north than anyone else.[58] 'Go further west along the Arctic Ocean!' the journalist from *Argumenty i fakty* exclaims after his voyage with the *Anadyr*, 'much further!' Space itself is often used as a powerful metaphor for and expression of Russianness, as we saw in Chapter 1. The 'boundless territory', the 'land with no edge', the 'flatness that curves around the horizon'[59] – that is what makes Russia Russia. And like the open territory, Russia is itself the ultimate expression of openness: openness of mind and openness of heart. The Russian landscape is wide, and so is the Russian soul, full of passion, generosity and recklessness 'in the constant need for a break-out'.[60] It's a wild ride; it's here-and-now and no-tomorrow; it's love and fun and spirituality, devoid of dull everyday life, the intolerable un-Russian *byt*.

And the wide soul implies a purity of heart found only in pure and holy Russia (or Arctic), long forgotten in the dirty, heretical West (or South). It belongs to the manly, authentic

North (or Russia) as opposed to the effeminate, artificial South (or West). The Russian Arctic is, after all, a man's world, with polar explorers, sailors and 'snow men', exercising 'the maritime right of the first night'.

The North is 'forgotten' and 'future', as we have seen; neglected and promising at the same time. It faces an imminent 'rebirth', which speaks of past glory and hopes of a bright future. 'Time' looms large in the Russian debate about the Arctic. 'This is our duty', says Medvedev, 'this is simply a debt we owe directly to *those who have gone before us*. We must firmly, and for the *long-term future*, secure the national interests of Russia in the Arctic.'[61] The *Anadyr* welcomes Chukotka back into the Russian fold, and Russia back into the Arctic's. And the quintessence of the debate: 'The Arctic *always has been* and *always will remain* Russian'. The Russian Arctic offers 'the ultimate test of our path towards timelessness'.[62] It is the 'land with no edge', in territory and in time.

Only rarely are these 'master narratives' challenged; the article in *Kommersant* titled 'Strike below the Pole' is one example, however. It reports the planting of the flag at the North Pole a couple of weeks after it had taken place. It starts by referring to 'the sensational achievement' of the 'Arktika-2007' expedition, 'the latest expression of the celebrated Russian national idea'. It reviews the scientific purpose of the voyage before the author remarks that Mr Chilingarov did not plant the flag to demonstrate support for Russia's claim to wider jurisdiction in the Arctic, 'but rather to promote his party political, propaganda and entertainment agenda, only lightly camouflaged as economic expediency'. It was not a one-man show, however; it was staged by the Russian elite to illustrate the idea of Russia as an immense, powerful country that can do whatever it wants, wherever it wants. It is not a country it is easy to like ('not exactly a jewel in your crown'), so it has little alternative but to stoke fear in the international community in order to gain respect. And then suddenly: 'we have already lived in a country like that, when the trees were higher and the water wetter' – and there's nothing to strive or yearn for. Reality will catch up with you anyway: 'if you repeat the word "halva" enough times, your mouth fills with a sweet taste, and a small country can look big by putting on the airs of a superpower'. The Soviet Union had global ambitions, but ended up 'ankle-deep in shit'. Recent events in Putin's Russia are 'blatant copies of Soviet advances', such as the Sochi Olympics, where 'friendship among nations' led to the expulsion of local inhabitants – in the mythical land where everything is built to go wrong (see Chapter 1). Oh, and Russia's old achievements in the Arctic are so touching – the SS *Chelyuskin's* ice flow, Schmidt's beard, Papanin's Mauser and Chkalov's non-stop flight – but would they have landed on the North Pole seabed had it not been for the Swede and the Australian on board the bathyscaphes? And how likely is it that Russia will have the capacity to exploit the riches of the High Arctic when it isn't even able to develop the Shtokman field in the Barents Sea without foreign assistance? The truth is, the emperor has no clothes.

This is Russia the miserable, the country plagued by 'everything from bad roads to the notorious Russian propensity to drink'. According to the nineteenth-century writer Nikolai Gogol, Russia is beset by two misfortunes: fools and bad roads. It is Anti-Disneyland and all that, but centre stage here is the foolish boldness, the lack of a sense of reality, the insistence on persuading oneself that one is something that one is not, and the desperate need to be that other. Russia is not even capable of learning from its mistakes. It repeats the grandiose gesturing of the Soviet Union in Sochi, at the North Pole, on Mars even. This is the backside of the happy-go-lucky, the here-today-gone-tomorrow, the unbounded urge to plunge beyond the horizon, the wild ride through territory and time.

*

The Russian debate about the Arctic is constituted by two major meta-narratives, which in Somers' (1994) typology (see Introduction) are the epic dramas in which we are embedded as contemporary actors in history. It is 'Russia vs the West', and 'Russia and the Arctic'. The two are not mutually exclusive, indeed, they are mutually reinforcing. Adjoined to the imagery of 'Russia and the Arctic' are the more subtle narratives (which can arguably be categorized as meta-narratives, too) of what it means to be Russian across space and time. It is the sense of vastness, recklessness, timelessness – in Hellberg-Hirn's (1998) words, 'soil and soul'. Then there are the far less frequent 'counter narratives', stories that question the premises of the 'master narratives'.[63] *Kommersant's* 'Strike below the Pole' ridicules Russia's Arctic ambitions specifically, and the country's inability to accomplish anything in the world more widely. It starts out as a public narrative, an account of the story-teller's cultural or institutional surroundings – here, contemporary Russian politics – but evolves into a meta-narrative of Russia's eternal fate. The author refers to Soviet grandiosity and misery, to Russian pride and unwillingness to learn from past mistakes – explanations of why Russia will always remain the land of 'fools and bad roads'.

Othering takes different but not necessarily incompatible paths in the various narratives. The most conspicuous act of othering we find in the narrative 'Russia vs the West'. Naturally, this goes in one direction only: the Other is the West. But there are nuances in the intensity of the othering. Journalists almost exclusively portray the West as the aggressor in the Arctic, with Russia being 'categorically against any militarization' of the region. But the West is interchangeably talked about as 'Cold NATO' and 'our neighbours'; when these foreign powers seek to maximize their interests in the Arctic, it is referred to either as a natural thing – what any reasonable state (or alliance) would do – or as outright offensive, reflecting the impudent behaviour of foreigners in Russia's backyard, or, rather, the country's core area. The latter clearly dominates the debate. Likewise, the 'soil and soul' narrative by its very nature places the West, or in principle anything non-Russian, in the position of the Other.

Russia points the finger of righteous indignation at the Canadians in response to the latter's 'harsh words' as in 'The Arctic has always been a part of us, it still is and always will be' and 'The Arctic is our country, our property and our ocean. The Arctic belongs to Canada.' Heard that before? The established Other is ridiculed for statements that sound strangely like one's own – the subconscious othering of oneself perhaps?

In the 'Russia and the Arctic' narrative, othering westwards is only indirect, implicit. If the Arctic is *'our* all', how can it also be somebody else's all? What are *they* doing here? It's not that we suspect their intentions, they've probably just not got it right – they've gone astray, but we will help them get back home. The real othering in this narrative takes place in *time*: The past of the Russian North is proud and its future bright – so why did we end up in this miserable situation? The Other is the present time itself, the 'here and now'. It took time to get here, and it will take time to get back on track. This is the slow ride home, the boring passage through time.

The 'fools and bad roads' narrative picks up the thread: there's a reason the Arctic has been neglected, like all other assets in the country. The reason is Russia itself, its never-failing ability to ruin everything that is good. Things are not the way they are because of accidental neglect, but by destined default. The Other is the hideous monster looking back at yourself in the mirror. The Other is also the picture of yourself that you present to the outside world; the image of Russia as a large, powerful country that can do whatever it wants, wherever it wants; the mirage on the horizon, your wishful thinking.

Soil and soul, fools and roads; combined they describe a 'fairy-tale life' of sorts, a noisy existence of extremes incessantly flying through the air, brutally categorical, nothing in-between. But Janus-faced and obscure; in Russia, reality is always up for grabs, but the choices are few and deceitful.

*

The dominant plot structure in the Russian media's tales about the Arctic lies somewhere between Ringmar's (2006) 'romance' and 'tragedy'. Russia is the hero determined to 'save the Arctic', although perhaps more for its own than the (global) common good. The 'romance' does not necessarily speak of an end to the story; it is the process that matters, the hero's journey spreading benevolence and good deeds. In the 'tragedy', the hero rebels against the established order but is himself destroyed in the process. In the Arctic, tragedy is looming, with signs of NATO arming up to take control – but Russia is intent on continuing the good fight: to avoid an armaments race in the High Arctic. Russia is the romantic hero that tries to pour cold (Russian) water onto hot (Western) blood. Russia is the one that has to remind the world that not only is there no war in the Arctic, or the war has been brought to an end; *there never really was one.*

The plots of the 'Russia and the Arctic' and 'soil and soul' narratives conform to the structures of the romance. Russia has a special mission in the world as the defender of the true faith, spirituality and goodness. It believes that peace can be maintained in the Arctic, and the prosperity of the Russian North restored, if only the Russians are given free reigns to put their sensitivity, morality and greatness to use for the good cause.

The 'fools and bad roads' narrative takes the form of the satire. Parasitic on the other forms of narrative, it reverses the plot structures, deconstructs and reassembles them into new structures. The 'sensational achievement' of the team that planted the North Pole flag is here turned into a reflection of Soviet megalomania, incompetence and inferiority complex. Chilingarov's heroic deed is mere propaganda and showing off, in reality performed by a Swede and an Australian. Past achievements might have had a veneer of success, but they actually left the Soviet Union 'ankle-deep in shit'. Holy Russia is not a country it is easy to like; it is not exactly god's gift to the world.

The ultra-simple plot of the story is: Hey, we're Russia. And let's face it – reality's going to catch us up anyway.

CHAPTER 3

DELIMITATION OF THE BARENTS SEA

'What can Putin do to get the Barents Sea back?' ran the headline of an article printed in several Russian newspapers in late winter 2013.[1] The author wanted the border between Norway and Russia in the Barents Sea, established by treaty in 2010, revoked forthwith. What's more, it's time the international community stood up to Norway and its management of the waters around Svalbard. The article attracted a lot of attention in the Norwegian media, too, as winter progressed into spring. It just goes to show, some said, we still have a Russian bear as a neighbour – it's best to be on our guard and expect the worst. The viewpoints expressed in the article were pretty eccentric, commentators suggested, but an anomaly, even a misunderstanding. What more could you say about such obvious absurdities? Let's be clear, the Norwegian–Russian maritime delimitation treaty is a binding agreement between two sovereign states. It was entered into in accordance with the principles of the Law of the Sea – it's not something you withdraw from at the drop of a hat. So the issue is not so much *what* Putin should do to recover the Barents Sea, but *why* the critics of the delimitation line want him to.

Endless negotiations, big compromise

By the early 1970s, it was plain that the world's fish stocks were buckling under the pressure of a growing and increasingly efficient fishing fleet. It was also plain that conflicts over marine resources could destabilize international relations. In 1973, the UN's Third Conference on the Law of the Sea convened to discuss, among other things, the possibility of allowing coastal states to extend jurisdiction beyond their territorial waters.[2] The question had been raised in 1958 and 1960 at the first and second Law of the Sea conferences, but the parties failed to unite behind an agreement. The time was now ripe and a couple of years later – the Third Conference on the Law of the Sea would go on until the 1982 signing of the Convention – the parties agreed to give coastal states a 200-mile economic zone. They would enjoy an exclusive right to explore, extract and manage marine resources within this zone, which for all practical purposes meant fish. Where fish stocks straddled the economic zones of two or more countries, governments were instructed to manage them jointly.

Norway and the Soviet Union both established their respective 200-mile zones in the winter and spring of 1976–7; the Norwegian as an economic zone, the Soviet as an interim fishing zone (formalized in 1984 as an economic zone). The parties were already known to differ on how the boundary between their respective zones should be determined. They had been talking several years previously on ways of dividing the continental shelf in the Barents Sea, that is the seabed and whatever lay below it. They agreed to base initial discussions on the 1958 Continental Shelf Convention. The Convention provided a three-stage rocket of rules regulating how governments should go about determining the border between their respective parts of a continental shelf. First, states can freely determine the boundary *by agreement*. This may sound patently obvious, but the point was to highlight the contractual freedom that applied in this area too, that is that parties can adopt whatever arrangement suits them best without worrying about external parties claiming the agreement is invalid, or indeed, unfair or biased. Second, if the parties cannot agree on a dividing line the *median line principle* will apply, that is a method whereby the dividing line offshore is determined by the direction of the boundary on land. More technically, a median line is a series of points at sea whose distance from land on both sides of the border is the same. Third, if *special circumstances* were to obtain, the Shelf Convention allows states to depart from the median line.

Norway pushed the median line principle in talks with Soviet representatives; the Soviets argued against it, referring to special circumstances. The special circumstances were the area's strategic importance to the Soviet Union – its largest naval fleet, the Northern Fleet, was stationed there with access to the Barents Sea. And there was a significant disparity in population numbers on either side of the border. By then, the Kola Peninsula had over a million inhabitants, more than ten times the number in Finnmark county on the Norwegian side. Moreover, the Soviets had claimed all the islands (and later waters) between the sector lines in the east and west of the Arctic Ocean as early as 1926. A sector line is a line of longitude that starts from the terminus of the land boundary and intersects the North Pole. This, then, was the Soviet Union's official stance vis-à-vis Norway. Put simply, Norway held to the median line principle, the Soviet Union to the sector line principle. Not surprisingly, the principle Norway preferred would give Norway a larger wedge than the Soviet Union, and vice versa.

Recognizing that an immediate solution was not likely, Norway and the Soviet Union agreed to an interim arrangement in parts of the disputed area – quickly baptized in Norway as the Grey Zone (in Russian colloquially referred to as the Joint Area). Within the Grey Zone, Norway could inspect Norwegian boats and third-country vessels with a Norwegian fishing license; the Soviets could control their own vessels and again third-country vessels to which they had given permission to fish. The Grey Zone is often confused with the disputed area, but it was simply a way of organizing the supervision of the two countries' fishing activities; it had nothing to do with oil and gas. Further, the Grey Zone and the disputed area were not coextensive geographically. Admittedly, the Grey Zone did overlap most of the southern parts of the disputed area, but a small wedge extended into undisputed Norwegian waters to the west (i.e. west of the sector line) and a smaller part into the undisputed Soviet waters to the east (east of the median line). This was primarily because

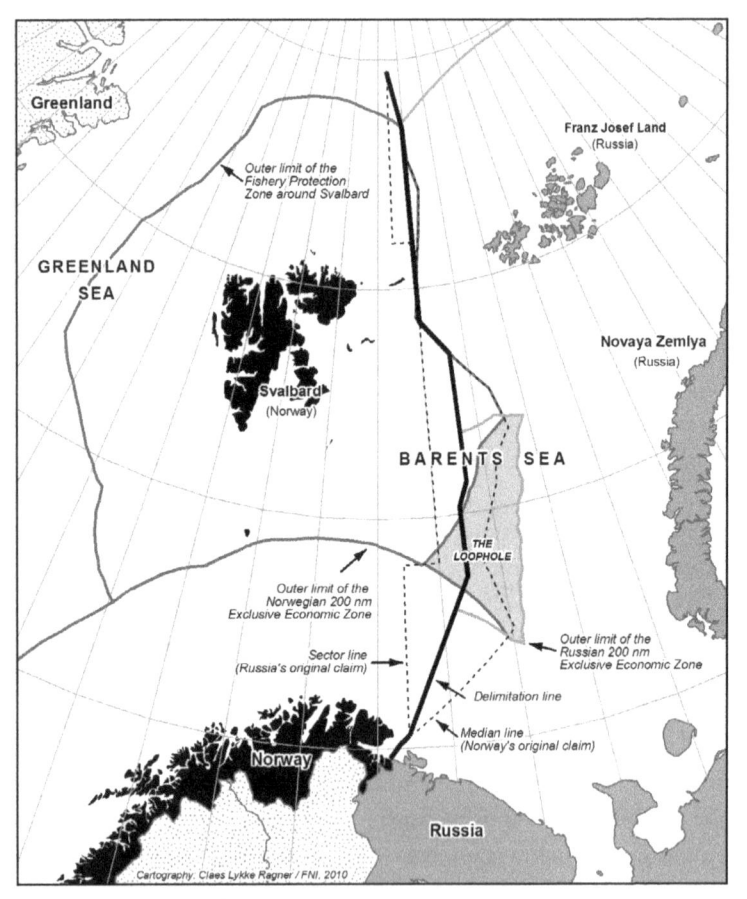

Map 3.1 Zone configuration in the Barents Sea
Source: Fridtjof Nansen Institute

Norway and the Soviet Union wanted the Grey Zone to cover the natural fishing grounds, that is, whole fishing banks without splitting them up.

Following the establishment of the economic zones, the maritime boundary became an item in the negotiations on the division of the shelf in the Barents Sea.[3] For years, Norway and the Soviet Union held talks on the Barents Sea border in deepest secrecy; there was no publicity nor leaks of importance to the media (at least right up until the home straight). All the same, it was widely known that the talks had been moving forward in the final years of the Soviet era, but had stalled again when the Soviet Union fell apart. In an extremely rare public statement from any political source, President Mikhail Gorbachev mentioned the delimitation negotiations when he visited Oslo in June 1991 to receive the Nobel Prize awarded to him the year before. A Norwegian journalist asked him at a press conference how the maritime delimitation talks were going. The parties, he said, had agreed on 80–85 per cent of the delimitation line; only the southernmost part of the line, down to the coast, remained in contention. In other words, the parties had drawn a boundary somewhere between the median line and sector line – a sort of compromise, which is what negotiating is all about. Progress was slow over the next 10 to 15 years, that is until a new coalition government took over in Norway in autumn 2005. The Labour Party's rising star Jonas Gahr Støre was appointed foreign minister and immediately declared the High North as his highest priority. December 2005 saw the start of a new round of boundary talks in Moscow; and it was announced this time in the media. There was no attempt to conceal that talks had recommenced. While the publicity could be construed as tempting fate, it also indicated that an agreement was a distinct possibility.

*

At around midday on 27 April 2010, prime ministers Dmitri Medvedev and Jens Stoltenberg, catching most people off guard, announced during an Oslo press conference that Norway and Russia had reached agreement on the maritime delimitation of the Barents Sea and the Arctic Ocean: 'We have agreed now on every aspect of this forty-year-old issue: the maritime delimitation line',[4] said Stoltenberg. 'The agreement will be based on international law and the Law of the Sea. It is evenly balanced, and will serve both countries.' 'The essence of our policy,' Stoltenberg continued, 'is not speed racing, but cooperation and mutual achievement, and today our two nations have reached an understanding in this regard.' Medvedev added: 'This has been a difficult issue and made cooperation between our countries difficult. Today we have reached agreement. We need to live with our neighbours in friendship and cooperation. Unresolved issues are always a source of tension.' How had they managed to keep news of the delimitation treaty secret, Medvedev was asked. 'In Russia, as you know, the conspiracy traditions are deep-rooted [laughter] and well-practised.'

On 15 September 2010, the Treaty on the Maritime Delimitation and Cooperation in the Barents Sea and Arctic Ocean was duly signed in Murmansk by foreign ministers Sergei Lavrov and Jonas Gahr Støre in the presence of Medvedev and Stoltenberg.[5] It was a compromise and divided the disputed area into two equal parts while also establishing a single common boundary to the continental shelf and economic zones. Entering into force 7 July 2011 it consists of three parts: the border agreement and two annexes on fisheries and 'transboundary hydrocarbon deposits', both of which are integral parts of the treaty. The fisheries appendix broadly commits the parties to the continuance of the Joint Norwegian–Russian Fisheries Commission (see Chapter 4). On a more specific note, the 1975 agreement between Norway and the Soviet Union on cooperation in the fishing industry, and the 1976 agreement concerning mutual relations in the field of fisheries, will remain in force for 15 years after the entry into force of the delimitation treaty. At the end of that period, both agreements will remain in force for successive six-year terms, unless one of the parties notifies the other at least six months before the expiry of the six-year term of its intention to terminate one or both of them. In the previously disputed area within 200 nautical miles from the Norwegian or Russian mainland, the technical regulations concerning, in particular, mesh and minimum catch size, set by each of the parties for their fishing vessels, shall continue to apply for a transitional period of two years from the treaty's entry into force. The appendix concerning transboundary hydrocarbon deposits provides instructions for so-called unitization in the exploitation of transboundary hydrocarbon deposits whereby such deposits shall be exploited as a unit in a way that both parties have agreed on.

'They'll squeeze us out, it'll be the end'

'In their talks with Norway, the Russian delegation failed to invoke Russia's preferential right to a coastline under the 1920 Svalbard Treaty, or to mention the historic borders of Russia's Arctic areas determined in 1926', writes Vyacheslav Zilanov, the author of 'What can Putin do to take the Barents Sea back'; he is former Soviet deputy fisheries minister and now a prominent political commentator in north-west Russia. The agreement, in other words, is seen as the result of negotiations between more or less equal parties – and the Russian side was under no compulsion when it signed over waters rightfully belonging to Russia. The effect of this 'outrageous' treaty could easily be to close off the entire western part of the Barents Sea where the biggest fish stocks are to the Russian fishing industry, leaving it to fish in the much poorer waters further east. It would also allow Norway to tighten the thumbscrews on Russian fishing vessels within the fisheries protection zone around Svalbard, a zone Norway unilaterally put in place in 1977 and Moscow has never officially recognized.

What we today call Svalbard was discovered by the Dutch explorer Willem Barentz in 1596. He was trying to find the Northeast Passage along Russia's northern coast but came to grief on an island with craggy mountains. He called it Spitzbergen. In the following centuries, Spitsbergen (which is the Norwegian and English spelling) attracted hunters from several European countries. Coal deposits were discovered in the late 1800s, and gave rise to the mining industry. It transformed the archipelago in the eyes of the international community from a no man's land of little consequence into a significant political issue. The trigger was something as prosaic as the need to establish a law enforcement agency to police the miners, especially on Saturday nights when they typically ended up in drunken brawls. In the early 1900s, three international conferences were arranged in the Norwegian capital, Kristiania (now: Oslo), on the Spitsbergen question, in 1910, 1912 and 1914 respectively, with the purpose of devising a system of government for the archipelago. It was not primarily about giving any particular nation sovereignty over Spitsbergen (on the contrary, delegates agreed *not* to tread that path) but about burden sharing. Plans for a fourth Spitsbergen conference were scuppered by the outbreak of World War I. At the Paris Peace Conference after the war, the question of Spitsbergen came up almost by accident. Count Wedel Jarlsberg, a rather meddlesome Norwegian envoy, persuaded the great powers to address Spitsbergen's status and give Norway sovereignty over the archipelago, partly in compensation for losses incurred by the Norwegian merchant fleet during the war. It was a politically feasible solution because Moscow, which doubtless would have objected given the archipelago's strategic importance, was not at the Paris Conference. Following the October Revolution of 1917 Russia made its own peace with Germany, and was therefore left out of the settlement talks. But a more important reason was possibly that the Bolsheviks, who had seized power during the final act of the Russian Revolution, were not recognized by the other great powers as Russia's legitimate rulers.

Norwegian jurisdiction over Svalbard came with three important provisos, however. First, military fortifications and any war-related activity were banned. Second, Norway could not impose higher taxation than it cost to govern the archipelago. Third – and this is the bone of contention about the status of the protection zone – citizens and businesses from all the state parties to the Svalbard Treaty should enjoy the same rights as Norwegian citizens and businesses to engage in maritime, mining and commercial activity on the archipelago. The Svalbard Treaty was signed in Paris in 1920 and came into force five years later. At the same time, Norway gave the archipelago the Old Norse name of Svalbard, 'the land of the cold coasts'.

The Soviet Union recognized Norway's sovereignty over Svalbard in 1924, without reservations, and largely because Norway as the first Western nation had recognized the Union of Soviet Socialist Republics as a state. The Union was established officially in 1922, when the Bolsheviks after civil war and economic chaos had consolidated power in most of the old Russian empire. It acceded to the Svalbard Treaty in 1935. The Soviets were already mining coal at a settlement called Grumant (which continued until the early 1960s), and opened new mines in 1932 at Barentsburg and in 1948 at Pyramiden. The Soviet communities and the largest Norwegian one – Longyearbyen, named after the mining community's first owner, John M. Longyear – lived within a stone's throw of each other on Svalbard for decades, but there was minimal contact. It was only in the early 1970s that the first tentative attempts were made to enforce Norwegian jurisdiction in the Soviet towns on what was, after all, indisputable Norwegian territory.[6]

Then came the upheavals in the Law of the Sea in the mid-1970s. The waters around Svalbard are the most important feeding grounds for the Northeast Arctic cod, and it was Norway's political position that it could also establish a lawful economic zone around Svalbard. Norway would be as entitled to oversee fishing activities there as it was in the economic zone around the mainland. But exploratory talks with other states with a tradition of fishing in the Svalbard area resulted in very little support for Norway's policy.[7] The Svalbard Treaty's provisions on equal treatment applied in the waters off Svalbard as well, they protested, not just on land and in the narrow strip of territorial waters along the coast. Norway, however, stuck to the actual wording of the Treaty, which says nothing about extra-territorial waters. That may be so, the other governments argued, but there was no deep-sea fishing in those waters when the treaty was signed in 1920, and if there had been, the area would obviously have been included within the ambit of the Treaty. Both sides of the argument find some support in international law. International tribunals may, after assessing all sides of the argument, choose to interpret the wording analogically, that is, extend the scope of relevant provision to areas about which the wording is silent but whose intended inclusion could reasonably be assumed to have been intended, or which, after taking policy considerations into account, could reasonably be assumed to fall within the scope of the provision.

Norway's middle-of-the-road solution was to create a 200-mile fisheries protection zone around Svalbard. Unlike economic zones, fisheries protection zones are not a clearly defined category under the Law of the Sea. As a practical expedient it is not forbidden as such, but it has no real substance in law. The Soviet Union withheld recognition, and to this day it remains the official Russian view that the waters around Svalbard are international. But the protection zone did provide a measure of protection for the fish in the area. Norway took responsibility for overseeing fishing activities here, something governments of other countries with interests in the area tacitly accepted. Their forbearance ended, however, whenever the Norwegian Coast Guard arrested their vessels (see Chapter 4). If they had not protested, Norwegian jurisdiction would gain legal plausibility, and the equal treatment provision of the Svalbard Treaty sidelined.[8] The Soviet authorities instructed their fishermen not to sign the inspection form used by the Norwegian Coast Guard, though they did allow the Coast Guard to inspect their vessels. As long as they continued to view the fish stocks as a common resource, their approach had a certain logic. Indeed, that the fish stocks in waters around Svalbard were protected benefited not only Norway, but the Soviet Union as well of course. As we shall see in Chapter 4, the Russians later maintained that a gentlemen's agreement had been concluded between Norway and the Soviet Union, whereby Norway inspects Soviet/Russian vessels but refrains from arresting them.[9]

*

Not only will the delimitation agreement in the Barents Sea treaty cost the Russians a great deal of money, according to Zilanov in 'What can Putin do to take the Barents Sea back' – the agreement is patently *unfair*. He wants a 'roadmap for the President', with instructions on how to 'repossess the Barents Sea'. It should include the appointment of a commission of Russian and foreign experts to assess whether the treaty can be said to be *reasonable* in the sense of Law of the Sea requirements. When the commission presents its conclusions, the President may then consider whether to have the treaty modified or amended, or even annulled. There should be a new 'Spitsbergen Conference' of the original signatories to the

Svalbard Treaty with a view to assessing the validity of Norway's fisheries protection zone around Svalbard. Both ideas are controversial from the Norwegian point of view, to put it mildly. The delimitation treaty is, as mentioned, a binding agreement based on the principles of international law on the delimitation of areas of sea between states. Of course, national parliaments do not always ratify treaties, but to go so far as to annul one is virtually unheard of. Nor are commissions usually appointed to consider an agreement's soundness in light of international law. States can agree to whatever boundaries they like, but once the agreement is in force they have to respect it. If being bound by the treaty becomes a cause of concern to one of the signatories, it can withdraw from the agreement if the procedures for doing so are in place. The usual option, however, is simply not to ratify the treaty rather than taking the trouble to annul it. In the event of interpretative disputes, the parties can bring the case before an international court, assuming both agree – either for this particular dispute or by prior agreement – to let a court, such as the International Court of Justice at the Hague, decide the issue. It is the courts which decide whether an agreement complies with the guidelines in international law, not an international commission of experts of the sort Zilanov proposes. And to call for a new 'Spitsbergen Conference' is also a radical ploy politically speaking, even though opinion is divided on whether the treaty applies to the *waters* around Svalbard.

Former president and current Prime Minister Dmitri Medvedev is the implied villain of the piece. The article starts by noting that the agreement 'which was signed during the presidency of Dm. Medvedev in 2010', meant that Russia lost 'huge fishing grounds to Norway'. 'The document', the article continues, 'which was approved by Dm. Medvedev, fails to satisfy the basic principles [under the Law of the Sea] of *justice and fairness*' (emphasis in original). Vladimir Putin, Russia's strong man over the past 15 or so years, you are needed. 'Putin, clear up the mess Medvedev left behind!', the article suggests. To an untrained eye, what the article says about Putin and Medvedev is a mixture of fact and ordinary political opinion. Medvedev happened to be president when Russia and Norway signed the agreement. Putin is in charge now. It was a bad deal for Russia – end of story. But to an eye trained in observation of Russian affairs, there's more to it. The article's author need not have mentioned the presidents by name, or at least to repeat their roles as if to emphasize a point. Medvedev was not personally involved in the negotiations, apart possibly from the run-up to the signing in Oslo on a few spring days in April 2010. The author could have asked the Russian government to look at the agreement again without calling on Putin himself. Medvedev and friendly relations with the West (represented here by Norway) are linked together in the article; reading between the lines, Medvedev comes across as at best naive, at worst a traitor – weaknesses to which Putin, apparently, does not succumb. True, many Russians, it is alleged, prefer having a 'strong man' at the helm – macho Putin against brainy, flabby Medvedev – but there is more to it than that. Putin is a 'real Russian' – indeed, many would call him an 'ideal Russian', echoing the sentiments of a song performed by a female singer during Putin's first term as president. Russian men are hopeless, she sings, 'What I want is a man like Putin, a man like Putin, full of strength, a man like Putin, who keeps off the bottle'.[10] Now, Medvedev is not known to be a drunkard either, but many Russians do feel there is something indefinably alien about him. Like the last Soviet leader, Mikhail Gorbachev, he is a man the West could 'do business with'. Can the Russians trust someone who gets on so easily with foreigners? Is he really one of them?

*

'So what d'you think? Is he having us on – or is he serious?' a colleague of mine had noted on a printout of a piece in a Russian newspaper that he had put in my pigeon hole a month after the signing of the agreement. 'They'll elbow us out eventually', predicted the article's headline in the business paper *Vzglyad*.[11] My colleague knew that Vyacheslav Zilanov, the primary source of the story of Norwegian plans to despatch the Russians from the

Barents Sea, was an acquaintance of mine and was wondering if I could explain what it all meant. A prank, perhaps? Or a massive misunderstanding?

'We've lost 90,000 square kilometres and the opportunity to fish in the western parts of the Barents Sea', said Zilanov, now deputy head of the Federal Russian Fisheries Agency's public chamber (a public committee all Russian federal authorities are obliged to have), and vice president of the All Russian Association of Fishing Enterprises and Fish Exporters (VARPE). Zilanov was exasperated with Russia's surrender of half of the previously disputed area with Norway and concerned about the huge losses to the Russian fishing industry as a result. While 210,000–215,000 tonnes are fished annually on average in the area east of the dividing line, 300,000–315,000 tonnes are taken in the area to the west. What's more, Zilanov protests, the waters around Svalbard – under the terms of the delimitation agreement – will all fall under Norwegian jurisdiction. 'We have lost territory, 60,000–90,000 square kilometres. We have lost the chance of fishing in the whole of the western Barents Sea – if not today, then tomorrow. They're going to force us out. It will be the end.'

> Interviewer: Did I understand you properly [when you said] the Svalbard Treaty is still in force, but only Norway can specify the fishery rules? That's to say, the Norwegians can easily 'throttle' our fisheries by, for example, banning 'outdated' fishing methods used by our Russian fishermen?
>
> Zilanov: We don't use 'outdated' methods. We use different methods to catch ground fish and pelagic fish in the Barents Sea: bottom and pelagic trawls, long lines and nets. The fisheries of Russia and Norway are asymmetric. What does that mean? Russia catches 95 per cent of its fish with bottom trawls and 5 per cent by line. The Norwegians use lines to catch 70 per cent; trawling only accounts for 30 per cent. So of course the Norwegians can introduce new rules

on trawlers and say 'this isn't discriminatory because they apply to Norwegian fishermen as well'. But our fishing fleet will bear the brunt. That was the first example. Example number two: Norway could ban bottom trawls in its waters. That would be the end of the Russian fisheries.

[...]

Interviewer: The agreement is hailed in Norway as a huge victory over Russia. Do you have any comments?

Zilanov: I wouldn't put it like that, that Norway has triumphed over Russia. We're not a an easily vanquished country. Let me put it like this. What Norway has done in the negotiations with the Russian Foreign Ministry is a glittering diplomatic, political and economic achievement. [...] No one with any practical experience was included in the Russian delegation, only officials who don't know the difference between Novaya Zemlya and Bear Island. [...] And there's another thing. This important intergovernmental document contains palpable grammatical and substantive errors. It feels like somebody was a bit unlucky with the translation – I don't know from what language – or the more likely explanation, it was all done by unprofessional people who had no conception of what they were signing.

Zilanov, in a later interview, expanded on his criticism of the treaty's language.[12] When the agreement speaks of mesh size – 'mesh size of what exactly', Zilanov wonders, 'trawls or nets?' And when it refers to 'the minimum [size of catches]',[13] he parries, 'minimum of what exactly – whales, fish, shellfish, crabs?' He also asks why the agreement fails to specify the coordinates of the disputed area. 'Are we supposed to get together with fishermen to solve the puzzle? "Oh no," the Norwegians are going to say, "you've got it all wrong; you're getting it completely back to front, this is the mesh size for drift nets, nor for trawls." I've discovered multiple examples of this kind of mumbo jumbo.' The points Zilanov is making here exemplify a long-standing difference between Norwegian and Russian legal prose. The Russians have predilection for minutiae, the Norwegians prefer brevity – and as simply phrased as possible with a view to helping ordinary people understand legal complexities. And anyway, why would one want to include the coordinates of a once disputed area in the treaty now that a new border was in place?

*

In the first few days following the signing of the agreement, the Russian media carried reports of the Oslo press conference with Medvedev and Stoltenberg and analyzed the background to the settlement. The gist of the analysis was: Norway was desperate to acquire new oil fields, and Russia wanted to get Norwegian support in its fight for the Arctic shelf, primarily against Canada (see Chapter 2) – hence the settlement. Some of the first comments on the delimitation treaty in the Russian newspapers refer to discord between Norway and Russia on fishery-related matters. *Kommersant*, for instance, writes: 'Completely unexpectedly, the leaders of Russia and Norway announced on 27 April that they had resolved an old dispute that has cost Russian fishermen 'quantities of blood, not to mention frayed nerves'.[14] Having explained that the dispute over the boundary had caused no significant problems historically, the quarrel, alleges the paper, 'did eventually lead to the wilful arrest of Russian fishing vessels in the disputed area', often for 'trivial offenses' as a result of 'the obstinacy of the Norwegian border protection service'. (For the record, Norwegian authorities have never arrested Russian vessels in the disputed area, so the author must be mixing the situation in the disputed area with the Svalbard zone.)

Norwegian and Russian fishery regulations are beset by 'numerous inconsistencies', writes *Rossiyskaya Gazeta* in its 28 April edition (an unfounded allegation as it happens; most monitoring and control procedures were harmonized in the 1990s). These contradictions include the 135 mm mesh size required by

Norway against Russia's 125 mm. (Russia and Norway split the difference in 2009; 130 mm is the size required by both countries.) Norway even arrests Russian vessels for using nets with a width of 125 mm (also not correct).[15] But the article is not entirely negative. It mentions some of the more positive things Russian fishermen can expect from the boundary agreement. For example, by adopting 'a uniform set of regulations for the fisheries [which had in fact nothing to do with the boundary agreement; a common set of regulations evolved over many years] the Norwegian Coast Guard will no longer be able to fine Russian fishermen significantly more than Norwegian fishermen for the same offence, a system which has been benefiting the Norwegian fishing industry no end.'

The tone sharpened around the time of the signing of the treaty. 'Today', declared the title of an article from the news agency *Regnum* on 15 September, the day the agreement was signed, 'Russia is giving Norway a chunk of the Barents Sea.'[16] In its 22 September edition *Argumenty i fakty* fired off the following salvo: 'Right up to the last minute, Norway did not believe the agreement would be signed, but Russia took this step which today is being described as a gigantic capitulation, even indeed an act of treachery.'[17] Vyacheslav Zilanov tells the newspaper, 'Seventy per cent of the Russian fishing fleet's annual catch is taken in waters where Norway from now on will have jurisdiction. Our fishing fleet will be consigned to an ice-filled backwater in the most eastern part of the Barents Sea.'

Like so many others, Vasili Nikitin, Director General of the Fishing Industry Union of the North, draws attention to the Soviet sector declaration from 1926 to explain the actual meaning of jurisdiction in the Barents Sea. The old declaration has still 'not been formally revoked', but with the treaty in hand, the Norwegians have all the 'leverage' they want to run Russian fishermen off the most abundant fishing grounds in the Barents Sea. Referring to the idea that the Russian fleet will never be able to meet the stringent Norwegian requirements, he concludes in some style, 'They will say to us: "We're not throwing you out, you've just got to be tall, well-built and fair-haired!'"[18] Only Nordics, in other words, may apply.

*

In an extensive piece in the 29 September 2010 edition of *Nord-News*, Zilanov offers a more detailed account of his take on the delimitation line and management of the Barents Sea fisheries.[19] The article's title is 'Lavrov and Støre's great breakthrough in the Barents Sea: A carbon copy of the Baker–Shevardnadze breakthrough in the Bering Sea.' He is referring to the 1990 Soviet–US Maritime Boundary Agreement establishing the boundary in the Bering Sea between the US and the Soviet Union. Most view it in Russia as an act of betrayal by Soviet foreign minister (and native of Georgia) Eduard Shevardnadze in agreeing to waive the sector line principle. There was no time to ratify the treaty before the Soviet Union collapsed, and it has not been ratified since by the Russian authorities.

Zilanov attacks the boundary agreement first under the paragraph heading 'The devil's in the details'. But what are these details, he asks. Well,

> Why don't the boundary agreement and appendices say anything about the fate of the fishing grounds that fall within the scope of 1920 Spitsbergen Treaty? Why is there not a single word about the fate of the borders of Russia's Arctic Ocean dependencies from 1926, which no one has annulled and which are on every map, not only Russian but foreign as well?

'I myself', Zilanov goes on, 'have defended my homeland's fishery interests as a member of more than 35 years' standing of the Russian delegation to the delimitation talks'. However, 'the precipitate events of the past five years have occurred without the participation of fishermen, experts or practitioners in Russia's northern fishery basin.' From his time as a negotiator he remembers

Norway presenting from the start an 'extraordinarily covetous median line proposal' even though they 'were well aware of the borders of our Arctic Ocean dependencies of 1926', and knew the Soviets 'would insist on the principle of fairness'. In the following years Norwegians let it be known 'in the corridors' that they would be going for a 50–50 division of the disputed area, which the Soviet leadership and the Russian Federation's first two presidents – Boris Yeltsin and Vladimir Putin – had the nerve to reject.

> [By the early 1970s] it was obvious to me that the Norwegian team had a well-defined, long-term national goal, namely to win acceptance for the median line principle as the basis for how the division of the continental shelf and the exclusive economic zones (which we then called fishery zones) should proceed. Their goal was to get the median line principle adopted in some document or another, if only informally and temporarily. And it can't be denied, they succeeded beyond belief [with the Grey Zone Agreement of 1978]. They are harvesting the fruits of this approach with their policy statement on the delimitation line: 50–50 split. So the question is, 'What area exactly is to be divided?' As it turns out, it is the area [measured] from the median line.

There is something suspicious about the Russian leadership, Zilanov seems to be hinting, for even accepting the Norwegian demand to base negotiations on the median line principle. (His annoyance would have been more understandable if the Russians had accepted the median line as the *outcome* of the negotiations.) The Norwegians are acting increasingly unilaterally in the Joint Fisheries Commission, Zilanov adds. The creation of a fisheries protection zone around Svalbard is a special case (an area to which he consistently refers as that 'covered by the Spitsbergen Treaty of 1920'). Acting on its own again, Norway increased the minimum size of mesh and fish in 1990; until then the parties had been content to have a uniform regulatory approach in the Barents Sea. After the collapse of the Soviet Union, Norwegian policy has increasingly aimed at 'impeding the work of the Russian fleet in the western Barents Sea and around Svalbard'. Under the headline 'Iraq syndrome in Russian overfishing' he takes issue with Norwegian allegations of Russian overfishing in the years 2002–8. Just as the Iraq war was in vain because the Americans found neither nuclear nor bacteriological weapons in Iraq, Norwegian allegations of Russian overfishing proved unfounded.[20] Russian fishermen were 'whipped monstrously' during these years, and inquiries were made at the highest level in Russia: 'Get those criminal fishermen out!' During the space of seven years Russian fishermen were supposed to have overfished their quotas by as much as 760,000 tonnes; in money terms between one and one and a half billion dollars. So why hadn't the market reacted? If the allegations of massive overfishing had been correct, prices would have fallen immediately. But they didn't. And apart from that, how would the fish stocks have survived this level of overfishing? The scientists say the cod population has grown consistently throughout the period during which this overfishing apparently took place. The seminal question is why the Norwegians wanted to start the debacle in the first place. It was obviously to 'compromise the Russian fishing industry in the eyes of the European market, making it difficult for our fishermen to sell their products. This is what's known as getting rid of a rival by means of "squeaky clean" methods.'

*

Criticism of the treaty was not a flash in the pan; it rumbled on and effectively delayed Russian ratification. The arguments noted above were rehearsed in an open letter to Foreign Minister Lavrov, 17 May, and to President Medvedev, 8 September. 'The coastal population in Russia's regions', warned the writers of the letter to Medvedev, 'will suffer harshly, socially and economically', if something isn't done to renegotiate the deal so that the interests of Russian fishermen are better protected. 'Revered Dmitri Anatolevich, do not forget the astute saying "measure seven times, cut once", nor the first commandment of our fishing fleet captains: "danger is never far away".'[21]

In October 2010, the Committee on Natural Resources Use and Agricultural Sector of the Murmansk regional Duma discussed the delimitation treaty. The event was reported by *Nord-News*, 18 October.[22] Several specialists from the regional fisheries were in attendance and repeated their arguments against ratification. In support of the alleged Norwegian plot to eject Russian fishermen from the western part of the Barents Sea, the lessons of the Bering Sea were mentioned. Although Russia has not ratified the Baker–Shevardnadze Agreement, Washington has used it to justify a number of unilateral measures, the effect of which has been to consign Russian fishermen to the worst fishing grounds, leaving them with only 'memories of fishing'. The same thing happened when Canada established its economic zone in 1976. They didn't actually throw the Soviet fishermen out, but the new regulatory regime was so rigorous, it just didn't pay to fish in Canadian waters. They are apprehensive the same thing could happen in the Barents Sea – indeed, there are tendencies in that direction already. Norway is pulling its own fishermen out of the Russian zone of the Barents, says Vasili Nikitin, Director General of the Fishing Industry Union of the North; it's only a matter of time before they tell the Russians to leave the Norwegian zone. Within two to three years, the Joint Norwegian–Russian Fisheries Commission will have lost its *raison d'être*. To back his argument, Nikitin points to the success of the 'greens' campaign in Norway to get the government to consider outlawing bottom trawling.

Igor Saburov, member of the Murmansk Regional Duma, remains uncommitted and asks the experts to say whether the Russian vessels can start using the longline method instead. In response, Andrei Ivanov, chair of the Committee on Natural Resources Use and Agricultural Sector, says converting the ships to line catching would cost half a billion dollars. Moreover, longline fishing has problems of its own, says Yuri Lepesevich, research director at the Knipovich Polar Research Institute of Marine Fisheries and Oceanography (PINRO). More small fish are caught and it has an adverse effect on seabirds and marine mammals. Nikitin is anxious: Norway could decide to relocate an established control point on the Norwegian–Russian border (where foreign fishermen have to report before fishing in the respective economic zones) closer to Tromsø, the city where 'Russian fishermen are taken by the Norwegian Coast Guard to face legal proceedings'. As they see it, Norway wants to 'streamline' the prosecution of Russian fishermen. It does not augur well, according to board chairman Vitali Kasatkin of the Fishing Industry Union of the North, 'these expressions of elation on the part of the Norwegians after the signing of the boundary agreement [...] as could be seen at the session of the Joint Norwegian–Russian Fisheries Commission'. The Duma committee then adopted a resolution urging the State Duma and Federation Council (the two chambers of the Federal Assembly, Russia's parliament) not to ratify the delimitation treaty. In the Regional Duma itself, the proposal also won a majority – but not unanimity.

Our common kitchen garden

On the same day the delimitation agreement was announced, former governor of Murmansk oblast, Yuri Yevdokimov, draws a generally sympathetic picture of Norwegian–Russian relations in an article titled 'This is Russia and Norway's promising kitchen garden':[23] 'Now that Russia and Norway are doing such a lot of things together, like extracting deposits in the Shtokman field [which was still at a preparatory stage] and the global nuclear safety measures, God himself has commanded us to get rid of the inconsistencies in the Grey Zone.' ('Grey Zone' is used incorrectly here for the disputed area; as we have seen, the two are not wholly co-extensive.) Yevdokimov admits he is not conversant with the details of the agreement and its likely impact, but he is confident the Russian negotiators have done what they can to defend Russian interests in the best possible way. Asked by a journalist whether Russia might not have got a better deal if they had played on the fact that Norway has practically run out of oil, Yevdokimov says:

No, that's not how I see it. The Norwegians are our neighbours – indeed, our very good neighbours – even if they do belong to a different defence alliance. They have extensive experience of working on the shelf. They have the gear and the technology. We don't. The sooner we can benefit from their lead, the better it will be for both countries. Apart from that, it was important for Russia and Norway to reach an agreement at this point in time. Many countries are looking at the disputed areas of the shelf, even countries with no connections to the sea. Everyone has something they would like to do there. In reality, the Barents Sea is our kitchen garden, useful today and promising for the future, because we are the only ones who border these immensely prolific waters. Now we have agreed that we alone can operate as rulers here, and we alone can set the rules of the game.

One month after the Murmansk Regional Duma had adopted a declaration that urged the Russian federal parliament not to ratify the delimitation agreement with Norway, the declaration was quietly withdrawn 'without explanation', according to *Nord-News*.[24] When a reporter asked what the reason was, Zilanov said, 'I can only tell you what I think. The federal government, Moscow, may have leaned [on the Regional Duma]. Besides, the voting in our State Duma makes it clear where the pressure came from.' He is probably referring to the decision of the presidential party United Russia, which had a majority in the Duma, which voted for a retreat. In a long interview with *Murmanski Vestnik*, 18 November 2010, Evgeni Nikora, then Speaker of the Murmansk Regional Duma, his deputy and United Russia faction leader, Igor Saburov, and Andrei Ivanov, chair of the Committee on Natural Resources Use and Agricultural Sector, are lavish in their praise of the boundary agreement.[25] Two months have passed, the article begins, since the agreement was signed. 'Passions have died down, and we can reflect more deeply about what the deal, after all, can give us.' 'The agreement', says the Speaker, 'is historic in character'; a 'serious step in a positive direction [and] a new platform for cooperation', his deputy adds. 'While Russians need to keep a close eye on how the Norwegians behave', says Igor Saburov, they 'should not anticipate anything untoward'. Last month's resolution by the Regional Duma was premature. Further delays in ratification would only give the Norwegians 'unhealthy food' to bring up in the talks ahead. 'Let's see how the agreement works in practice before we do anything', is the advice. The chair of the Committee on Natural Resources Use and Agricultural Sector explains why he changed his mind:

> Having had several important meetings in Moscow, I came to the conclusion that fishing is not the most important thing in this respect, not by a long way. The big issue is the division of the Arctic shelf; the 'race for the Arctic' has a lot of competitors already. We also need to remember the implications on the strategic national interests of the whole country, and our children and grandchildren will hopefully be grateful for the decisions we make today. The agreement will, of course, be ratified, but the work of correcting it is already in progress. We and Norway 'breathe in sync' in many areas. We understand each other, just as the residents of the [Soviet] communal apartments [*kommunalki*; council tenements where several families shared the same kitchen and bathroom] would argue and then make up again. If a broken gas valve needed replacing, they pulled together – because if the flap fell out, none of them would be safe. I don't think we should worry too much whether the Norwegians are going to institute particularly draconian measures. They are a reasonable people and would never do anything like that.

*

The State Duma ratified the delimitation treaty on 25 March 2011. Three hundred and nine Duma members (all of whom were members of United Russia) voted in favour of ratification, while the 141 representatives from other parties abstained.

The principle of fairness, the ultimate betrayal

Two very different perceptions of what constitutes Russia's relations with its north-western neighbour are reflected above; let me use Vyacheslav Zilanov and Yuri Yevdokimov, both long-time observers of joint Norwegian–Russian ventures in the North, as representatives of the respective approaches. Zilanov has been involved in the joint Russian–Norwegian fisheries management system since it began in the mid-1970s. He led the Soviet delegation to the Joint Commission for several years in the 1980s and has since been a fisheries advisor to the Federation Council and the Governor of Murmansk. He has retained close ties with the Norwegian fisheries community, and visits Norway regularly. Yevdokimov, for his part, was the first elected Governor of Murmansk oblast. That was in 1996, but he was re-elected three times before President Medvedev fired him in 2009. Various reasons were given by the president's administration and party United Russia, but he was mainly accused of being too chummy by half with the Scandinavian countries. Medvedev had allegedly given him 'one last warning' and told him to concentrate on domestic problems instead of 'fooling around abroad'.[26] Yevdokimov had indeed spent time and effort promoting cooperation with the Nordic countries in the Barents region, and was even appointed Commander of the Royal Norwegian Order of Merit by Norwegian King Harald in 2007.

According to Zilanov, the delimitation agreement was bad for Russia. First, because the Russian leaders had given ocean territory to Norway that rightly belonged to Russia. Second, the treaty would effectively banish the Russian fishing fleet from the richest fishing grounds in the Barents Sea, leaving them with the 'ice-filled backwaters' in the eastern part of the sea. The first allegation is demonstrably incorrect; the second disputable at best. The bit of the Barents Sea Norway got as a result of the delimitation treaty did not belong to Russia; it was internationally recognized as *disputed* territory, and both countries accepted that the disagreement could only be solved by negotiation. Zilanov disregards this fact, preferring instead to cite a declaration from 1926 delineating Soviet Arctic possessions to prove that the waters east of the sector line were Russian. Disregarding subsequent dramatic developments in the Law of the Sea, he refers to the sector principle as *the principle of fairness*, unknown for what reason. The claim that Russia will lose fishing grounds as a result of the agreement is unfounded. Norway has the legal right to bar foreign fishing boats from the Norwegian economic zone, but it has no *interest* in doing so. The mature cod are found in the western parts of the Barents Sea and it is clearly in Norway's interest that as much as possible is fished here rather than in the ice-filled eastern waters, where the fish are much smaller. In addition, it is better for Norway if the Russians fish in the Norwegian zone because Norway can keep an eye on what they are doing. In the Russian economic zone, policing and enforcement of the regulations are believed to be less stringent.[27] Be that as it may, the point is that the delimitation agreement has not changed any of this; it merely adds a small slice of water to the Norwegian economic zone (as indeed it does to the Russian zone, too). Norway could have expelled the Russians from the Norwegian zone any time in the past, but never did. Russian fishermen have depended on Norwegian 'good will' for nearly 40 years to operate in the best fishing areas of the Barents Sea, areas which are much larger and richer than the part of the disputed area which is now Norwegian.[28] Finally, Zilanov seems to be implying that Norway's 'victory over Russia' in the delimitation question has given Norway the confidence to act in the disputed protection zone around Svalbard as it sees fit. As one of the participants in the debate put it, Norway doesn't have to close off the Svalbard zone to foreign fishing vessels, it can simply require fishermen to be 'tall, well-built and fair-haired' – a metaphor for what Russians see as an overly precautious regulatory environment. As long as the talks went on, Russia had a card up its sleeve. 'If you tighten the screw in the protection zone, we'll pay you back in the delimitation negotiations.' In this sense, the dividing line could actually be seen as making a difference. But even that idea depends on Norway *wanting* to act unilaterally and without consideration.

Zilanov inscribes himself into a narrative in which Russia is always pitted against shrewd, calculating Westerners. The plot of the story is that incompetent Russian negotiators fell prey to the clever Norwegians, and the Russians will therefore be wiped off the strategically and economically important part of the Barents Sea map. It is a 'tragedy' in Ringmar's (2006) sense, where the narrator assumes the role of the hero who – proudly and passionately – rebels against the established order (the current political leadership in Russia; Russia's pragmatic approach to the West) and relentlessly fights for his country's interests, only to see himself marginalized in the political play. Even his likeminded comrades in the Regional Duma saw their views on the delimitation agreement turned upside-down after a quick trip to Moscow; he and his allies are forcefully driven back. The West is established as the significant Other, but the external othering westwards is not of a particularly malign character. Norway is presented as a foreign country that simply pursues its own economic interests; what they did in the delimitation talks with Russia was 'a glittering diplomatic, political and economic achievement'. It is what any country would strive for, rather than a palpable act of evil – but more of this in Chapter 4.

There are other forms of othering here, too, internal othering and othering in time. Zilanov repeatedly draws a line between the new delimitation agreement and the old Soviet declaration of its Arctic possessions. Implicitly, he 'others' the entire time span between these two events, a period during which the Law of the Sea changed considerably, especially from the late 1950s and, in particular, the mid-1970s – developments he himself has witnessed, and participated in. He forgets to mention Russia's global commitments under the 1958 Continental Shelf Convention and the 1982 Law of the Sea Convention; instead, he refers to the unilateral Soviet declaration of 1926 which established what he calls the *principle of fairness*. Since subsequent events are by implication *unfair*, Zilanov has tasked himself with the restoration of the old order. It is a quest for a certain form of Russian identity, a national self-image of Russia as independent, prepared and proud, as opposed to weak, unpatriotic and subservient to or envious of the West. It might not be a conscious, calculated strategy – or even a genuine fear that Norway will go mad in its desire to dominate the Barents Sea – but in its reference to past pride and future doom, the story about the big compromise between Russia and the West is given a recognizable and meaningful coherence, assembled with the various pieces available in this narrative toolbox, for this specific place, at this specific time.

Zilanov's argumentation includes moreover a strong internal othering, implicating other Russian interest groups, other Russian individuals. Former president Medvedev is the big villain of the story, Putin the hero, the saviour. Medvedev gave territory away; Putin will hopefully get it back. Medvedev's name is irrevocably linked to the cession of land, the ultimate betrayal. Behind Medvedev stands a line of incompetent Russian negotiators – notably from the Ministry of Foreign Affairs – who 'don't know the difference between [Russian] Novaya Zemlya and [Norwegian] Bear Island', are capable of 'palpable grammatical and substantive errors', mutter all kinds of 'mumbo jumbo', and had 'no conception of what they were signing'. In Russian politics, the Ministry of Foreign Affairs is considered, not unsurprisingly, to be one of the most outward- (and westward-) looking political institutions in the country, as opposed to, for example, the power structures, where the Eurasian (see Chapter 1) outlook dominates (Mankoff 2012). The Russian fisheries establishment is also believed to be rather 'inward-looking', concerned, among other things, with reducing the export of Russian fish and increasing supplies to the home market (Hønneland 2004; Jørgensen 2009). The internal othering in this specific case is more malign than the external othering. While Norway's behaviour is fully understandable, the Russian negotiators either would not or could not defend Russian interests (the former, of course, being the far more suspicious of the two) and instead orchestrated 'a gigantic capitulation'. Beware of foreigners, beware of the new times; this narrator speaks Russia 'inwards, backwards'.

Former Governor Yevdokimov calls the Barents Sea 'Russia and Norway's promising kitchen garden', where 'God himself commanded us to get rid of inconsistencies'. The Norwegians are 'our good neighbours – indeed, our very good neighbours'. Upon their return from Moscow where they were whipped into line, members of the Murmansk Regional Duma praise the delimitation treaty. It is 'a serious step in a positive direction', they say, and 'a new platform for cooperation'. There is no reason to 'anticipate anything untoward' from the Norwegians; they are not going to 'institute particularly draconian measures'; they are 'a reasonable people'. In fact, Russians and Norwegians 'breathe in sync', and understand each other like the residents of the Soviet *kommunalka*, where people fight but make up, where they are acutely aware of how much they depend on each other, and offer help when necessary. The plot of the story is that 'we thought our negotiators had betrayed us and we initiated this incredible hullabaloo in the Regional Duma, but we were fooled by our emotions and luckily our leaders in Moscow cleared up the misunderstanding – our grandchildren will be grateful to us for that'. The plot structure is that of the *comedy*, where oppositions and misunderstandings are resolved in the course of the narrative thanks to some fortuitous intervention, where the different twists and turns eventually lead up to a happy ending. The common good prevailed, the catastrophe averted. In hindsight, back from Moscow, cool-headed and relaxed – 'we count ourselves lucky and can laugh about what happened'. The specific kind of Russianness reflected in this narrative is the image of Russians as playful, unpredictable, emotional and game for a lark (see Chapter 1), as opposed to the boring rationality of the West.

The 'kitchen garden narrative' is rather weak in its othering. It goes with the genre; comedy ridicules, but more subtly. This specific comedy is light-hearted; there are the mellow Moscow heroes, who gently intervene when misunderstandings reach a level of absurdity, but there are no real villains. Yet the Norwegians are not unconditional 'friends' either. Yes, they are good neighbours – very good neighbours even – but they 'do belong to a different defence alliance'. And while nothing untoward should be expected, 'Russians need to keep a close eye on how the Norwegians behave'. The West is not an enemy here and now, but they cannot be fully trusted.

But is it really a comedy, this story about the naughty Duma members from Murmansk who were summoned to Moscow to be reprimanded by the headmaster? Isn't the unexpected praise for the treaty a bit 'over the top'? The agreement isn't just 'ok after all', according to the reborn Duma members; it is suddenly 'historical in character'. Might the unexpected level of praise for the delimitation treaty, and the story about how the Duma members changed their opinion overnight, actually be a satire, a genre that assumes an ironic distance to the world, turns plot structures inside-out, upside-down? One possible interpretation is that the Regional Duma members dared challenge the political establishment in Moscow, but quickly realized they had nothing to show against Putin and his men, and returned home with their proverbial tails between their legs. Instead of expressing their (assumed) frustration or (any amount of) remaining doubt upon return home, they engage in a convulsive tribute to muscovite wisdom. Well aware that regional authorities enjoy practically no authority in Putin's Russia, and that their own Duma seats in reality depend on federal goodwill, there is no other narrative option than hallelujah and applause, the implicit satire. Continued protest isn't just against the interest of individual Duma members; it is something there is (practically) no word for. This is also a story of Russian absurdity, just like the comedy, but of a more malign sort. It is the story of Russian lawlessness, lack of democratic values and respect for the individual's (including the politician's) autonomy. It is the story of a Russia where criticism isn't tolerated, at least if you have even the modest level of political ambition; where lying in public isn't condemned (either by the narrator or the audience), but expected. It is the story, as we said in Chapter 1, of a country 'where everything that can go wrong, will go wrong'. The satire, in turn, isn't necessarily (and in our case probably isn't) an open and conscious ridicule. As I imagine it, the regional politicians seem neither explicitly or implicitly disillusioned when they inform the local press about the happy news from Moscow; that would be a breach with narrative convention.

*

There is no material reason why Russian fishers would oppose the delimitation agreement with Norway; it doesn't change the *quota ratios* or any other important aspect of the bilateral fisheries management regime. It only gives Norway the opportunity to *inspect* Russian fishing vessels in a *marginally larger area* of the Barents Sea than before – and Russia to inspect Norwegian vessels in an equally larger area. By repeating the story of the dismantling of old Soviet practices, how the Cold War never really came to an end, 'Soviet' identity is re-created and maintained in the form of a tragedy. The post-Soviet period has been a 'formative moment' in Russian history when new metaphors have been launched, when new stories have been told about Russia's place in the world, when what passes as meaningful is 'up for grabs' – and, some would say, Russia has lost face geopolitically. Zilanov and his companions perform a forceful defence of traditional Russian (at least Soviet) identity, in the face of radical change: Something's wrong – we don't know exactly what, but it's something about the new times, things going too fast. To come to grips with this fluidity, the opponents of the delimitation agreement – consciously or subconsciously knowing how a story is expected to be composed – read into the plot a structure that it, strictly speaking, does not have, crafting a story that hangs together, makes sense and gives your actions credibility; narrating a sense of meaningfulness here and now, in-between past and future.

The comedy-slash-satire is less prevalent in the public debate about the delimitation treaty; it is also 'lighter' and less tangible than the forceful tragedy. The story of the Duma members who happily return from Moscow with new insight about a bright future, is more difficult to grasp. The explicit shorthand plot of this story is the same whether we understand it as a comedy or a satire: 'misunderstandings cleared up, everything fine now'. The *implicit* plot of the satire variant is, 'Hey, this is Russia, you know how it is.' Inherent here are different expressions of Russian absurdity, either good or bad.[29] It is the Russia where people are able to, and sometimes forced to, change position at the drop of a hat; where black and white predominate the narrative platter; where narrative convention fosters categorical expression rather than doubt and nuance – though the inherent plot of the story is that in Russia reality is never what meets the eye. It is a Russia where everything is seen through a veil, where the colours are unclear, where black is white and right is wrong, where stories circulate at ever-greater speed. Where you can't do anything but freeze the frame, live in the present, raise the glass.

Societal fluidity is tackled at a distance, as it were, but in recognizable patterns. The narrated sense of meaningfulness is, in fact, a Russia of meaninglessness.

CHAPTER 4

MANAGEMENT OF MARINE RESOURCES

Just before the Joint Norwegian–Russian Fisheries Commission was to hold its annual session in autumn 1999, marine scientists at the International Council for the Exploration of the Sea (ICES) announced that errors had been made in their calculations of the number of Northeast Arctic cod.[1] With the revised figures in hand, and a declining cod stock, they had no alternative but to reduce the recommended quotas from 490,000 tonnes in 1999 to 110,000 tonnes in 2000. The news shocked the Norwegian fishing industry, not so much because ICES had lowered the recommended quota, but *by the size of the reduction.*

During the Commission's session in Murmansk in November that year, the Norwegian delegation proposed giving the assembled scientists as much time as possible to explain the severity of the decline in the fish stock. The first day in plenary is typically spent on the agenda and probing the parties' initial policies on the various matters to be discussed in the working groups over the following days. The Norwegian scientists spent more than an hour explaining the scientific basis for ICES's quota recommendations and why the Commission should act accordingly. A Russian scientist then mounted the podium. In less than two minutes and with minimal scientific evidence to back up his claim, he told the meeting there was no substantive reason for reducing the quota. He looked somewhat bedraggled and the Norwegian scientists said later it was a tragedy to see how the professional integrity of their Russian colleagues was undermined by their own head of delegation. The head of the Russian delegation on this occasion was a young shipowner from Kaliningrad, not much older than 30.

During breaks, the Norwegian Commission members had a chance to catch up with the regional newspapers. The lead story knocked them sideways. By proposing to cut the Barents Sea quotas so drastically, the headlines thundered, Norway was attempting to put Russia out of business. They had persuaded their Western cronies at ICES to agree to an artificially low quota; now you see the result! What they want is to hit Russia as hard as possible because it is always in a state's interest to harm another state. Even if it makes it worse for yourself, as long as the other state suffers more, it is worth the effort. Norway is a wealthy nation that can offset the lower quotas by boosting the production of farmed fish; Russia is in the grips of a damaging financial crisis and entirely dependent on fishing to maintain social stability in the north-west. Let it be known: we have not a single fish to give away.

It was a worrying day for the Norwegian Commission members, albeit memorable. (I was there myself.) There was chaos in the corridors as members of the Russian delegation jumped around with aggressive journalists who were trying almost physically to cart off Norwegian negotiators to their editorial offices for interrogation; a more than half-drunk Russian interpreter was sitting and weeping in the hallway – he hated his job so much (and was eventually relieved of it). Further down the corridor a well-known regional politician was hitting the air with clenched fists, shouting, 'Down with Norway! Down with Norway!'

The Norwegian delegation left the negotiating room. For the first time in the history of the Norwegian–Russian Fisheries Commission, negotiations had collapsed in mid flow.

Our common future

The rich marine resources of the Barents Sea have traditionally sustained human habitation along its shores, especially in northern Norway and the Arkhangelsk region of Russia. After the 1917 Russian Revolution, the city of Murmansk on the Kola Peninsula became the nerve centre of the Barents Sea fishing industry in Russia. One element of the Soviet push to industrialize the economy after World War I involved 'colonizing' the Kola Peninsula, a process which accelerated rapidly in the early 1930s. Within the space of a few decades, the population multiplied from a few thousand to well over a million. Fishing was main industry, at least in the city of Murmansk. Most of the important fishing associations and processing plants had been set up in the 1920s, followed by the construction of a reasonably modern trawler fleet. After World War II, the fleet sailed the seven seas — or at least the seas off the coast of Africa and South America. But the Barents Sea remained the fleet's backyard, and for some time after the war, Norwegian and Soviet vessels dominated fishing activities in the Barents Sea, with the UK making up a good number three.

With the major upheavals in the Law of the Sea in the mid-1970s, Norway and the Soviet Union eyed an opportunity to manage common fish stocks in the Barents Sea in partnership. The idea had already been discussed by Norwegian and Soviet fisheries ministers at several meetings. Management of the area was then conducted by the multilateral North East Atlantic Fisheries Commission (NEAFC), whose reservation arrangements and frequent use of majority decision-making procedures — for example, a fishing quota needed the support of two-thirds of the member states to be adopted — impeded an efficient regulatory practice. It was only in 1974, towards the end of its tenure, that NEAFC actually succeeded to set a quota on Barents Sea cod; until then, it had limited itself to regulating technical matters such as mesh size. The 200-mile economic zone agreement gave Norwegian and Soviet fisheries authorities the opportunity to sign a bilateral accord in 1975 under which the two countries would together manage the marine resources of the Barents Sea. The accord thus established the Joint Norwegian–Soviet Fisheries Commission. It met for the first time in January 1976.[2] Norway and the Soviet Union had already agreed to divide the commercially most important fish stocks in the Barents Sea, cod and haddock, equally. Norway had initially wanted a larger percentage for itself because there were more fish in Norwegian than in Soviet waters. But the Soviet Union was a superpower, after all, and dividing equally would prove psychologically useful (at least later) in getting the two parties to see the resources objectively as part of 'our common heritage'. This would have been harder otherwise.

*

One of the substantial difficulties in the almost 40-year-old lifetime of the Norwegian–Russian fisheries management regime arose in the years around the turn of the millennium, when the precautionary approach to fisheries management was taking hold in the international community. The total allowable catch (TAC) from the cod stock had reached a record-breaking 850,000 tonnes in 1997. Back then, marine scientists had started to worry about the accuracy of their models, which they suspected might be inflating estimates of stock size. They therefore decided to cut the total stock size estimate by 200,000 tonnes. In the following two years, the TAC was reduced further to 654,000 tonnes and 490,000 tonnes, respectively.

The essence of the precautionary approach adopted by both the ICES and the Joint Commission is that lack of scientific knowledge shall not stand in the way of efforts to prevent the degradation of the environment or depletion of common-pool resources. Whereas protective measures used to be invoked only when there was a palpable, scientifically proven threat to the environment or resource base, the precautionary approach reversed the procedure: only when science showed beyond reasonable doubt that preventive measures were *not* necessary could they be postponed or disregarded.

Despite the significant decline in stocks in 1998 and 1999, quotas remained acceptably high, from the perspective of the two countries' fishing industries at least. It was in the autumn of 1999 that ICES sounded the alarm about their faulty models. They now believed the cod stock had actually declined to a disturbing level, with spawning stock biomass as low as 222,000 tonnes, less than half the precautionary reference point for spawning stock as defined by ICES. From the point of view of outside observers, there was never a better time to invoke the precautionary approach. ICES' primary TAC recommendation for 2000 made with a view to helping the spawning stock to recover to acceptable levels within three years – was, as mentioned, 110,000 tonnes, nearly five times less than the 1999 quota. In the final minute of its Murmansk session in 1999 – negotiations had been on hold for several days – the Joint Commission agreed on a TAC of 390,000 tonnes, almost four times higher than the scientific recommendation. The following comes from the minutes of this session:

> The Norwegian party notes that the level of the cod quota is alarmingly high in consideration of the available stock assessments and the recommendations from ICES. Taking into account the difficult conditions of the population of Northwest Russia [...], Norway has nevertheless found it possible to enter into this agreement.[3]

It was clear that precaution had not prevailed in the Joint Commission, to the disappointment of the Norwegian side.

It wasn't looking at all good for the new millennium; then the story took a turn few had predicted. By autumn 2000, the young, affluent, myopic and aggressive members of the Russian delegation, who were mostly from the regional level in the north-west, had been replaced by experienced officials from Moscow. The Russians were still uneasy about Norway's motives, but the constructive atmosphere had returned. The first decade of the new century was characterized by pragmatism and compromise. An agreed three-year quota was set in 2000, giving both parties breathing space. A harvest control rule followed in 2002. The purpose of the harvest control rule is to ensure average quotas remain within ICES's precautionary reference points for spawning stock size and fish mortality in each rolling three-year period. It also gives the fishing industries in the two countries a level of predictability inasmuch as cod quotas may not be changed by more than 10 per cent year on year, and haddock quotas by more than 25 per cent, unless an emergency of a predefined nature threatens the stocks. The harvest control rule had a massive effect on procedures at the Commission by mechanizing quota setting. Delegation leaders now had time to attend to all the other matters pertaining to the Commission's work. Renewed overfishing by Russian fishermen was prevented by the introduction of stricter inspection and monitoring rules both bilaterally and multilaterally via NEAFC. The end of the decade saw renewed willingness to meet each other half way: Greenland halibut was defined as a new common stock, and after 30 years of negotiations, minimum fish and mesh sizes were finally adopted. A few months later, Russia and Norway agreed on the Barents Sea delimitation line.

Gentlemen's agreements and NATO raids

Behind Norway's disappointment with the 2000 TAC levels approved by the 1999 session of the Joint Commission, lay a fundamental disagreement on how to interpret scientific advice from ICES and how to understand its implications. In Norway, the TAC cut was generally considered sensible and legitimate, and both government and industry were prepared to adhere to it, if not necessarily wholeheartedly. The dilemma was between long- and short-term interests. Should more fish be taken now at the expense of future fisheries, or should less be taken at the expense of today's fishing industry? There was a certain amount of indifference in Russian fishery circles, where these questions were hardly discussed at all. What was discussed, however, was the rivalry between the two states involved, Norway and Russia, and their interests.

The Russian delegation made it clear that it was not ready to accept further reductions to the year-on-year cod quota.[4] The local media carried a story ahead of the session:

> At a meeting in the regional administration with representatives of the fishing industry and scientists from PINRO [...] the tactics and strategy of the Russian party [to the Joint Commission] were discussed. The principle that 'ours' should follow in the establishment of TACs for cod and haddock was adopted unanimously: not to relent on a single kilo.[5]

Second, the Russians appeared to see Norway as a rational, unitary actor whose TAC policy was based essentially on economic considerations. That the Norwegians insisted on complying with internationally accepted principles of fisheries management, such as sustainability and precaution was in fact a smoke screen hiding their real intentions.

> Norway's administrative system is highly rational and the political environment highly stable. Before last year's quota negotiations, the Norwegians calculated exactly how much their fishing industry could bear to lose, made plans for compensating those who did lose out using revenue from the aquaculture sector, and decided to go in for a reduction in the cod quota at this level.[6]

> Right from the start, the Norwegian delegation pursued a hard line, based on ICES' recommendations which, to put it politely, are 'a bit more precautionary than necessary' as far as the assessment of the cod stock is concerned. Here, it should be observed, some experts do not exclude the possibility that one of the factors behind these recommendations, with all due respect for this indisputably highly respected organization, has been the interests of Norway and the EU countries, whose representatives constitute the majority of the members of

the ICES working groups. And it is quite possible that the Norwegian delegation has pressed for sharper reductions in the cod catches as a means of maintaining the high price of the country's fish exports. [...] This is the third year in a row the Norwegian delegation has tried to gain acceptance for a lower cod quota, and it is far from inconceivable that their reasons lie in the recently started artificial cod breeding industry. In two to three years' time, the production of this artificially bred cod could approach 180,000–200,000 tonnes a year, almost as much as Norway's share of the 'wild' cod quota. And in order to maintain price levels, it would make sense to 'freeze' catches at this level. Whether one likes it or not, the Norwegians at the session [of the Joint Fisheries Commission] gained additional support for their argument by the demands of the 'greens' and parts of the local press.[7]

There is also another reason why the Norwegians urged the setting of a fixed cod quota three years in advance. The Russian participants at the session were told behind the scenes [of the negotiations] that Norway expected to reach production levels of artificially bred cod in precisely three years, and that would allow them to cut quotas of this stock quite dramatically.[8]

Third, the Russians refer explicitly to (what they perceive as) Norway's decisive economic calculation as 'natural'. The first quotation below continues where the extract above depicting Norway's use of the ICES for its own economic motives, left off.

[I]t is quite possible that the Norwegian delegation has demanded stiff reductions in the cod catches simply to maintain the high price of the country's export of fish and fish products. In principle, there is nothing unusual about this – every country defends its own interests with the means available to it.[9]

Norway does everything it can to destroy the Russian fishing industry. And that's good. That's how it should be. It's just a pity the Russian state isn't strong enough to defend the interests of its inhabitants in the same manner.[10]

Fourth, there is a clear tendency in the Russian press and among actors involved in Russian fisheries to refer to the work of the Russian delegation to the Commission primarily in terms of defending Russia's national interests.

'There's a deep misunderstanding that Russia won this year's fishery negotiations in Murmansk,' says [deputy director] Vladimir Torokhov of Sevryba. The opposite is the case, he tells the newspaper *Rybnaya Stolitsa* in Murmansk, it was Norway that got its will. 'Our crafty neighbours had right from the start the same quota figures in their heads as the negotiations ended with. [...] We didn't learn the lessons of the previous negotiations and defended our national interests badly.'[11]

Of course, it's necessary to mention the arguments presented by the Russian scientists in the negotiations [of the Joint Fisheries Commission], which, to a considerable extent, made it possible to achieve the many acceptable results for the members of our northern fishery complex. [...] Our scientists really did a good job at the negotiations.[12]

[In the Joint Fisheries Commission, the Russian scientists] defended the Russian positions in a precise and well-prepared manner.[13]

In summary then, representatives of the Russian fishing industry and management system appear to agree that the Norwegians should be seen as rivals, not as partners:

Fishery entrepreneurs and scientists of the Northern basin have held a 'round table' session in Murmansk to work out recommendations for our national delegation to the coming sessions of the Joint Russian–Norwegian Fisheries Commission. 'It's about time for us to think of the Norwegians as rivals rather than partners, in competition for marine bioresources,' said Gennadi Stepakhno, head of the Fishing Industry Union of the North, at the opening of the meeting. Indeed, this seems to have been the general feeling of the meeting – along with the view that 'there is plenty of fish in the sea, and we must press our case for an increase in the total allowable catch'.[14]

*

The fishery protection zone around Svalbard forms a particular jurisdictional and regulatory complex (see Chapter 3). Since the turn of the century simmering conflicts have flared up and exposed the different perspectives of the Norwegian and Russian fishery authorities.[15] Most of the fishing vessels operating in the zone are Russian.[16] Although Russia has not formally recognized the fishery protection zone, Russian fishers have largely complied with Norwegian fishery regulations in the area and also complied with less formal requests of the Norwegian Coast Guard to fish in areas where there is less likelihood of catching too many juvenile fish. Russian vessels do not report to the Norwegian fishery authorities what and how much they catch in the zone, and Russian captains refuse to sign Norwegian Coast Guard inspection forms following inspections on board. However, they do welcome the Norwegian inspectors, who follow the same inspection procedures as in the Norwegian economic zone. To avoid provoking other states, Norway for many years applied a soft approach to regulatory enforcement in the zone, where oral and written warnings were given for violations, but where offenders were not penalized further. Up until the turn of the millennium, force had only been used against vessels from states with no fishing quotas for the Barents Sea.[17]

In the summer of 1998, the Norwegian Coast Guard arrested a Russian vessel for failing to act on requests to leave a certain area where too many juvenile fish were being caught. The conflict was resolved through diplomatic channels between the two coastal states before the vessel reached the Norwegian port. However, Norway's 'softly, softly' policy was severely strained after the Norwegian Coast Guard in April 2001 arrested a Russian trawler, the *Chernigov*, in the Svalbard zone for what was now known as 'environmental crime'. The offence was so grave – *Chernigov*'s crew had attached a false trawl (with a mesh size smaller than half the permissible width) to the cod end of the main trawl, catching large quantities of undersized fish – the Coast Guard felt it had no option but to arrest the vessel. In an attempt to avoid detection, the crew had cut the trawl wire, though the nets were later salvaged by the Coast Guard and could be measured. The Russian government protested. The arrest, they alleged, had taken place in international waters. All practical collaboration on fisheries management was immediately put on hold and the Russian delegation walked out of a meeting of the permanent committee under the Fisheries Commission. The highest levels of the Russian fisheries sector reacted strongly. The chairman of the State Committee for Fisheries (now the Federal Fisheries Agency) stated notoriously that Russian naval vessels should sink Norwegian Coast Guard vessels in the Svalbard zone and not bother to rescue the crew.[18] Fishing circles in Murmansk saw it as another Norwegian attempt to exorcize Russian fishermen from the waters around Svalbard; by arresting *Chernigov* Norway had broken the old *gentlemen's agreement* between the two countries. According to this agreement, Norway may carry out inspections in the Svalbard zone but not arrest offenders.[19] Norway wouldn't have dared to act like this if the Soviet Union had still existed; they're taking advantage of a politically and economically weakened Russia, it was said. It was also seen as an element in the West's attempt to perpetuate the Cold War in the form of a 'Cold Peace', as exemplified by NATO's expansion eastward, which was also a breach of the *gentlemen's agreement* whereby Russia allowed former Soviet republics to become independent in return for the West not expanding its sphere of influence eastwards. Another example was NATO's attack on Russia's sister state Serbia in spring 1999.

On 18 September 1999, a Russian newspaper printed a report by Vyacheslav Zilanov (who would later become deputy head of the Federal Russian Fisheries Agency's public chamber; see Chapter 3), where he accused Norway of exploiting Russia's present troubles to its own advantage in the fisheries sector.[20] Norway, you see, requires trawlers to carry a fish sorting grid, a device which puts Russian fishermen at a particular disadvantage since they use trawls while Norwegians use longlines. The inspections by the Norwegian Coast Guard are far too stringent and discriminatory, and fishing grounds are closed arbitrarily. 'Our management system has broken down. But that notwithstanding, does that give the one party the right to exploit the other's failings and seize more than what rightfully belongs to him?' The reports below show how this issue was framed both before and after the arrest of *Chernigov*.

> There is still disagreement on the Russian–Norwegian fishery in the Svalbard zone. According to the Paris Convention, signed more than sixty years ago,[21] our country has the right to conduct and expand industrial activity there. However, the Norwegians have recently introduced a range of measures aimed at pressing Russian vessels out of this area.[22]

> Russia wants extensive changes in the 200-mile fishery protection zone around Svalbard. 'Norway cannot continue to squeeze our fishers out of the area,' says leader of the catch department of the Murmansk-based fishing company AO Sevryba, Vladimir Torokhov. [...] 'The leadership of Sevryba has continuously addressed our State Committee for Fisheries with demands that the Ministry of Foreign Affairs engage in the issue. It is high time the disagreements [between Russia and Norway] were resolved.'[23]

The same year as the *Chernigov* episode, Norway passed a new law regulating use of the natural environment on Svalbard. The law requires all commercial actors to maintain high environmental standards on Svalbard and makes it particularly difficult for them to establish new operations for the purpose of extracting natural resources. My former colleague Jørgen Holten Jørgensen (2003) has shown how the law was broadly perceived in Russian political circles — as a disguised attempt by Norway to expel Russia from Svalbard.[24] 'The environmental law is more about politics than the environment', said a Russian diplomat in an interview with Jørgen. 'Immense areas are protected and closed off for commercial activity. [...] The fact is, Norway wants to be the only player in town on Svalbard, that's why they've pushed the law through.' Inconveniently for Norwegian authorities, the law was adopted when it was already known the Russians were thinking of starting a new mining operation on Svalbard, in Coles Bay. Using powers provided under the new law, the Norwegian Governor of Svalbard proposed the creation of a plant protection zone precisely in Coles Bay — proof to many Russians that the law was part of a wider strategy to remove the Russians from Svalbard. Deputy Director of the Russian mining company Arktikugol explains:

> First, they presented the new environmental law just after Arktikugol had announced plans to start mining in Coles Bay — hardly a coincidence. Second, the Grumant coal mine was in operation for 68 years, and there was never any talk of rare plants in the area. And third, Arktikugol's claim area amounts to no more than about 1 per cent, that is, 500 square kilometres of Svalbard's 50,000 square kilometres. And just this percentage is included within the scope of the new plant protection scheme. Virtually all the places where Arktikugol might consider mining have been declared plant protection zones.

Deputy Chairman of the State Duma Foreign Affairs Committee draws a connection between the Svalbard Environmental Protection Act and the arrest of *Chernigov*:

> If you Norwegians had really bothered about the environment, you would have regulated activity in Barentsburg long ago. We have cars with prehistoric technology, we have rubbish floating all over the place, and a coal power plant which spews out the worst shit. You could easily come up with regulations to prevent pollution, but instead you go on about a few plants in Coles Bay! [...] Before, Norway and Russia used to have a *gentlemen's agreement* in the fisheries protection zone; we agreed to disagree. Norway agreed that Russia did not recognize the fisheries protection zone, while Russia tacitly went along with Norwegian policy in the zone. Recently, though, Norway has adopted a more aggressive tone, directed against Russian fishermen. [...] Norway is doing the same on Spitsbergen and trying to squeeze Russia out. Norway can only get away with it because of Russian weakness.

As far as the Russians are concerned, Norway's Svalbard policy and NATO membership are two sides of the same coin. As a vice admiral of the Northern Fleet argued in an article in *Voennaya mysl* in 2000, what is happening on Svalbard is evidence of an attempt by 'Norway and its NATO allies to secure the rights to the disputed areas at whatever cost and limit Russian presence in the Barents Sea and indeed in the Arctic to the barest minimum.'[25] Murmansk Governor Yuri Yevdokimov, who was removed a decade after this for allegedly having too close ties with Norway, wrote in an article in 1997:

> The behaviour of Norwegians towards Russians on Spitsbergen has changed in recent years. It's obvious they are trying to get us to leave the archipelago voluntarily. Well, in my opinion, it is to be expected — that's how the cookie crumbles: when a country is temporarily weakened, its neighbours will seek to profit from it. But we must not forget that in this case it is not just about losing a few concessions; it is a catastrophic erosion of Russia's strategic defence

potential, the possible destruction of nuclear parity, the annihilation of the nuclear triad which forms the basis of our defence doctrine. Why do we forget that our neighbours on the planet are not overjoyed at the prospect of Russia's resurgence? Some of them have political and economic interests in the continued deterioration of our country. It would make it easier [for them] to solve the problems of the Caspian Sea to their own advantage. It would be easier to throw the Russians off Spitsbergen altogether.[26]

*

The work done by Norwegian and Russian marine scientists in collaboration is often seen as the linchpin of the bilateral fisheries management regime in the Barents Sea. For one thing, the scientific component of the Norwegian–Russian partnership on fisheries management is the one with the longest history.[27] While collaboration on fisheries regulation started in 1975 and on enforcement in 1993, the first steps towards scientific cooperation had been taken as early as in the late nineteenth century and the partnership was gradually formalized during the 1960s.

Around the mid-2000s, a schism in Russian fisheries science became evident. The federal fisheries research institute, VNIRO, launched an attack against ICES and the regional institute in the Russian north-west, PINRO.[28] Russia's regional fisheries research institutes became formally independent of VNIRO in the early 1990s, though their scientific work is still reviewed by the federal institute. At the same time, PINRO and the Norwegian Institute of Marine Research expanded their collaboration, in line with relaxed East–West relations in the European Arctic more widely – and substantial Norwegian funds to support a 'starving' bureaucracy in Russia's north-west. VNIRO was not part of the international scientific community in ICES to the same extent as PINRO (and had not received as much financial support from Norway as the regional institute had), but now VNIRO scientists began questioning the scientific credibility of the models ICES employed to estimate fish stocks in the Barents Sea. This disagreement is not mentioned in the minutes of the Joint Commission, but from the early 2000s VNIRO scientists' questioning of the ICES models became an 'annual performance' at the plenary sessions of the Commission, as a member of the Norwegian delegation put it. At first, VNIRO seemed to lack legitimacy in the Russian delegation, at least in its upper echelons, but by the second half of the 2000s Norwegian scientists were afraid VNIRO's approach might actually prevail.

According to VNIRO, too much weight was given to the relationship between recruitment to the stock and the size of the spawning stock in ICES models; environmental factors such as natural fluctuations caused by swings in temperature and ocean currents are far more important. Hence, there is no need to worry about keeping the spawning stock at a specific level. In the preface to a report from a joint Norwegian–Russian scientific workshop in 2006, VNIRO's director stated: '[the] use of completely unreal models which are based on recruitment dependence on abundance of the spawning stock could be treated as *prophesying voodooism* rather than developing scientifically-based assessments of the state and dynamics of the fish stocks'.[29]

A central point in VNIRO's criticism of ICES is found in the latter's own figures of the catch pressure on (or fishing mortality of) Northeast Arctic cod. Except for a very short period around 1990, fishing mortality since the 1950s has been well above the level defined by ICES to secure the long-term viability of the stock, the so-called target reference point. Since the 1970s, fishing mortality has largely been at or above the limit reference point. At this level one risks the total collapse of the stock (admittedly only for one in twenty theoretical runs of the entire existing time series for the stock, which VNIRO failed to mention). Well, the stock hasn't collapsed. 'If the reference points and ICES models had been correct, there wouldn't have been any fish in the Barents Sea today', one VNIRO scientist noted in an interview.[30] He further explained: 'The only logical explanation of the divergence between ICES' models and the fact that we still have fish in the Barents Sea, is that the estimates are wrong. We underestimate the [cod] stock, and the reason is to be found in the traditional methods.'[31]

Before the interview, the director of the research institute had welcomed me and my co-interviewer: 'It's horrible', he said, 'what's happening in the Barents Sea at the moment.' It was a commonly heard phrase in the Norwegian fisheries debate at the time, in 2007, and the Russians were to blame for the overfishing. What the VNIRO director implied, however, was the exact opposite: he was complaining because the Barents Sea fish stocks, in his view, were *underexploited*. Since the ICES models underestimated the stocks, TACs were artificially low, to the detriment of the Russian and Norwegian fishing industry. He continued to complain about the recently introduced precautionary principle in international fisheries agreements, which he described as Western inventions aimed at harming the Russian fishing industry, or Russia in general. 'The FAO Fish Stocks Agreement [from 1995, introducing the precautionary principle as the basis for fisheries management] was written by Greenpeace, with money from the CIA, aimed at destroying the Russian fishing industry.'[32]

The runaway captain, the bucket on the mast

In the autumn of 2005, the Norwegian Coast Guard arrested the Russian trawler *Elektron* in the Svalbard zone on suspicion of chronic overfishing. It had been fishing in the so-called Loophole, a sliver of international waters north of the Russian and Norwegian economic zones, and out of bounds for Norwegian enforcement authorities,[33] but when it entered the protection zone the Coast Guard struck. While being escorted to a Norwegian port, the Russian vessel changed course and headed off for Murmansk, with two Norwegian inspectors on board. The Coast Guard arrested several more Russian vessels in the Svalbard zone in short succession. According to the Russian press, Norway was behaving like a 'trawler terrorist', targeting Russian ships in Barents Sea. Under the pretext of safeguarding marine resources, they argued, Norway was trying to purge the Svalbard zone of foreign vessels, at least of Russian ships. 'We have a clear impression [Norway] wants to make life as uncomfortable as possible for our fishermen', General Director of the Fishing Industry Union of the North, Gennadi Stepakhno, told *utro.ru* on 1 November 2005.[34] In the same article Foreign Minister Sergei Lavrov is reported as saying there was an agreement in Soviet times that Norway would inform the Soviet government in the event of 'problems' in the protection zone. 'That's how it's been until recently', he said. 'It is obvious', the author of the article continues, 'that Norway's "trawler terrorism" is a guinea pig in the great game of dividing up the Arctic. If that is the case, it is – whatever they might say in Oslo – no private conflict.' And behind the scenes lurks the US: Norway will challenge Russia in the future as well in the Barents Sea 'since they know they can rely on the support of the United States. And [the US] is obviously not supporting the descendants of the Vikings out of a concern for the fish.'

The captain of the runaway trawler was convicted in a Russian court for illegal fishing, but acquitted of charges of kidnapping the Norwegian inspectors. He immediately became a popular hero, not just locally but in other parts of Russia as well. As reported by *Kommersant*, 'The actions of the *Elektron* captain are considered heroic not just by the inhabitants of Murmansk oblast – the regional administration continuously receives letters from different regions across the country with support for [the captain].'[35] The Regional Duma in Orenburg oblast, for example, urged the Murmansk court to drop the charges against the captain because he had 'saved the trawler from the pirate arrest performed by the Norwegian Coast Guard'. As a result of his sudden fame, the fugitive captain was elected mayor in one of Murmansk's satellite towns.

*

But 'trawler terror' was not the only angle on the arrest of Russian ships. Speaking to *Vzglyad* in January 2008, Andrei Kraini, head of Russia's Federal Fisheries Agency – who has backed Russian fishermen's complaints about Norwegian control in the Barents Sea on several occasions – does nothing to allay suspicions of backroom deals in the Russian fishing industry.[36] Not only does he admit to widespread, systematic criminality in the fishing industry, he identifies the real culprits behind the illegal fishing. 'In this country, unorganized illegal fishing doesn't exist. The fishermen are all in someone's pocket: veterinary services, Ministry of Interior, FSB and all manner of other government agencies.' In other words, government agencies have vessels of 'their own' to do their illegal fishing for them.

'The idea that Norway is trying to eject Russian fishermen from the Norwegian maritime zone,' said the head of the Federal Fisheries Agency – and head of the Russian delegation to the Norwegian–Russian Fisheries Commission at the time – to *Regnum* in October 2005, 'is wrong'. 'Norwegian and Russian fishermen are joined at the hip.'[37] 'Like a band of brothers of the sea, Russians and Norwegians', the head of the Norwegian delegation adds. In an article of 20 October 2010 entitled 'The bucket on the mast', and subtitled 'Why Norway has started a campaign against Russians involved in illegal fishing even though it's not in Norway's best interests', *Novaya Gazeta* reasons as follows. Norway deserves praise, it says, for taking its control responsibilities in the Barents Sea seriously.[38] The 'bucket on the mast' is a device used by Russian fishermen to disable the statutory satellite tracking system, which is indispensable in the monitoring of the fisheries. Russian fishermen are described as members of 'the international fishing mafia'. Having pointed out that overfishing benefits Norwegian fish processing plants (where much of the Russian fish is landed), the journalist asks why Norway is determined nonetheless to stop illegal fishing.

> Well, it's down to the national idea! In our country we have the steppe, tundra, taiga and volcanoes, while little (on our scale) Norway is simply known as 'the country of fjords'. The national idea of this country is the role Norway is playing in Europe as a leading Arctic power. Only Norway can bring order to the Arctic, declare the Norwegians. Not only do they

declare this, they have also shown their ability to fight crime: three Norwegian inspectors conducted a raid last summer in three European ports and discovered three thousand tonnes of illegal Barents Sea fish. Of course, it might just be a PR stunt. That is, if we were to look at it from our Russian point of view. But from a Norwegian point of view ... for the fifth consecutive year, Norway is the most prosperous country in the world. And prosperity affects one's worldview and is reflected in one's behaviour. Given its status, Norway cannot be seen to cover up crime. Their only mistake is to have counted on our support. There is one sea, but two countries [...] The Norwegians are so well-mannered, they comply with the law.[39]

The article goes on to contrast Norway's efforts to prevent illegal activity with the slovenly attitude of the Russian authorities, where the minister of agriculture (who at the time was also responsible for the Russian fisheries) is more interested in opening a racetrack in Kazan than fighting illegal fishing. 'We are a big country – we have both taiga and steppe [...] But our sailors fish under the Mongolian flag. [...] It would be intriguing to know: Is there a fisheries minister in Mongolia?'

In oil and gas industry circles, Norway is depicted as the small country that evaded the resources curse. *Nezavisimaya Gazeta* asks in a piece entitled 'Not by oil alone' what would happen if Norway were suddenly to lose its oil and gas.[40] 'Nothing really bad', it suggests. 'The money Norway has squirreled away will fund another century of affluence. The oil and gas industry will not grind to a halt, and people will not freeze in their homes – and this is all because the country's power industry does not depend on oil and gas.' In an article from August 2006 called 'Descendants of the Vikings on the Russian shelf', *Rossiyskaya Gazeta* mentions President Putin's desire to see a partnership between Russia and Norway on the Russian shelf because the Norwegians 'hold a leading place [in the world]', their 'infrastructure in the North is highly developed', they are 'objective without looking down their noses at you'.[41] Rather than allowing themselves to be sidetracked by 'deals with empty words', Norwegians have created a programme to utilize oil and gas deposits in the Barents Sea, including plans to lay oil and gas pipelines along the coast – and in the direction of the Russian deposits. The Norwegians are ready to go, on their own if need be 'if, as usual, Russia is too late off the mark to join the partnership séance'. Reference is made to how the Norwegian companies have expanded their footprint in different parts of the world, and that teaming up with them could give Gazprom new legs to stand on abroad. It would generate valuable spillovers in areas such as energy conservation, alternative energy sources and environmental protection. 'On the whole', the *Gazeta* concludes, 'we have often underestimated our closest neighbours.'

Naive *muzhik* meets cunning Viking

It is striking how closely Norwegian–Russian relations in the management of the Barents Sea fish stocks mirror the wider tides of Russian foreign policy. Westernization in the early 1990s was followed by a degree of 'introversion' on either side of the millennium, which itself was succeeded by a pragmatic turn in the 2000s. Almost until the end of the 1990s, Russians were happy to comply with whatever new fishing regulations Norway wanted to bring in – just as they in the wider picture flirted with NATO. In reference to the Cold War, they told the West, 'you won, we lost'. By the end of the decade this period of camaraderie was definitively over. Now the sentiment was: we'll just have to get on with things as best we can, as we have always done in Russia. And after all, NATO was not very interested in giving Russia a place at the table, though it was ready to welcome former Soviet satellite states in Eastern and Central Europe, even the Baltic republics. Russia had been tricked – the Cold War had not ended, it had just morphed into a Cold Peace.[42] Coordination of technical regulations in the fisheries sector – considered such a success in Norway and worthy of emulation elsewhere – was nothing but a ruse by a conniving neighbour to trick unsuspecting Russians to accept offers of help that ultimately were not in their interest. Norway had got its Western allies on the ICES to recommend small quotas around the turn of the millennium because they knew it would harm Russia where it really hurt. And Norway had also arrested a Russian vessel in the Svalbard zone – that had never happened before – and passed a new environmental law for Svalbard, establishing a nature reserve precisely where Russia was planning to set up a new mining operation. Coincidence or what?

Compared with the volatile 1990s, relations between Norway and Russia the following decade were excellent. It was still possible to hear echoes of the 'introverted' opposition, but as in foreign policy in general, pragmatism was the new watchword. Cooperation on fisheries enjoyed a new golden age. Several milestones were passed, such as the harvest control rule, elimination of overfishing and a wide range of new compromises – the boundary agreement being the most important of them. The Russian press did not stop criticizing Norway, but it did at least print reports about Norwegian accomplishments in technology and the economy – a role model for Russia perhaps? The Norwegians are 'so well-mannered, they comply with the law'. That's why the money they've put in the piggy bank will be enough for another 'hundred years of prosperity'. Norway is the country where people should not have to freeze in their houses, thanks to the generosity of the state. Norway is the country with its own house in order and where the 'national idea' is to maintain order in the Arctic. For Russia, Norway is not (just) 'West' – Norway is 'neighbour' and 'North', the 'Siamese twin'; the two countries are like a 'band of brothers of the sea'.

Norway is, however, a country that observes international treaties, but breaks *gentlemen's agreements*. Norway is the neighbour that sends money to Russia and says nice things, but 'is far from happy about the prospect of a resurgent Russia'. Norway is the small state one has long underestimated. Norwegians do as they please, always ready to do service for NATO. They move stealthily in the Norwegian–Russian project landscape, ears to the ground. They are wise and objective and 'they don't look down their nose at you'. They also dislike empty chatter. They have their sophisticated strategies, what with the sorting grid for small fish and nature reserves — the West's foreign policy toolbox is full of gadgets.

The Russians, on their side, are habitually too late to the collaboration party, fooled by their worldly-wise neighbour to install stupid catch technology, reduce quotas and give up their fishing grounds. Russia is the good-natured, portly old yokel (*muzhik*), the short Mongol who'll never turn into a tall, blond Viking. Russia is the land of taiga and steppe, oil and cod, but — let's be honest — the bucket on the mast and illegal fish in the trawl. Russia is the country where the minister responsible for the fisheries would rather go horse racing in Kazan than fishing in the Barents Sea. Russia is the country where the fishermen do not violate the law of their own free will, but at the request of the supervising authorities themselves. Russia is the country with 'prehistoric cars', 'rubbish all over the place' and 'the worst of shit'. Russia is the country where everything that can go wrong, does go wrong.

*

Two related forms of Russian identity are narrated in these accounts, both with Russian tragedy as the more or less obvious end result. Russia's destined tragedy follows either from ever-present Western malice or from its own eternal inability to maintain order, possibly a combination of the two. Norwegian cunning is praised and despised at the same time. According to the most forceful narrative, the crafty Vikings conduct raids on behalf of NATO with the purpose to break Russia's neck, economically and ultimately also politically. All types of subterfuge are allowed; the rules of the game are those of the intelligence world, not petty international law. The more benign version sees Norway as a country that is civilized beyond Russian comprehension and is only concerned to defend its interests as well as possible. Russians are either the innocent victims or careless ne'er-do-wells.

The story of Norwegian NATO raids in the North is narrated as a tragedy in pure form. Russia fights for its legitimate rights, but is driven back, step by step. The story of Russian incompetence and carelessness speaks of Russia's tragic fate as well, but follows the narrative structure of the comedy. It is a story of pirates and police, heroes and 'terrorists', the good and the bad. The comic element lies in the twists and turns, oppositions and misunderstandings, fugitive captains and buckets on the mast – and, ultimately, in the sudden realization that the stranger's intentions weren't bad after all. The Western villain of the story turns out to be the good guy, who saves the fish stocks from degradation, despite Russian suspicion and ingratitude. 'We Russians made all this fuss about the Norwegian Coast Guard arresting our vessels in the Barents Sea, but we were wrong: they're out to save us all, thank God.' The key words of the plot are not so much 'Norwegian cleverness', but 'civilization beyond Russian comprehension'. How can any state care so much about the sustainability of the fish stocks that they sacrifice the economic interests of their own fishing industry? We didn't believe it was true, but it was. Misunderstandings resolved, catastrophe averted, curtain falls.

The Other is not necessarily the West, the Other is actually ourselves.

CHAPTER 5

REGION BUILDING, IDENTITY FORMATION

Late one Thursday night a few years ago I found myself at one of Murmansk's more popular nightspots in the company of a foreign delegation and our local facilitator and interpreter, who we can call Ignat.[1] Ignat is a typical product of the Barents Region development scheme: an exchange student in Norway, followed by studies and jobs in various other European countries. We were celebrating a successful week in Murmansk before travelling home on the Friday. Ignat was talking to the various foreigners in flawless Norwegian and English. The situation could hardly be more different than it was in the early days when we worked with post-Soviet Union authorities, and the Russians were unknown quantities in dark suits whose interpreters spoke 'dictionary Norwegian'.

Ignat suddenly left his place at the other side of the table and, looking mischievous, sat down beside me on the sofa and whispered in my ear, 'Pssst – Norway has acted very shrewdly in the Barents Region. You've got your hands on every public office. So when the Russian Federation falls apart [. . .], you can quietly go ahead annex the whole of the Kola Peninsula.'

Our common history

BEAR came into being in 1993, the result of a Norwegian initiative.[2] It is based on and encourages cooperation between

Norway, Sweden, Finland and Russia in a number of fields including the arts, student exchange, business development and infrastructure, at regional and national levels. The general idea is to dismantle the barriers between East and West in the North erected by 70 years of communism and revive what before the 1917 Russian Revolution was lively cross-border interaction and trade, the so-called Pomor trade.

The concept of 'region building' has evolved in the IR literature as an alternative to defining regions 'inside-out' or 'outside-in' when discussing what constitutes a 'natural' region (Neumann 1994). Whereas the 'inside-out' approach sees regions essentially as entities sharing certain linguistic, cultural, and social characteristics within a defined geographical area – with the accent on internal, 'centripetal forces' – the 'outside-in' approach looks at trans-national regions largely as the outcome of the preferences of hegemonic states. The two approaches converge, however, in their focus on regions as given entities (with some kind of common identity, in the former case, or dominant international power structure, in the latter). They aspire to explain the existence of regions *a priori*, ignoring the capacity of individual and collective actors to define them from other vantage points.

Criticizing these older approaches for lack of self-reflection, region-building theorists claim that political actors are capable of defining the parameters of what counts as inside or outside a region. Drawing on nation-building literature, they claim that politicians, bureaucrats, researchers, artists and others can contribute to defining and developing regional entities. According to this view, regions are not given by either cultural similarities or international power structures, but have to be actively formed through a region-building process similar to earlier European nation-building projects. In Neumann's words (p. 58),

> When an elite has formulated a political programme which hinges on the existence of a nation, it is [always] possible, to construct for it a prehistory which will embody it in time as well as in space. This is done by identifying, and thus making

relevant to the identity of the human collective in question, a host of political ties, cultural similarities, economic transactional patterns etc. Of course, such a political process will always be imposed on a geographical area which is already, in a number of respects, heterogeneous. The point made here is simply that these similarities and dissimilarities are processed politically by nation-builders, and it is *these political actors* who decide which similarities should be considered politically relevant, and which should not.

Political actors will likewise invoke historical events to bolster the construction of a notion of community within an area. Regions may therefore be taken as 'imagined communities' (Anderson 1983), cognitive outcomes of deliberate political ambitions. In other words, they are 'talked and written into existence' (Neumann 1994: 59).

Several authors have noted the suitability of the North for region building in post-Cold War Europe.[3] In an article addressing the 'state of northernness' shared by Finland and Russia and the establishment of BEAR, Medvedev (2001: 92) claims that 'whereas the East, West and South have more or less fixed meanings, and are interpreted as relatively populated and explored, the North appears as a mythological domain, a semiotic project, a constructed identity.' A more prosaic claim would probably be that the geographical category of the North could be cultivated to deconstruct the established East–West divide in Europe that had been reinforced during the Cold War.

Browning (2003) identifies two sets of representational practices in discourses underlying region building in the European North. Region-building attempts in the first set, such as BEAR and the EU Northern Dimension, move the European North towards a more variegated politics by breaking down discursive structures of self and otherness regarding Russia. In the second category, these integrative moves are challenged and marginalized by a more traditional discourse:

Whilst the region builders of the 1990s took on board the postmodern understanding of the constructed nature of social reality as a liberating moment to reconstitute their own regional environment, they have been less observant of the way in which the representational practices they have utilised in order to promote change have, in many respects, only served to re-inscribe the very world they have sought to transform. Thus, whilst aims to construct an egalitarian relationship with Russia in order to break down traditional negative self–other depictions are clearly to be welcomed, Russia, in fact, often continues to occupy negative positions in the underlying discourses of region-building projects that serve to re-inscribe Russia's difference from the 'West' European 'us' in negative terms. In short, and to the detriment of its stated objectives, the new region building often resonates badly with a 'West' European legacy that constitutes Europe as a unified civilisational empire. This offers Russia the option, either of being imperialised within its folds, or alternatively of remaining marginalised on the periphery of Europe. In particular, in this discourse Russia remains construed as the object to be acted upon, the diseased that needs to be cured. (p. 48)

*

'Region building' refers essentially to efforts to 'create' a political region by deliberately speaking and acting as if the chosen area was a 'natural' entity already, from which a region would eventually emerge.[4] Now, as the politically correct 'Barents region builders' frequently point out, any remaining cultural differences in the region are the result of the hermetically sealed border between East and West during the communist era. When the borders opened again, the peoples of northern Norway and north-west Russia would re-discover their similarities, formed by centuries of living in the same unforgiving environment, and harsh northern weather, not to mention a shared experience of the periphery's historical traumas. Learning each other's language and improving the general infrastructure, one hoped, would remove any remaining Soviet sand in the machinery of cooperation.[5]

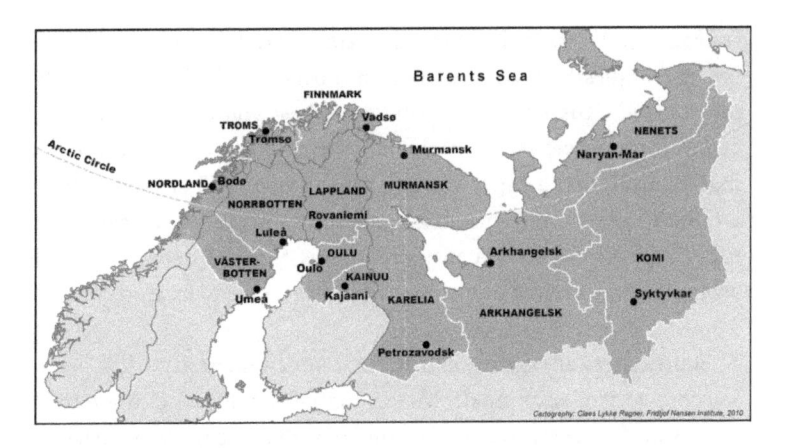

Map. 5.1 The Barents Euro-Arctic Region
Source: Fridtjof Nansen Institute

Building the region did not go as smoothly as anticipated. People-to-people cooperation flourished, but in the business sector failures were soon mounting up. For instance, as soon as various high-profile projects began operating with a profit, the Russians turfed the Norwegians out, creating a good deal of ill-will. Soon, even the most adamantly enthusiastic region-builder had to admit that language courses and road construction works would not persuade the people of Kola and northern Norway to feel united as Barents region citizens with the same frame of reference, worldview and situational understanding.

In a Barbie world

In a series of in-depth group interviews, I investigated how Kola inhabitants spoke of themselves as northerners and Russians, in contrast to (Russian) southerners and Scandinavians, respectively. My interviewees offered a fairly uniform description of what they felt it meant being a (Russian) northerner: northerners are competent (with a high level of education), cultured, calm and considerate – they paint a picture of 'the good life in the north'.[6] The labels my interviewees use to characterize Russian northerners resonate quite strongly with the 'Arctic myth' and ideals of the Soviet conquest of the north. This in contrast to the harsh life in the uneducated (Russian) south, where the best you can hope for – as one of my interviewees (female, late thirties) put it – is 'a job on a market stall, and a bit of trading on the side'. Where southerners are loud, impulsive, emotional and tight-fisted, life in the north teaches people to show consideration, as they all depend on each other. In the words of one of my interviewees (female, mid-forties):

> Southerners are different from us temperamentally; they are more active, emotional. We are compelled by the climate to be more conservative, even-tempered. Because of the weather we've learned to take things as they come, so we're more patient than southerners. They can't take criticism; you can't say anything negative about them, but here, people say whatever they like about you. Me, for example, I never quarrel with people I don't know, fellow travellers for instance, and I don't often see others involved in quarrels of that sort, because I live here in the north.

Then how about Scandinavians, I ask, in particular the *Norgs*, as people in Murmansk affectionately (and perhaps a bit condescendingly) refer to their neighbours to the west?[7]

The striking thing here is that most of my interviewees seem to have far less to say about Scandinavians than about southerners; they don't even seem to have a common set of characteristics to give structure to the discussion. The range of descriptive expressions they can choose from to depict southerners is far wider and variegated. When it comes to Scandinavians, many seem unsure of what to say or how to respond. Some are categorical, but don't really say very much. A few – those with personal experience – have a richer, more balanced repertory to choose from.

While many interviewees have no personal experience of Scandinavians, they have seen them on the streets of Murmansk or heard stories about them. They tend to characterize them as 'different', even 'strange', based on physical appearance or reported demeanour. In many instances, interviewees talk first about the difference in appearance before offering their own assumptions of 'how they are over there'. Many are struck by the foreigners' look, which seems to express curiosity and interest (as opposed to Russians who stare at a fixed point in front of them). Foreigners walk slowly and apparently aimlessly (as opposed to Russians who need to get from point A to point B without dawdling). Foreigners are helpless when it comes to dressing. They choose the wrong clothes for the weather (go without a fur hat in winter, for instance) and for the occasion (they don't wear suit and tie when it is expected of them). They seem incapable of observing even the simplest rules of proper dress, like buttoning up your jacket ('jackets undone', as several of my interviewees observe). Aleksandr and Tatyana (both in their early thirties), who are colleagues and personal friends, talk about clothes, roads, Scandinavian dullness[8] and respect for the law[9] in this brief extract:

Interviewer:	What do you know about our northern neighbours? How would you describe the difference between people in Russia and people in Scandinavia?
Aleksandr:	I wouldn't live there for love or money. It's excruciatingly dull, in my opinion. And the roads are so narrow! As an experienced driver, I'm amazed to see how enormous transport vehicles negotiate the roads [moves some glasses around on the table to illustrate his point].
Tatyana:	On the other hand, vehicles stop if you're at a zebra crossing to let you over. [Addressing Aleksandr] As a driver, you form your own opinions, but I look at it from the pedestrian's point of view. It'll never be like that here.
Interviewer:	What about the people over there, what d'you think of them?

Aleksandr:	Frost-resistant [laughs]! We wear fur, they wander round in casuals, jackets undone. This is an example from everyday life. They're also extremely honest. They don't like getting involved in anything fishy.
Tatyana:	Best not to even try, because they are also extremely law-abiding. It wouldn't occur to them to try and con anyone. Anything goes wrong, they give themselves up, intestines and all.

Viktoria and Julia, two women in their late twenties, blame Scandinavians' poor posture and inability to dress on the welfare state:

Viktoria:	There's no two ways about it – they're pofigists [*pofigisty*, people characterized by indifference to and disregard for the feelings and opinions of others]. And their clothes are dreadful. You can spot them a mile away from the clothes they're wearing. Even though everything is available in the shops, they still can't dress properly.
Julia:	It's because they don't have a clothes cult. You said yourself they're all pofigists [impersonates Viktoria]. And it's really true, they sort of lumber around all floppy like. The government's given them everything, so they don't have to keep fit. Not like here.

Elena and Nikolay, an elderly couple who describe themselves as hostages to the north because they cannot afford moving to the south, tell a story purporting to illustrate the different ways Russians and Scandinavians tackle everyday challenges.

Interviewer:	Since we're on the subject of abroad, what do you know about your northern neighbours? Are the people who live in Scandinavia like us?

Elena:	Well, I think their life's a lot easier than ours.
Nikolay:	They don't need to use up all their energy on all sorts of everyday problems. Living there's more enjoyable. [...]. They're wilting under all that wealth. Here, it's like this: if you can't find a screwdriver, you use whatever you've got at hand. *They* call the local service station.
Elena:	Ay, d'you remember what our friends told us? Some foreigners came here with flies to fish with, probably Finns or Norgs. They board this helicopter, and off they fly to the tundra. They'd brought along a piece of Swiss cheese, but forgotten the knife. [Parodying the fishermen, she throws out her arms in an expression of helplessness] A disaster! One of our boys, the helicopter mechanic, seeing their horrified expressions thought something really serious had happened. So what does he do? He cuts a length of wiring, fixes a piece of wood at either end, and uses this contraption to carve up the cheese. He'd probably never felt more proud of his own people than at that moment.

People with personal experience of Scandinavians have a more nuanced approach. Valeria (female, around forty) and Katya (female, early twenties) work at the international department of an institution of higher education and have visited the Nordic countries on a number of occasions.

Interviewer:	Both of you know a lot about foreigners from personal experience. Could you tell me what you think about the differences between people living in Russia and Scandinavia respectively?

Valeria:	Well, I mix with foreigners mainly out of interest. It's always interesting to learn new things about people living nearby. They're sort of next door [pointing in the general direction], but their worldview couldn't be more different. In the very beginning, after I'd started going around with foreigners, a lot of things shocked me. For instance, what I found weird was normal to them.
Katya:	You're right, but after you've met a few of them and got to know them, you realize they're human just like us. And you start accepting these foreign bodies as they are instead of trying to get them to be like us.
Valeria:	But that's something you learn from experience ... [exhales audibly, as if she is thinking of something with regret]. So many thoughts whirling around ... To start with you think everything here is just how it's supposed to be and not there. But then everything seems good there, but not here [gestures right and left as she speaks]. I'll tell you about the washing machine – all my friends know this story. [Recounts the story with great passion.] I'd been dreaming about buying a washing machine, because I DIDN'T HAVE ONE. Finally I managed to buy one – I'm pleased as Punch and tell a Finn. I mean, I tell him how much time I'm saving, and how my hands will benefit etc ... Then he asks me twice in a row, 'so you've bought a dishwasher.' And I say 'not a dishwasher, no, not me nor any of my friends or acquaintances – that's a luxury for us.' So he says, 'I can't imagine how anybody can live without a dishwasher. Whenever ours stops

	working I call the repair man immediately or have to go and get a new one. Otherwise there'll be mountains of dirty dishes in the house.' I can tell you, I felt really, really put out! On the one had (in what way am I worse [=*this is unfair!*]), and on the other, how can you not wash dirty dishes for days on end?
Katya:	Precisely. That's how they raise their kids too. And it's not right!

Finally an extract from an interview with three young men who had little personal experience with Scandinavians – an example of the very derogatory way of describing the Western neighbours, of which there are quite a few in my interview sample:

Tolik:	Some friends once showed me a picture [from Norway] of eight people. Only one of the faces had the merest glimpse of intelligence. The others, some had disproportionately large heads, others disproportionately small. It wouldn't be insulting to call them completely deformed.
Kolya:	And the intelligent-looking guy, he wasn't Russian by any chance?
Tolik:	Precisely! Didn't I say? But you're right. It was the first time I saw the photo. Since then it's been explained to me scientifically. To put it briefly, population density in northern Norway is extremely low, so there's a particular blend of blood and what have you.

As we can see, the subject of Scandinavians evokes a range of different views among my interviewees. Scandinavians are different and strange; OK when you get to know them; gentle and naive. But they're also seen as mentally and physically impaired. Underlying these different descriptions, a theme can be distinguished, a common thread in almost all of the narratives in my sample. It is the idea of 'the good life in the West'. Many interviewees are explicit about what they believe is the prosperity of the Nordic countries. People over there are positively 'wilting under all that wealth'; they 'live in an incubator', are 'given everything by the state' and 'don't lift a finger if they don't have to'. Even the least impressed interviewees seem to imagine Scandinavians as a rich and comfortable bunch. The three young men who found hardly a trace of intelligence among the *Norgs* portrayed in a photograph, believed their Western neighbours 'take planes like we take taxis'. Later in the interview, they added, 'something has to be wrong with them too', indicating that by and large Scandinavians are pretty well off. And two psychologists (female, early forties, and male, around fifty), who claim Scandinavian countries are withering on the vine from lack of fresh blood, agree that it would be a good idea to settle there if one had the chance.

But while 'the good life in the north' is an ideal to strive for (or an idealized reality they had been promised by Soviet authorities), the 'good life in the West' is a good life *in scare quotes* for my Kola inhabitants. It is – at least in its extreme version – a hollow 'good life', like a horror film, the heaven you don't want to end up in, a sanitized Barbie world. And with so much in-breeding, 'they're all sisters and brothers', as the female psychologist claimed. Life in the West, including Scandinavia, is a 'life in plastic, it's fantastic'.[10] High levels of personal wealth and highly organized, *but with no soul*. One of my interviewees (female, around forty) in fact likened Scandinavia to the classic American soap opera *Santa Barbara*, notorious for its glamorous but cardboard characters and the 'slow motion' of its plot. It is a place of 'extraordinary dullness' and monotony, where parents are unable to stay awake at the wedding of their own children,[11] where people eat for the sake of nutrition, not for pleasure,[12] where schools produce 'degenerated children',[13] where you can hardly tell the difference between a man and a woman,[14] where people are incapable of handling unexpected situations – like how to divide the cheese when you've forgotten your cheese knife, or what to do with the dirty dishes when the dishwasher breaks down. The way people move shows you how weak they have become. But they don't have to keep in shape because the state literally supports them. What they need is a strong dose of Russian zest, initiative and spirituality. As formulated by one of my interviewees (male, early thirties): 'They're completely normal people. But they should visit us more often and let their hair down. There they sit, turning sour. They need to add a bit of zest to their lives. We're always ready to help, right?'

'The good life in the north' is well within the bounds of accepted Russianness, although it is also a way to distinguish oneself from outright *ordinary* Russianness, characterized by a lack of *kulturnost*, the alleged bane of the south. 'The good life in the West', on the other hand, is the exact opposite of what is considered the essential quality of the good Russian, their *shirokaya dusha*, or 'wide soul', comprising passion, generosity, open-mindedness, hospitality, unlimited kindness and a certain amount of recklessness.[15] 'The good life in the West' is, in this sense, a representation of 'Anti-Russia' – for better (a certain amount of law and order is in principle desirable), but most of all *for worse* (it's not worth it if a soulless society is the alternative).

On the whole my interviewees are more likely to define themselves by othering southwards than westwards. They all seem to have a very distinct idea of what it means to be a Russian *northerner*, and how that identity differs from that of southerners. My interviewees have a harder time pinning down the Scandinavians – some have nothing to say at all, some are quite categorical in their opinions but lack the supporting evidence; only a few have experienced Scandinavians face to face and can put flesh on the bone. Hence, narratives about life in Scandinavia might serve to shape north-west Russian identity by confirming pre-established images of Russianness, though presumably with less force than narratives about southerners. Even in my scattered sample, a thread runs through the interviews, an image of relatively wealthy Scandinavians, but spiritually impoverished in comparison with Russians. The othering westwards might be less outspoken than southwards, but the conclusion is no less clear: even those who, given the chance, would settle in the Nordic countries (which quite a few of them have, in fact), express the same sentiment: 'this is not what we want *for Russia*'.

*

Then, when I introduce a new topic for discussion, the environmental situation in the country, all this is turned upside-down. From a conversation with two women in their twenties:

Interviewer: Do you have any thoughts about nuclear safety on the Kola Peninsula?

Tanya: Well, we live in a peaceful nuclear environment. In inverted commas, I mean, obviously. In my view, we've had a run of good luck so far. Russians in general are a lucky bunch of people. Foosht! Foosht! [spitting twice over her left shoulder].[16]

Sveta: Not to mention superstitious. Touch wood! There's a lot they don't tell us in general. There's probably a ton of problems on those submarines and elsewhere too. There are nuclear powered vessels in the middle of town, and we've got the Kola power station in our back yard.

[...]

Tanya: Live and die in blissful ignorance, tra, la, la. We depend on a good dose of Russian *avos* [faith that nothing unpleasant will occur], and, I might add, on our European neighbours.

Interviewer: In what sense?

Tanya: We still believe 'foreigners will come to our aid' [old expression]. They aren't particularly keen on dying just because we're idiots. So they're keeping an eye on the environment. And our leaders aren't interested in international scandals. So we're better off than the other regions.

On the topic of the environment, then, the Scandinavian countries come in for praise. Some ridicule foreigners for worrying: 'only foreigners are afraid of all that' (female, around thirty). Nevertheless, many appreciate the work done by the Nordic countries to monitor radiation levels in the area. As articulated by Valeria, the woman with the washing machine above: 'They've got their ear to the ground all right. At least, that's what people secretly hope'. And by Tanya: 'We still believe foreigners will come to our aid. They aren't particularly keen on dying just because we're idiots. So they're keeping an eye on the environment.' In the opinion of one young woman, Russians are incapable of overseeing nuclear safety, 'I'd say the mentality is different in other countries. In Russia, safety regulations will always be broken.'

Interviewer: What do you know about the radioactive waste deposited underground in the Kola Peninsula, and how do you feel about it?

Olga: I'm *categorically* [*ka-a-a-ategoricheski*] against it. It would've been much better in my opinion if we weren't making the stuff in the first place — we can't use the waste and don't need it. The environment round here is already saturated with poisonous substances. In our country, you know, everything is for sale. That's just how it is. Someone makes a decision, and the waste is dumped underground. They don't ask us.

Valentina: That is so true! Russians as a nation are all for sale [*prodazhny narod*], and especially the bureaucrats. They ... er, I mean Russians ...

obviously have their good points, but putting them into practice is difficult. I personally, my roots are Jewish, and I feel closer to the Jews, despite being Russian as well, strictly speaking.

Olga: Russian or not, you don't want to live in Russia do you?

Interviewer: Is it like that? And if it is, why don't you?

Valentina: [Exclaiming loudly] I loathe Russia as a state! They're pumping up oil both in Norway and here, but they have different attitudes to sharing the pickings. Just compare the Norgs with us, just as an example. [Bangs her fist on the table top.] [. . .] So I'm looking for a nice place in Old Europe [*v Starushke-Evrope*] for my daughter. And I'm investing stacks of money in her education. I can't see any future for my kid in our country.

Completely different narratives are invoked when the discussion shifts from 'our Scandinavian neighbours' to 'our northern environment'. Most people are protective of Russia and what they conceive of as Russianness when asked to share their impressions of Scandinavians. The subject of the environment, on the other hand, gives them an opportunity to complain about everything that goes wrong in Russia, but which the Scandinavian countries, in contrast, are good at. The term *avos* is used to describe Russian unpredictability and excitement, which in discussions about the foreigners carries a positive connotation. Sometimes the stakes are too high, though. When no one takes responsibility and everything is for sale, it could just as easily end in disaster. While Scandinavian discipline and diligence might add up to utter boredom, they might, in certain situations, save your life. The positive accounts of Nordic diligence provide a specific way to reproduce Russianness. The important thing is not so much which conclusions are drawn on particular issues – whether northerners are cultured or not, whether Scandinavia is boring or not, or whether there is something wrong with the Kola environment or not – but that your opinion is drawn from a specific set of recognizable narratives, keeping certain types of stories 'in the air'. And we have learned something about the situations that are more likely to evoke specific narratives. If you want a Kola inhabitant to say something nice about people on the other side of the border, don't ask him what he thinks about foreigners, ask him about nuclear safety.

Separatists, beware

BEAR was invented by the Norwegian Ministry of Foreign Affairs, with good help from Oslo's IR research circles. The then Minister of Foreign Affairs, Thorvald Stoltenberg, launched the idea of a joint transnational East–West partnership in the European North in spring 1992; he already persuaded Russian Foreign Minister Andrei Kozyrev of the idea's merits. By the time the partnership was formalized in January 1993, its history had already been written: cooperation in the Barents region, according to the Ministry, is simply a continuation of eighteenth- and nineteenth-century trade relations between the coastal populations of Norway and north-west Russia, which had been going on for nearly two centuries until the Russian Revolution, and mainly involved the exchange of Norwegian fish for Russian grain and wood. Relations between Norwegians and Russians had several aspects, including a pidgin language of some 400 words of use in trading and bargaining. The Russians usually arrived in northern Norway as soon as the ice had melted in the White Sea, and in the summer season, there was a good deal of commercial and social interaction. Many of the Russians returned to the same places in Norway every year, thus establishing more or less permanent relationships with the locals.[17]

In Norwegian, that historic form of trade with Russia is called the Pomor trade. With the establishment of the Barents region, 'Pomor' became something of a buzzword in Norwegian foreign policy circles. And in people's everyday lives as well: shops, museums and festivals in northern Norway were soon baptized *Pomor* this or that – and quite a few drinking establishments too. (Discos or clubs tended to be named *Gorbie*, in tribute, of course, to the man who opened the border.) 'Pomor' became synonymous with the new times, the end of the Cold War and friendship across the border. In Russian, however, 'Pomor' refers to 'people who live on the shore', in practice those who inhabited the Russian northwestern shores before the Soviet expansion – the 'conquest of the north' – set in after World War I. Following the Norwegian 'cultivation' of the concept of Pomor, it was picked up by the few Russians whose predecessors had lived in the region for generations. The majority of the population was either first, second or third generation 'immigrants' from other parts of the Soviet Union.

Since 'Pomor' did not gain much resonance among Russian decision makers, the term gradually lost its significance as a metaphor for cross-border collaboration. It did come to stand for a narrower channel of cooperation, however, between the old 'Pomor capital' in Norway, Vardø, and groups in Arkhangelsk who wanted to revive the concept. Vardø, practically no more than an old fishing village on the north-eastern tip of Norway, was in dire economic straits in the 1990s, with sky-high unemployment and accelerating depopulation. The town milked the Pomor brand for all it was worth. With financial assistance from the Barents Secretariat, which manages the Norwegian funds for joint projects with north-west Russia on behalf of the Norwegian Ministry of Foreign Affairs, ties were forged with Russian Pomor-friendly groups in the cultural, economic and political spheres. At the 2012 Pomor Festival, Thorvald Stoltenberg, 'father' of the Barents Region partnership, was given the title of 'Honorary Pomor'. On visiting Arkhangelsk the year after, he proposed the establishment of a new department at the Northern (Arctic) Federal University, dedicated to the study of Pomor culture. On the same occasion, a Norwegian–Russian Pomor Agreement was signed, and Stoltenberg was appointed Honorary

Doctor at the University. The Director of the new Pomor Institute of the Indigenous Peoples and Minorities in the North, Ivan Moseev, said,

> A special thing about the Institute is that for the first time we will study not only indigenous peoples and minorities included in the official list of indigenous peoples and minorities of Russia, but also other indigenous peoples who do not have the status of a minority.[18]

*

In autumn 2012, the Russian Federal Security Service (FSB) accused Ivan Moseev of working with Norwegian secret services to destabilize Arkhangelsk oblast socially and politically, a charge carrying a 20-year sentence.[19] Charges of high treason were dropped when the case came to court; instead he was accused of incitement to ethnic hatred. The charge was originally brought because Moseev was believed by FSB to have posted a piece on a newspaper website in which Russians were referred to as 'scum'. According to the editor of the website the comment had been sent from Moseev's IP address, which Moseev denied. A group of Russian patriots had gathered outside the court, carrying banners on which Pomors were accused of being separatists and traitors of Russian national interests. One of them read, 'Is Arkhangelsk oblast the big, sovereign Russian North or Norway's Pomor colony?' Another, 'Say NO to Pomor fairy-tales in Norwegian orchestration!'

Two years before, a book called *Pomor Fairy-Tales* had been published in Norwegian and Russian, financed by the Norwegian Barents Secretariat – free copies were distributed to schools in northern Norway and north-west Russia. Around the time of Moseev's trial, the book suddenly attracted the attention of the media. In an article that goes to some lengths to ridicule the book's attempts at adapting modern Russian to 'Pomor style', its author speaks of the publication as 'a Norwegian–American attempt at destroying the Russian ethnos'; the message being transmitted to

Russian schoolchildren is, 'Be a Pomor – that is, DON'T BE RUSSIAN'.[20] In another article – entitled '"Pomor hysteria": When will Norway "negotiate with the Pomors", and not with the Russians?'[21] – the fairy-tale book is referred to as 'propaganda' aimed at 'defending Norwegian interests [...] against the interests of the Russian people and the Russian state'. Moseev is referred to as a 'perpetual activist, with no constructive work to his name, no real [standards of] professionalism, a noisy person who loves the [sound of] loud words of the "civil society organizations"'. The author quite correctly observes that the word Pomor is used differently in Norwegian and Russian, a result, which he explains, either of Norwegians' ignorance of the word's real meaning, or as a determined effort by Norway to create chaos in Russia in order to get hold of Russian natural resources. Norwegian attempts to 'create a positive northern identity' necessarily imply a perception of 'traditional Russian identity [as] something "negative"'.

Yet another article attacks the premises of the entire enterprise – both the fairy-tale book and Barents regional cooperation as such – which is reflected in the book's foreword: the Barents region is portrayed as a 'common home' of Norwegian and Russian northerners.[22] The Barents region, the author argues, is not a historical region; the concept was invented by the Norwegians for political purposes (and not very benign ones). Northern Norway and north-west Russia are united 'artificially' in a regional structure to promote collaboration. The claim that northerners on both sides of the border are fundamentally similar is a lie, and an insult to the north-west Russian population: northern Norway is the 'utmost periphery' of Europe, known for its 'deepest provincialism' – the old trade across the border in no way involved any 'spiritual relationship'. And insofar as Norwegians are described as 'the closest Europeans' to the Russian Pomors, the author asks: 'Who were we then: Asians or Arctic Papuans? Would have been interesting to know.' The Pomor fairy-tales are 'not fairy-tales at all, but plain Russophobia'. The inanities of the book would have been amusing, were it not for 'the author's convulsive attempts' to influence the mindset of the coming generation.

Ivan Moseev was found guilty in early 2013 of violating Article 282, part 1 of the Russian Federation Criminal Code, concerning actions aimed at inciting hatred or enmity, as well as abasement of dignity of a person or group of persons on the basis of nationality or origin with the use of mass media.[23] He was fined 100,000 roubles (about 2,500 euros), lost his right to be a member of any Russian public organization and to have a bank account. By order of the procurator, he was also dismissed from his post at the university, and put on Russia's list of 'terrorists and extremists'. He appealed the verdict in higher courts, but to no avail. In late 2013, he filed a complaint to the European Court of Human Rights that he was denied the right of a fair trial.[24]

Norgs and pomors

BEAR was a targeted and determined effort to create a region, to be 'talked and written into existence' by reference to history and space. This chapter does not evaluate those region-building efforts in detail, but a certain pattern emerged in my interviews with ordinary people on the Kola Peninsula, conducted around one and a half decades after the transnational partnership was launched. Few interviewees, if any, speak of similarities between Russian and Norwegian northerners – quite the opposite, as we concluded above. Norgs and Russians are different – for better, but most of all for worse. Norgs differ from Russians physically and mentally, even though it's hard to pin down exactly how: they're frost-resistant but floppy; eyes agaze but niggardly; naive but cunning: 'They're sort of next door, but their world view couldn't be more different.' They live their lives in a northerly *Santa Barbara*, all predictable and in slow motion. They have everything you can dream of, but do not know how to enjoy life. It's 'excruciatingly dull', it's monotonous and rational. Life in plastic, no soul.

Interestingly, Scandinavian rationality and dullness are framed differently depending on the topic of discussion. They have negative connotations when the question concerns how Scandinavians compare to Russians in general, but positive ones the moment the conversation turns to a more practical field, like environmental protection. Different kinds of Russianness are narrated in the two situations: 'holy Russia' and 'land of idiots'. The genre is comedy: My interviewees apparently try to outdo each other when they speak of Scandinavian vacuity or wealth, Russian spirituality or madness. Norwegians are 'wilting under all that wealth' and 'take planes as we take taxis', they're 'all brothers and sisters' and their schools produce 'degenerated children'. Russians are the exact opposite, but at the same time they 'live and die in blissful ignorance, tra, la la'. Sometimes a Scandinavian 'Other' enters the frame and puts things into perspective, shows you what's important in life and what's not. There is the Finn who doesn't know what to do with the dirty dishes when the dishwasher breaks down – 'that's how they raise their kids too – and it's not right!' There are the fly-fishing foreigners, 'probably Finns or Norgs', who don't know how to divide the Swiss cheese when they have forgotten to bring a cheese knife to the tundra. 'Our boy [...] probably never felt more proud of his own people than at that moment.' But it's also the Scandinavians who turn open the 'inverted commas' of the Russian 'peaceful nuclear environment', who come to the rescue when Russian incompetence becomes all too evident, who show people that the emperor has no clothes.

Everyday Russian chitchat about Scandinavian neighbours is a cheerful genre, a blissful mix of comedy's aha-moments and satire's playfulness. It is a place where you can throw out exaggerations, absurdities, whatever comes to mind in the situation, twist and turn established truths, laugh and provoke. It is a joyful commonplace for the cultivation of Russianness.

The Other is the West, loud and clear. But it is not a fixed entity; it changes with circumstance, evades definition. It's not actually so important who the Other is, it just has to be someone. And the West is always there to play with.

*

The Barents regional cooperation continues to this day, albeit on a smaller scale than its heydays in the 1990s. Growth in cross-border contact is, by any thinkable measure, impressive. But the story behind the collaboration is no longer that of the Pomors. Norwegian foreign policy in the European North – declared in the early 1990s as 'Barents policy' – was re-branded 'High North policy' after the turn of the century, and in recent years increasingly as 'Arctic policy'. The Pomor adventure has tapered off, and is now represented by the occasional joint festivity between a wind-swept decaying Norwegian fishing village and a small group of local patriots in Arkhangelsk. The old slogan remained in circulation until Ivan Moseev was accused of high treason and later convicted for incitement to ethnic hatred – against the Russians. Herr Stoltenberg the elder – Thorvald is the father of long-serving Norwegian Prime Minister Jens Stoltenberg – occasionally travels around his old northern empire, unveiling a statue of himself here, receiving an honorary doctorate there. In 2012, he was appointed Honorary Pomor in Arkhangelsk.

The story of Moseev's arrest is the 'NATO raid tragedy' plot in distilled form. It is the story of a NATO with no inhibitions whatsoever, which peddles fairy-tales to indoctrinate innocent children, to disrupt the patriotism of the coming Russian generation, to ultimately destroy the Russian ethnos. It is also a satire over Norwegian Barents rhetoric. So you want to 'create a positive northern identity' – that means the old Russian identity isn't good enough? So you think we're two of a kind – oh, yeah! Well, we did trade with each other a hundred years ago, but there was no 'spiritual relationship' involved. You consider yourselves Europeans, where you sit in the 'outermost periphery', and in 'deepest provincialism'? And what are we then – Arctic Papuans? Norway's Pomor colony?

*

In March 2014, Stoltenberg Jr was appointed Secretary General of the North Atlantic Treaty Organization. Do I hear: 'What were we saying?'

CHAPTER 6

ARCTIC TALK, RUSSIAN POLICY

What is the Arctic's role in the story about Russia? How does the Arctic fit in with the other building blocks of that story? How does it all make Russia 'ready for action' in the Arctic, in terms of foreign policy? This is the simple way of putting what I've been attempting to answer in this book. Of course, there's a multitude of stories about Russia and the Arctic doing the rounds, just as there are about Russianness in general – and these stories interact in mysterious ways. So do the various explanations of Russian foreign policy, drawn from the complex tool box of IR theory. And there's the 'whose story?' question too: there's a plethora of story-tellers in the field – I'm one of them.

*

The point of departure for this study is the assumption that our sense of who we are, whether as individuals or states, is narratively constructed. And further, that this sense of self, or identity, is part of the fabric that constitutes action, foreign policy included. We become who we are by telling ourselves stories and acting them out; it is how we make sense of the world and give our lives coherence and direction. When we recount our actions, we consciously or subconsciously seek to adopt the story-teller's position, rather than just that of a character. If I ask you what you have been doing, for example, you will often not just chronicle a series of events (with yourself as one of the characters), but make it sound coherent and reasonable (as the story-teller). You craft a story that hangs together and makes sense, a story that goes to show that your actions are credible and legitimate. Knowing the ways in which stories are normally expected to be composed (and knowing that you will often have to recount what you do to others), you sometimes adapt your actions to these conventions. In Carr's (1986: 61–2) words, to act is 'to make the constant attempt to surmount time in exactly the way the story-teller does. It is the attempt to dominate the flow of events by gathering them together in the forward-backward grasp of the narrative act.' The key words here are 'to dominate the flow of events' – 'in exactly the way the story-teller does'. So, while sometimes we change a story to accommodate the events, 'sometimes we change the events, by acting, to accommodate the story' (ibid.).

Past experiences suffuse our perceptions of the present and our expectations of the future, but they have to be 'storied' in order to become intelligible. In our efforts to make sense of the world, we read into the past a narrative structure that it doesn't really have; beginnings and ends are randomly set. Present and past function together in our perception of time, like foreground and background, or focus and horizon, in our perception of space. Narration is not just a passive recounting of events but is informed and influenced by our knowledge of the past end expectations for the future. Narration is our modus operandi as human beings when we try to come to grips with our here and now, in-between past and future.

A community exists wherever there is a narrative account of a 'we' which has continuous existence over time. Such a community is 'constantly in the process, just like the individual is, of composing and re-composing its own autobiography. Like the autobiography of an individual, such a story seeks a unifying structure for a sequence of experiences and actions' (p. 163).

A state can be such a community. A common thread in the IR literature on narrative and foreign policy is the link between identity and interest: foreign policy can be explained as the result of state interest (in addition to, not in place of, the international power game; see Introduction); but such interest is determined by narratively constructed identities. As claimed by Browning (2008: 46), action only becomes meaningful in the process of narrating a constitutive story of the self: 'By establishing a linear story from whom we were in the past up until the present a narrative framework is created within which experiences become intelligible to ourselves and to others, and future action becomes meaningful (ibid.).' In brief, it is only by telling stories about who we are that it becomes possible to say what we want.

According to Carr (1986), claiming that we first act and then tell about what we have done, 'seated around the fire as it were', is a simplification – we cannot separate our actions from stories previously told and stories yet untold. My Russian story-tellers talk and act, they act and talk. As the author of this book, I myself act (in writing the book) and talk (or write), but I am not a character in the stories captured in the chapters above; therefore, at least in principle, I do not have to play the role of the narrator who consciously or subconsciously tries to avoid being the ingenuous chronicler of stories in which he or she also plays a part and establishes him- or herself as a story-teller. Admittedly, I am not just a chronicler – I select events based on their relevance for my story, and I strive to give an organized, coherent account rather than reporting events as they apparently happen – but I can make an attempt, at least, to focus on the events and strip my story of justifications and explanations. So let us sit down for a minute, by the fire.

Seated around the fire

Now this is what happened, as far as I'm concerned:

The Arctic is getting warmer, in more than one way. The ice is melting and scientists are uncertain about how it will affect the Arctic ecosystems. Political discussions are also heating up. Who, people are asking, actually owns the Arctic?

In the aftermath of the Cold War, the Arctic became a site of collaboration between East and West. European governments were keen to draw the young Russian Federation into new forms of transnational institutional arrangements aimed at reducing the potential for future East–West conflict. In the European North, BEAR was established following a Norwegian initiative in 1993. The partnership between Norway, Sweden, Finland and Russia spanned a number of functional fields, with infrastructure, business cooperation and environmental protection at the core. At the circumpolar level, the Arctic Environmental Protection Strategy (AEPS) was created in 1990 by the 'Arctic eight', at Finland's suggestion. Canada soon proposed the establishment of an Arctic Council. After some initial opposition from the USA, the Council was created in 1996, with the AEPS programmes subsumed under the new structure. Indigenous peoples' associations were included on the Council as 'permanent participants'.

During the first decade of its existence, the Arctic Council remained a forum for coordinating environmental monitoring and science in the Arctic. At the same time, the regional BEAR collaboration was struggling to meet the initial expectations of thriving East–West cooperation on trade and industry. The partnership also had a declared region-building objective, which included creating a common northern identity among the inhabitants in the eastern and western parts of the European Arctic. These Arctic political partnerships, whether circumpolar or regional, many considered to be 'a thing of the early 1990s': early post-Cold War initiatives that ultimately failed to attract sustainable high-level political interest.

This changed when members of a Russian scientific expedition planted a Russian flag on the seabed at the North Pole in August 2007. It was widely perceived in the international community as a demonstration of power by the Russians in the Arctic, even indeed as a brazen attempt to lay claim to the North Pole itself. It happened at a time of mounting interest in the prospects for extractive industries in the Arctic, and for the use of the new ice-free waters as shipping lanes. The global media started talking about a 'scramble for the Arctic', and there was a marked surge in political interest. In the Arctic Council, member states began to deploy delegates of increasing seniority: the 2011 biannual ministerial meeting was the first to host a convocation of all eight foreign ministers. Non-Arctic states also showed an interest in Arctic affairs, especially Asian nations. In 2013, China, Japan, Singapore and South Korea, among others, were accorded status as permanent observers in the Arctic Council.

*

The 1982 UN Convention on the Law of the Sea (UNCLOS) had introduced the concepts of economic zone and continental shelf, giving coastal states exclusive jurisdiction over the exploration, management and extraction of natural resources. All coastal states may establish an economic zone and continental shelf of 200 miles. They can also claim sovereignty over their continental shelf *beyond* the 200 nautical mile line, but only if the extended shelf is a natural prolongation of the area within the 200-mile limit. The shelf can extend up till 350 nautical miles from the shore, or 100 nautical miles beyond the 2,500 metre isobath. In contrast to the economic zones and the continental shelf within 200 miles, however, jurisdiction is not granted automatically. Governments must file a claim with the international Commission on the Limits of the Continental Shelf in New York, along with scientific evidence that the area beyond 200 miles is, in geological terms, a prolongation of the landmass. The Commission is neither a court of law nor a political body, but an expert panel tasked with assessing the validity of the scientific documentation provided by the coastal states. And states have only the one opportunity to get the international community to agree to an extension of their continental shelf beyond the 200-mile limit: governments have to file the claim within ten years of ratifying the Convention on the Law of the Sea. As many governments did not ratify the Convention until the mid-1990s and later, the clock marking the countdown to their submission deadlines did not start ticking until 1999.

Russia was the first Arctic state to file a claim, as early as 2000. Considered lacking in several respects, it was quickly rejected by the Commission. The Russians had included large areas of the continental shelf between the eastern and western sector lines. Part of the area extended to the North Pole itself. After having their submission rejected, the Russians intensified their exploration of the Arctic shelf. Norway filed its claim in 2006; it was approved in 2009. In addition to agreeing with Norway that the seabed under the Barents Sea and the Norwegian Sea beyond 200 nautical miles from land belongs to the continental shelf (i.e. is not deep sea), the Commission agreed that a small sliver of seabed beyond the 200-mile limit north of Svalbard also qualified as continental shelf. In other words, Norway was not making any claim to a shelf in the High Arctic. The Danish claim, which also covered the North Pole, was submitted in December 2014 and will be deliberated by the Commission at the September 2015 session. Canada was due to submit its claims in 2013 at the latest, but the Commission has not enforced these deadlines strictly. Russia has no definite time limit to worry about since its first submission was rejected, but Moscow apparently has plans to make a new submission in 2015. The US has yet to ratify UNCLOS.

Russia adopted its first Arctic policy document in 2001; the document focused mainly on the region as a potential zone of conflict involving the great powers. As global interest escalated, each of the Arctic powers hammered out their own Arctic strategy. Russia's Fundamentals of the State Policy of the Russian Federation, published in 2008, was the second to be issued by a member of the 'Arctic Five', after Norway's High North Strategy from 2006. The main objective of the Russian strategy is to transform the Arctic into the country's most important strategic natural resource base by 2020, and to preserve Russia's role as a leading Arctic power. It calls for the development of the Russian Arctic in a number of fields, most notably resource extraction, transport (primarily the Northern Sea Route) and other forms of infrastructure, but also 'softer' policy areas such as science and environmental safety. It presupposes a new Russian continental shelf claim by 2015, and also the formation of a new Arctic military unit for combating terrorism, smuggling and illegal immigration in the region. While the Russian strategy is considered somewhat 'harder' than those of the other Arctic states, with its explicit emphasis on national interest and sovereignty, it downplays the potential for international tension in the Arctic. The need for international collaboration to preserve the Arctic as a zone of peace is among the priorities of the strategy. A follow-up strategy appeared in 2013, covering more or less the same priorities as the 2008 strategy, but in a somewhat more realistic and dispassionate tone than its predecessor. Acknowledging that Russia will not be able to effectively explore the energy resources in the Arctic by itself, the document recognizes Russia's need for domestic and foreign private sector investment and experts to develop the country's northern regions.

There are no signs that Russia will not continue to fashion its claims to the Arctic shelf under the established Law of the Sea regime. In the Russian debate, Russia is presented as the guarantor of law and order in the Arctic, while identifying the Canadians and their overly aggressive rhetoric as the chief trouble maker.

*

In the Barents Sea, Norway and the Soviet Union had already established their respective 200-mile zones, in 1976–7, but they disagreed over how the boundary between them should be determined. They had been talking for several years about different methods of dividing the continental shelf in the Barents Sea. They agreed to base their initial discussions on the 1958 Continental Shelf Convention. The Convention set out a three-stage procedure governments were expected to follow to determine the border between their respective parts of a continental shelf. First, the Convention allows states to freely determine the mutual boundaries by simple agreement. Second, if the parties cannot agree, the median line principle will apply, according to which the dividing line offshore is determined by the direction of the boundary on land. Third, in the event of special circumstances, the Shelf Convention allows states to depart from the median line approach.

Norway lobbied on behalf of the median line principle, while the Soviets argued against it, referring to special circumstances. The special circumstances were the area's strategic importance to the Soviet Union – its largest naval fleet, the Northern Fleet, was stationed there with access to the Barents Sea. And there was a significant disparity in population numbers on either side of the border. Moreover, the Soviets had claimed all the islands (and, later, waters) between the sector lines in the east and west of the Arctic Ocean as early as 1926. A sector line is a line of longitude that starts from the terminus of the land boundary and intersects the North Pole. This, then, was the Soviet Union's official stance vis-à-vis Norway.

For years, talks between Norway and the Soviet Union on the Barents Sea delimitation line were held in deepest secrecy; there was no publicity, nor indeed, leaks of importance to the media. On 27 April 2010, prime ministers Dmitri Medvedev and Jens Stoltenberg, catching most people off guard, announced that Norway and Russia had finally reached an agreement on the maritime boundary. It was a compromise solution which divided the previously contested area of the Barents Sea into two equal parts. On 15 September of the same year, the Treaty on the Maritime Delimitation and Cooperation in the Barents Sea and Arctic Ocean was signed in Murmansk by foreign ministers Sergei Lavrov and Jonas Gahr Støre. Entering into force 7 July 2011, it consists of three parts: the border agreement and two annexes on fisheries and 'transboundary hydrocarbon deposits', both of which are integral parts of the treaty. The fisheries appendix broadly commits the parties to the continuance of the Joint Norwegian–Russian Fisheries Commission, established in 1975–6. The Commission sets total allowable catches for the main fish stocks in the Barents Sea, including the world's largest cod stock, and divides them 50–50 between them. The appendix concerning transboundary hydrocarbon deposits provides instructions for so-called unitization in the exploitation of transboundary hydrocarbon deposits whereby such deposits shall be exploited as a unit in a way agreed by both parties.

The agreement was met with domestic criticism in Russia, in the fishing industry, in parts of the regional political establishment and, eventually, within the opposition parties at the federal level. The Russian negotiators had failed to defend Russia's interests, the critics argued. As a result, ratification took longer than anticipated. The State Duma ratified the delimitation treaty on 25 March 2011, with only members of the 'presidential party' United Russia voting in favour.

*

Another issue of contention in the Barents Sea, one which is still unresolved, is the status of the fishery protection zone around Svalbard. Norway claims the right to establish an economic zone around the archipelago, but has so far refrained from doing so because the other signatories to the 1920 Svalbard Treaty have signalled that they will not accept such a move. They hold that the non-discriminatory code of the Svalbard Treaty must apply to the ocean area around the archipelago as well. Norway refers to the wording of the treaty, which only mentions the land and territorial waters of Svalbard. The waters around Svalbard are important feeding grounds for juvenile cod, and the protection zone, determined in 1977, represents a sort of 'middle way' aimed at protecting the young fish in the area from unregulated fishing.

To avoid provoking other states, Norway refrained for many years from penalizing violations of the protection zone regulations. Russian vessels do not report their catches in the area to Norwegian authorities, and Russian captains consistently refuse to sign the inspection forms after onboard inspections by the Norwegian Coast Guard. But the Russians do welcome Norwegian inspectors on board, and the same inspection procedures are pursued in the Svalbard zone as in the Norwegian economic zone. Norway's lenient enforcement practice hardened somewhat in relation to Russian fishers in 1998. The Norwegian Coast Guard had observed a Russian vessel fishing in an area that had been closed off because of the density of juvenile fish, and decided to arrest and escort it to a Norwegian port. The journey was interrupted, however, before they reached a Norwegian harbour, as a result of diplomatic exchanges between the two countries. In 2001, the Coast Guard arrested another Russian vessel in the Svalbard zone. It had committed a serious environmental crime, according to the authorities, having violated a number of fishing regulations. In the opinion of the Russians, on the other hand, Norway had illegally detained a Russian vessel in international waters, and in the process broken a *gentlemen's agreement* between the two countries of nearly 25 years' standing, whereby Russia accepted Norwegian monitoring of fishing operations in the Svalbard zone (including physical inspections of Russian fishing vessels), as long as Norway did not behave as if it had formal sovereignty in the area. The arrest of the Russian vessel was taken as an indication that Norway indeed considered itself as having such formal jurisdiction. The next time Norway attempted to arrest a Russian vessel in the Svalbard zone was in 2005 – again, for serious violations of fishing regulations, including overfishing. And again, the procedure came to an abrupt halt, though for different reasons than in the 1998 incident. The captain of the Russian fishing vessel simply decided to make run for it for a Russian harbour – taking along the Norwegian inspectors who were still on board. He was later sentenced in a Russian court, and official Russian reactions to the Norwegian move were much milder than in 2001. In 2009/10, the Norwegian Coast Guard arrested a handful of Russian fishing vessels in the protection zone around Svalbard, without any official response from the Russian authorities. They lodged a protest following an arrest in 2011, but not because it had taken place in waters where Norway had no formal jurisdiction. Instead, the Russians accused the Norwegian Coast Guard inspectors of brutal behaviour, which was not in the collaborative spirit of the delimitation line agreement signed a year earlier.

*

The BEAR alliance was the brainchild of the Norwegian Minister of Foreign Affairs, Thorvald Stoltenberg, in 1992. It was officially established by multilateral agreement a year later. While BEAR projects initially prioritized the building of common infrastructure and the development of East–West business cooperation, the underlying motive – at least as seen from the Norwegian side – was to revive a cross-border northern identity and thereby, hopefully, ease tensions between the two sides of the Cold War. The prerevolutionary Pomor trade between northern Norway and the area around Arkhangelsk in Russia was the perfect tool for this dedicated region-building effort. The mantra was that 70 years of Communism in Russia was an historical parenthesis; Russians and Scandinavians could finally get back together again, like long-lost cousins. Judging from my interviews with inhabitants of the Kola Peninsula, the results are mixed. Kola people both admire and loathe their Scandinavian cousins, but most of them would not want to be like them. 'The good life in the West' is an 'Anti-Russia' of sorts – for better or worse, mostly the latter. The rhetoric extolling the Pomor past – the word Pomor has different connotations in Russian and Norwegian – was eventually scandalized when the authors of the book *Pomor Fairy-Tales* were accused by Russian authorities of inciting ethnic hatred – against the Russians.

*

Which acts of Russian foreign policy can be observed in these accounts?

In the Arctic Ocean:

- Russia filed a claim with the UN Continental Shelf Commission in 2000, which was quickly rejected. Russia accepted this rejection and continues scientific exploration of the Arctic shelf.
- Russia published a new Arctic strategy in 2008, with the objective to transform the Arctic into the country's most important strategic natural resource base and to preserve Russia's role as a leading Arctic power. Acknowledging that Russia is not capable of effectively exploring the energy resources in the Arctic by itself, the document recognizes Russia's need for domestic and foreign private sector investment and experts to develop the country's northern regions.

- (Members of a Russian expedition planted a Russian flag at the seabed on the North Pole in 2007.)[1]

In the Barents Sea:

- Russia agreed to a delimitation line with Norway in 2010, splitting the previously disputed area into two equal parts.
- Russia has cooperated closely with Norway for 40 years on the management of the Barents Sea fish stocks.
- Russia disputes Norway's claim of a 200-mile zone around Svalbard, but accepts inspections of Russian fishing vessels by the Norwegian Coast Guard there. In the few instances where Norway has arrested Russian vessels in the zone, Russia earlier protested on the grounds that Norway had made the arrest in international waters. They no longer do that.

In the Barents region:

- Together with Norway, Sweden and Finland, Russia established BEAR in 1993. The regional cross-border collaboration continues to this day, with Russia as an active partner on a par with the Nordic countries.

That was my summary of events. Now let's hear what the characters in this account have to say – let's hear their own stories.

Enter the story-tellers

So this is what happened, as far as we're concerned, us Russian story-tellers:

> *The Arctic always has been and always will remain Russian. We are not at all convinced of Canada's peaceful intentions – the Canadians construct new military bases in the Arctic; they build new ice-going patrol vessels for use in the region; and they conduct military exercises there. On top of that, they claim that the Arctic*

always has been and always will remain Canadian – they cannot be trusted, and the rest of the Arctic nations will have to keep a watchful eye on them. Canada's worst – we just cannot stand how they're constantly banging on about the Arctic – but when you come to think about it, they are, of course, lined up with their NATO allies. Canada, Denmark, Norway and USA are pursuing a coordinated policy to prevent Russia access to the riches of the Arctic shelf. To that end, foreign intelligence are intensifying their activities in the border areas with Russia. They use their scientists for that purpose; they use their NGOs – no one can be trusted. By declaring the Arctic as strategically important for the alliance, NATO is meddling in the ongoing diplomatic conversations among the 'Arctic five', adding to them an element of power and thus increasing the risk that diplomacy will give way to military demonstrations. We are categorically against any militarization of the Arctic. The Arctic is our destiny, the Arctic is our everything.

But what the heck: you and I both know that there was once a country where the trees were higher and the water wetter – hubris and escapism, secrets and lies. We're Russia, let's face it.

This is a story told mainly by the journalists themselves – and it can be interpreted in the context as a specific journalistic genre. There's the occasional reference to a statement of the President, Prime Minister or FSB director, but only to support the journalist's own description of the situation (or the other way around: journalists tell stories they know the political elite would like to hear). My own account about the process of the establishment of the outer limits of the continental shelf under UNCLOS is mentioned, but only briefly, mostly as a factual background to the 'real' story about heroes and villains in the Arctic power game. Russia plays on the side of international law, while NATO operates without restraint in the background to take control of the Arctic, not very smartly, though – less like a threat than a nuisance. The 'story' itself isn't really a story; it's more of a statement about how the world is: Russia vs the West, black or white. There's a thin line between bold exclamations and the nervous retreat: we take it all back, we know our place in the world, and we know everybody knows. The mirage on the horizon, our fairy-tale lives.

Conspicuously, actual foreign politics at the time did not reflect this apparently widespread opinion that Russia should do whatever it wants in the Arctic, and whenever it wants to. Russia complies with the guidelines of the Law of the Sea, down to the last detail.

*

On 15 April 2010, we were all completely taken by surprise. Our President, Dm. Medvedev, had reached a most treacherous agreement with Norway on the delimitation of the Barents Sea. Out of the blue they had drawn a boundary dividing waters that have been indisputable Russian territory for nearly a century; with the stroke of a pen we handed over a large segment of our Arctic possessions to our Western neighbour. Yes, the two countries have been negotiating, but only because Norway was impudent enough, back in the 1970s, to claim the right to a significant share of Soviet waters in the Barents Sea. The Norwegians presented the extraordinarily covetous median line principle to support their claim, although they were well aware of the borders of our Arctic dependencies from 1926, and that we, naturally, would have to insist on the principle of fairness: what you have acquired under customary law cannot be taken away from you.

Seventy per cent of the Russian fishing fleet's annual catches in the Barents Sea are taken in waters over which Norway from now on will have jurisdiction. The Norwegians have been chasing us for years with their arbitrary inspections, and now they have the leverage they need to complete their long-standing strategy of getting rid of us in the Barents Sea once and for all.

But who knows, maybe the Norwegians aren't preparing draconian measures after all? They are our good neighbours – indeed, our very good neighbours – even if they belong to a different strategic alliance. And with the other NATO members casting their eyes on the Arctic riches, Norway could be a good ally.

The dominant voices in the Russian debate about the Barents Sea delimitation agreement are representatives of the Russian fishing industry who are well connected politically, primarily with the legislative branch of government, at both regional and federal levels. They engaged in a vigorous media debate and political campaign causing a significant delay in the Russian ratification of the delimitation agreement; and only the presidential party voted in favour of ratification. At the regional level, Murmansk Governor Yevdokimov was part of President Medvedev's delegation to Oslo, where the final agreement was reached in April 2010, and he supported the agreement publicly. The regional Duma was initially sceptical and adopted a resolution urging the State Duma and the Federation Council – the two chambers of the Federal Assembly, Russia's parliament – not to ratify the delimitation agreement. One month later, however, the resolution was withdrawn, and the Duma members now stepped forward with lavish praise of the agreement. Passions had died down, they declared, and it was time to reflect more deeply on the positive sides of the agreement; several meetings in Moscow had convinced them of that. Those responsible for the delimitation agreement, primarily the legal department of the Ministry of Foreign Affairs, but ultimately the President himself, were conspicuously absent from the domestic debate.

These stories are seemingly contradictory. On the one hand, Norway has always tried to harm Russia's interests in the Barents Sea and should be recognized for what it really is: the extended arm of NATO in the region. On the other hand, the Norwegians have initiated a good many collaborative ventures and displayed a genuine wish to cultivate good relations with Russia in the Barents region – they are actually an amicable and probably trustworthy neighbour. To an even larger extent than was evident in the debate about wider Arctic politics, there is also here a thin line between apparently opposing narratives. Again there's the bold exclamation followed by the nervous – or rather happy – retreat: we were categorically against the agreement, now we're categorically in favour of it. But, well, us Russians – we often act without thinking, led by our profound emotions and vibrant soulfulness. Luckily for us, though, there are a few level-headed people among us who can take the lead (although admittedly we're not an easy flock to lead).

Further, the fiercest defenders of the anti-Western approach have themselves close connections with Norway through long-standing professional partnerships and personal friendships. This is not reflected in the media material on which this investigation is based, but it's something I know from personal experience. The two most prominent figures in the debate, former Soviet Deputy Minister of Fisheries Vyacheslav Zilanov and Director General of the Fishing Industry Union of the North, Vasili Nikitin, are the most good-natured elderly men you can think of – yes, I know them personally – both are thoughtful, receptive and friendly; they often express their deepest respect, moreover, for the Norwegian people and how they have organized their society.

In the Russian discourse, there is no contradiction between talking about someone as a (genuine) friend and an (equally real) adversary, at one and the same time. Particularly, in international politics states are continuously trying to make life hard for each other, and there is nothing wrong in that. I have investigated these things in some depth earlier (Hønneland 2003) – there was, for instance, the Russian Minister of Fisheries who told his Norwegian counterpart in all seriousness: 'you're doing everything you can to destroy the Russian fishing industry, and for that, I respect you', giving the minister a clap on the shoulder as if to say 'you're my sort of man, now let's go and get ourselves a good vodka and talk about life'. (It would never occur to a Norwegian to use terms like these; a Norwegian minister would most likely have said something about mutual benefits, sustainability and win-win.)

Second, and even more important for the context of this book, Russian talk is liable to rapid jumps back and forth between seemingly incongruous conclusions. This was something I noted in my interviews with people in my investigation of Russian northern identities (Hønneland 2010). At the time I called it 'narrative juggling'. A person may say Murmansk is the best place in the world to live, only to indict the Soviet authorities of a crime against the Russian population by building a city of half a million people in this inhospitable northern outpost. One and the same person may call Scandinavia the most boring place on earth, and shortly thereafter say they would like to build a future there. Murmansk governor Yevdokimov called the Barents Sea 'our promising kitchen garden' but characterized what Russians perceived as a Norwegian attempt to prevent the Russians from fishing in it as completely natural, just as a decade earlier he had asked the Scandinavian countries for humanitarian aid, while in the same breath complaining in the Russian newspapers about misguided helpfulness.[2] As I speculated in Chapter 3, where the delimitation line was at issue, it is always a question of 'either/or' – anything 'in-between' would be in breach of narrative convention.

*

The main story in Chapter 4, about the management of natural resources in the Barents Sea, provides an important backdrop to our understanding of Russia's criticism of the delimitation agreement.

It all started in the 1990s, when Russia lay prostrate with a broken back and the Norwegians knew to take advantage of it. Within a few years they had trapped us into agreeing to a new set of fishery regulations that are clearly to the disadvantage of our Russian fleet – we found out that too late. Then it all culminated in 1999, when the Norwegians used their Western allies in the International Council for the Exploration of the Sea to secure majority for an artificially low cod quota recommendation for the Barents Sea, clearly motivated by the prospect of striking a blow against our already struggling fishing industry. For their part, the Norwegians could make up the quota reductions by increasing the production of farmed cod. Besides, a few years of lower catches wouldn't hurt their thriving economy, which is more than you can say about us. And it was all so obvious: at exactly the same time, they broke our old gentlemen's agreement not to arrest Russian vessels in the Svalbard zone – God knows, they wouldn't have dared back in the days when we were a superpower – and they suddenly introduced a new environmental law on Svalbard just after our coal company had announced plans to open a new mine. A coincidence? It hasn't got anything to do with environmental concerns – there's plenty of Russian shit around on Svalbard they could have taken us for if they wanted – no, what they want to prevent is the development of a prosperous Russian industry. And why is that? Norway and its NATO allies are determined to reduce Russia's presence in the Arctic to the barest minimum, at whatever cost.

And it continued in the years that followed, with trawler terror and pirate arrests. That said, our own fishing industry isn't exactly clean – our boys out at sea hold to the highest professional standards, but they're all in somebody's pocket. In this country, unorganized illegal fishing doesn't exist. So when you come to think about it, who else can keep things in order in the Barents Sea if not the Norwegians? They're a cunning lot, but their merit list is impressive: year after year, Norway is named as the most well-governed country in the world. Prosperity affects your worldview, I guess. And the head of our delegation to the Norwegian–Russian Fisheries Commission tells us that it's wrong to think Norway is trying to push us out of the Barents Sea, for whatever that's worth.

The characters who appear in stories about fisheries management in the Barents Sea are themselves story-tellers in the Russian media: representatives of the Russian fishing industry at both regional and federal levels. But again it is primarily the journalists who take the lead; it is the journalists who most fervently (and frequently) defend the view that Norway is after Russia in the Barents Sea, and it's the journalists who (admittedly rarely) question this claim. Political actors at higher levels (i.e. the Federal Fisheries Agency, which is subordinate to the Ministry of Agriculture) are occasionally referred to in the media, and similarly express both views: Norway and Russia are political adversaries, but a band of brothers at sea. And again, any praise there may be for Norway is inevitably followed by laments of Russian incompetence, the country's eternal fate.

The Barents regional cooperation, the topic of Chapter 5, is sometimes mentioned in my media material, but mostly in a factual way: neutral reports from joint Nordic–Russian projects, like cross-border winter sports festivals and student exchange schemes, or, more frequently, official visits by dignitaries from the other side of the border. It was 'storied' with the publishing of the book *Pomor Fairy-Tales* in 2010, described as a 'Norwegian–American attempt at destroying the Russian ethnos'.

*

As we saw in the Introduction, most IR studies of identity presuppose some form of othering, either external (of other states), internal (within the state) or historical (in relation to previous and future selves). In our case, external othering comes through loud and clear. In Chapter 2 on general Arctic politics, 'a Polar bear went out to hunt' – and it was not Russia. Canada is Russia's quintessential Other in the Arctic, with the other NATO countries lined up behind. In the subsequent chapters on the delimitation line and resource management in the Barents Sea, and on regional collaboration in the Barents region, Norway is the obvious Other, again with NATO indiscreetly lurking in the background. But the West is not a uniform and static Other – I will have more to say on that below. Internal othering is limited in the cases covered by this book, but there is an explicit othering of Moscow in regional criticism of the delimitation line in Chapter 3, and of the Pomor protagonists in Chapter 5. More pronounced is the othering in time, especially in Chapters 2 and 3: we are not what we used to be, and we will strive to become someone else than who we are now (in practice return to our former self). And, most conspicuously, throughout the chapters we find an 'inverted' othering: the Other is actually ourselves – all this, too, I discuss in the concluding sections of this chapter.

I have repeatedly referred to Ringmar's (2006) literary categories of romance, tragedy, comedy and satire. Only in one instance did I find the plot structure of the romance, but that was in the most fundamental story about Russia and the Arctic. Russia is the hero who is determined to 'save the Arctic'; Russia believes peace can be maintained in the region if only Russians are given free reigns to use their sensitivity and morality for the greater good. The most forceful narrative in the book takes the form of the tragedy. It is less prevalent in the general story about Russia and the Arctic, where Russia is still proactive, but all the more powerful in the stories about Russia and Norway in the Barents Sea region, where Russia has been referred to a more defensive role. This is somewhat ironic since Norway is at the same time spoken of as the good neighbour, the most trustworthy of the 'Arctic five', all of which (except Russia, of course) are members of NATO. The comedy is not very prevalent in my narratives, but there are subtle reflections of this genre in the stories of Russian absurdities, the blurred line between good and bad, the unexpected twists and turns. Satire does not occur frequently either, but it is blatant and noisy when it does: hey, who do we think we are really: God's gift to the world, or what?

In brief, tragedy and satire dominate – that sums up the story about Russia.

Defending the other self

This book says something about the narrative environment in which Russian Arctic politics is formulated, but it provides only bits and pieces of the analytical framework needed to explain Russian foreign policy. Theory on narrative and IR is actually quite simple – it claims that the available narratives form state identities, which in turn determine state interest, which then determines action. Alternatively, 'interest' is left out of the equation: in some situations, states simply act in defence of their identity, without explicitly considering whether it is in their 'interest' to do so. Typically, such actions take place at the expense of apparent political and economic gain. It could arise, for example, if Russia decided to flout the recommendations of the Continental Shelf Commission and unilaterally establish the limits of Russia's Arctic shelf. It would certainly lead to economic sanctions (in some form or other) and raise tensions between East and West. (Needless to say, we're already there since Russia's annexation of Crimea and involvement in the conflict in Ukraine from 2014 on, but unilateral action in the Arctic would not improve the situation.) An 'annexation' of the Arctic would clearly not be in Russia's political or economic interest – yes, it would secure Russian jurisdiction over potential reserves of oil and gas in the High Arctic shelf, but these resources are practically inaccessible and at least not economically viable to extract at the moment. (Most of the Arctic's hydrocarbon resources are on land and on the shelf within 200 nautical miles from the baselines, and therefore much easier to extract). And the foreign experts Russia needs to develop even the most accessible resources beneath the shallow waters close to land would leave the country (which they have already done in response to the Ukrainian crisis, but it would reduce the chances of Western companies to resume their work on the Russian shelf).

Such an action would have nothing to do with political or economic interests – it would be an action, perhaps more spontaneous than considered, performed in defence of the self: what would Russia be without (dominance in) the Arctic? Russia would not be Russia. We must act to ensure the survival of who we are, whatever the cost. The stories people tell about Russian heroism in the Arctic (ranging from the great eighteenth-century Arctic expeditions to the Soviet conquest of the North) must be kept alive. Only action can keep this constitutive story about Russia alive (and that is even more important since one of the other constitutive stories, that of Russia the great power, evaporated with the dissolution of the Soviet Union). By acting, one makes 'the constant attempt to surmount time in exactly the way the storyteller does [...] to dominate the flow of events by gathering them together in the forward-backward grasp of the narrative act' (Carr 1986: 61–2). We change the events, by acting, to accommodate the story.

As we saw in the Introduction, Ringmar (1996) emphasizes the importance of *recognition* for state identity. Identity is a precondition of interest, and in certain situations identity-driven explanations of foreign policy can substitute for interest-driven explanations altogether. This can happen, for instance, when a state has experienced loss of recognition under humiliating circumstances ('lost face'), or at 'formative moments' when new metaphors are launched and individuals tell new stories about themselves, and new sets of rules emerge through which identities are classified – in short, 'when the very definition of the meaningful is up for grabs' (p. 85). At these moments, there is an urgent need to have one's own constitutive stories recognized. Needless to say, Russia lost face when the Soviet Union (or the old Russian Empire) fell apart. It lost face, domestically and abroad, when it lost its capacity to take care of its Arctic possessions: infrastructure disintegrated and the population fled. New stories about the self were in the air – about a 'new Russia' totally different from the old – but things didn't work out, and the old stories provide a safe heaven, away from contemporary chaos.

So far, however, Russia has opted for the opposite strategy in the Arctic: openness to the outside world, strict adherence to the rules of international law and other norms of good political behaviour. As we have seen, this is not in opposition to the narrative where the West is out to get Russia in the Arctic. Incorporated in this narrative is the idea of Russia as the guarantor of law and order in the region. One might speculate whether the political elite actually wanted to add a new layer to the old narratives in order to ensure popular support for the chosen policy: to act responsibly in the Arctic despite overt Western aggression. The scales could easily have tipped, with the other variant of this overarching narrative determining the actions of the President: the West is out to get us, they cannot be trusted, so we should shun them. As we saw in Chapter 3, the Ministry of Foreign Affairs is generally outward-looking while the power structures in Russia tend to be more inward-looking. In Arctic affairs, the hardliners have been rewarded by increased security investments in the region. But the views of the Ministry of Foreign Affairs have determined action: strict compliance with the country's international obligations (which was Putin's more general foreign policy outlook up to the Ukrainian crisis; see Chapter 1). The power structures are not necessarily against this, but they would probably be less concerned were Russia to pull out of the international club.

The same goes for the Barents Sea delimitation agreement. In the opinion of almost all the public debaters, it was a bad deal for Russia, and it was largely seen through the lens of East–West conflict. And this is not just a debate that emerged with the conclusion of the delimitation line agreement – stories about Norwegian aggression in the Barents Sea have flourished for years. But action went against the (implicit) recommendations of these stories: Norway was to be trusted, according to the country's leadership, and a compromise was warranted. The accepted explanation in the Western foreign-policy literature is that Russia agreed to the delimitation line in order to further strengthen the status of the Law of the Sea in the Arctic.[3] By acting according to the principles of the Law of the Sea in establishing a delimitation line with a neighbouring state (following the guidelines of the Law of the Sea Convention to find *equitable* solutions, in practice a compromise), it would be harder for other states to challenge these principles in the establishment of the shelf's outer limits (i.e., the political costs would be higher the stronger the international norm). Interestingly, this explanation was not mentioned in my media material; slightly reminiscent, though, is the claim that the agreement was necessary in order to ensure Norwegian support to the future primacy of the existing Law of the Sea in the Arctic.

Similarly, the dominant narrative has not determined Russian action in the Barents Sea fisheries management. While the anti-Western narrative is clearly dominant in the public debate, Russian behaviour has been markedly accommodating. Russia is a constructive participant on the International Council for the Exploration of the Sea, the Northeast Atlantic Fisheries Commission and, not least, the Joint Norwegian–Russian Fisheries Commission. Even in the contested Svalbard zone, Russian authorities let the Norwegian Coast Guard inspect their vessels. They have also stopped protesting against Norwegian arrests of Russian vessels in the area.

Where does all this land us, in theoretical terms? Is my study a refutation of the claim that narrative equals identity equals (interest and) action? Of course not; reality is never that simple, nor is the theory. Narrative doesn't operate alone – a full explanation of a state's foreign policy requires a variety of theoretical tools (not a very bold statement; see the Introduction), including, not least, a study of internal power struggles at the domestic level. Moreover, narrative theory's fundamental claim that narratives define (or at least contribute to defining) identities and that understanding who we are influences our understanding of what we want, can hardly be refuted. This is not only for epistemological reasons (how can it be falsified?), but also ontologically most IR theorists would arguably agree that identities (possibly determined narratively) can influence interest and action (even hardcore realists would agree; they just have their analytical focus elsewhere). The question is what explanatory *force* it has. And even constructivists, among whom narrative theorists are normally grouped, would stop short of claiming that foreign policy in general can be explained by discourse, identity or narrative alone. As we saw in the Introduction, realists are normally content to explain a few important things in international politics (often state security and international economy), and leave the rest of the IR field to others. Constructivists, on the other hand, have no intention of taking over the whole field, but of enriching it, filling in the nooks and crannies overlooked by the 'grand theories' and, perhaps, of modifying their conclusions.

The lack of apparent congruence between the dominant narratives and actual politics makes for two further comments. First, there is the temporal aspect: a narrative that maintains its force over time will not necessarily display a high 'impact' on action (here: foreign policy) incessantly – it will fluctuate. And the impact of an emergent narrative can be either immediate or gradual, if it has any effect at all. Second, and this is one of my main points: acting (consciously or subconsciously) in opposition to a particular (e.g. dominant) constitutive story of oneself may imply acting consciously in defence of another (e.g. challenging or declining) constitutive story. Not playing by the rules of anti-

Western rhetoric in the Arctic, Putin has acted in defence of another story about Russia: we're not the backyard of Europe; we're a normal country.

In-between past and future

There are four meta-narratives in the Russian public debate about the Arctic – as we called them in Chapter 2: 'Russia vs the West', 'Russia and the Arctic', 'soil and soul' and 'fools and bad roads'. Most conspicuous is the story of NATO chasing Russia in the Arctic, fiercely, persistently and often surreptitiously. Othering westwards is present in all four case studies, but it grows in strength throughout the chapters, as the topics under discussion become more specialized and less highly profiled. In the general debate about the Arctic, with the imminent division of the Arctic continental shelf as the main issue, the Western states – especially Canada – are accused of acting improperly. The Russian response, however, is more righteous indignation than outright anger. When the Canadian Minister of Foreign Affairs said at a press conference the Arctic war was now over, his Russian colleague corrected him. There had never been any war in the Arctic. 'Fellow journalists smiled, while the slightly bemused Canadian nodded his agreement.'[4] Othering of the West is more distinct, and possibly harsher, in the public debate about the Barents Sea delimitation agreement, but it is still milder than the internal othering of those in Moscow responsible for the agreement (primarily the Ministry of Foreign Affairs). Norway does what it can to take advantage of Russian incompetence – that's natural; it's Medvedev who has committed the ultimate act of treachery. In the debate about the management of marine resources in the Barents Sea, the tone is even sharper. Norway conducts raids on behalf of NATO with the purpose to break Russia's neck. All forms of subterfuge are allowed; the rules are those of the intelligence world, not petty international law. In the story about the Pomors, the 'NATO raid tragedy' is presented in distilled form. It is the story of a NATO with no inhibitions whatsoever, aimed to indoctrinate innocent children in order to undermine Russian patriotism and ultimately destroy the Russian ethnos.

The anti-Western position reflected in the 'Russia vs the West' narrative is taken for granted as a point of departure for further discussion, but it can be reproduced, nuanced or challenged. The point is, it is here the story starts, whether the conclusion is in line with this narrative or in opposition to it. You can praise the Barents Sea delimitation agreement or Norwegian diligence in managing the marine resources for the good of future generations, but you first have to refer to the prevailing truth about NATO–Norway and its determination to get you, *and actively distance yourself from it.* The West is the axis around which Russian identity production revolves, just as it has been for centuries. But it is not a fixed entity. As we concluded in Chapter 5, everyday Russian talk about Scandinavian neighbours allows for exaggerations, absurdities, whatever comes to mind in the situation, twists and turns, making light of established truths, laughs and provocations. The Other is the West, but it changes with the circumstances and evades definition. Narratives can be juggled, oppositions combined – it's a thin, thin line. It's not actually so important who the Other is, it just has to be someone. The West is always there to play with.

*

'Russia and the Arctic' represents a temporary low, between a glorious past and a promising future – 'fools and bad roads' are Russia's eternal fate. 'Russia and the Arctic' is the story of the Arctic as the shrine of Russia's national idea; it was exactly where 'Arktika-2007' planted the titanium flag. The Arctic is a new political and spiritual continent, a promised land, Russia's cosmic destiny. Russia is the land with no limit, territorially or temporally. It stretches infinitely, it lasts eternally. The Russian landscape is wide, and so is the Russian soul – full of passion, generosity and recklessness. Russia is the ultimate expression of openness: openness of space and openness of heart – 'soil and soul'. The Arctic is all that; the Arctic is more Russian than Russia itself. The Arctic is the picture you present of yourself to the outside world, your wishful thinking:

Russia as a great power that can do whatever it wants, wherever it wants. But the Arctic is also the monster returning your gaze in the mirror: rubbish, decay, corruption, incompetence – hubris and escapism, secrets and lies.

This is the 'fairy-tale life', the noisy existence of extremes incessantly flying through the air: brutally categorical, nothing in-between. This is Russia the Janus-faced, the obscure – where reality is never what meets the eye but the choices are few and deceitful. So you move along the plain, exhilarated and numb at the same time, always part of the intense Russian drama.

*

The Arctic is the ultimate commonplace for the cultivation of Russianness. It is no place for the intolerable lightness of being, the unbearable un-Russian boredom. It is the venue for the big epic dramas in life, a ballroom floor for the wild Russian dance – through the ages, across the plains.

NOTES

Introduction

1. Borgerson (2008), who largely spurred the debate by his article 'Arctic Meltdown' in *Foreign Affairs*, spoke of 'a new scramble for territory and resources' and a 'great Arctic gold rush' (p. 63). Many of the books that followed on the subject had similar titles, like Anderson's (2009) *After the Ice: Life, Death and Politics in the New Arctic*, Howard's (2009) *The Arctic Gold Rush*, Sale and Potanov's (2010) *The Scramble for the Arctic* and Zellen's (2009) *Arctic Doom, Arctic Boom*.
2. This and the next paragraph draw on Hønneland (2010: 5–7).
3. Cameron (2001: 10ff) defines discourse as 'language above the sentence' or 'language in use'. The term is widely used throughout humanities and the social sciences and its meaning varies with academic discipline and epistemological stance.
4. Gubrium and Holstein (2009: xviii, emphasis in original) do not make the distinction between narrative and story, and provide a more commonsense definition of the terms: 'we use the terms *narrative*, *story*, and *account* interchangeably to refer to spates of talk that are taken to describe or explain matters of concern to participants'.
5. As an empirical example Gergen (2001: 254–5) refers how American adolescents characterize their life stories according to narrative conventions – happy at an early stage, difficult during the adolescent years, but now on an upward swing – that do not reflect actual events in their lives, or their perception of them, as accounted for when asked upfront: 'In these accounts there is a sense in which narrative form largely dictates memory. Life events don't seem to influence the selection of the story form; to a large degree it is the narrative form that sets the grounds for which events count as important' (p. 255).
6. Carr here understands narrative more narrowly than Czarniawska (2004) and many others (especially linguists) in that he assumes that a narrative singles

out only the most important in a series of events, those that are of importance to the coherence of the story at the time of narration. (He does not go as far as to presuppose a plot, like many do in their definition of a story.) '[T]he chronicler simply describes what happens in the order in which it happens. The narrator, by contrast, in virtue of his retrospective view, picks out the most important events, traces the causal and motivational connections among them, and gives us an organized, coherent account. The counterpart of the chronicler at the level of small-scale events would be the radio announcer giving us a live description of a baseball game: "There's the pitch ... the batter swings ... line drive to center field!" etc. The story of the game, by contrast, is told afterwards and in full knowledge of who won. It will mention only the most important events, especially those that contributed to scoring points and thus to the outcome (p. 59).'

7. Typically, recent commentators on identity tend to start with a declaration such as, 'Culture and identity are staging a dramatic comeback in social theory and practice at the end of the twentieth century' (Lapid 1996: 3); 'Identity [...] has become a major watchword since the 1980s' (Paasi 2003: 475); 'Identity is back. The concept of identity has made a remarkable comeback in the social sciences and humanities' (Goff and Dunn 2004a: 1); and 'Research on language and identity has experienced an unprecedented growth in the last ten years' (De Fina et al. 2006: 1).
8. This does not mean that students of identity disregard the role of power in international relations. Nau (2002), for instance, holds national power and identity as two separate and independent factors defining national interests and influencing foreign policy behaviour.
9. The Russian word for 'house' and 'home' is the same: *dom*.
10. See Hønneland (1998) and Browning (2003).
11. See, for instance, Harders (1987), Stokke (1990), Roginko and LaMourie (1992) and Caron (1993).
12. See, for instance, Scrivener (1999) and Young (2002, 2005).
13. See, for instance, Neumann (1994), Hønneland (1998) and Aalto et al. (2003).
14. Exceptions include the constructively oriented contributions on identity and region building (Neumann 1994, Hønneland 1998, Keskitalo 2007, Craciun 2009 and Dodds 2010).
15. See, for instance, Harders (1987), Hoel (2009), Brosnan et al. (2011), Stokke (2011) and Young (2011).
16. See, for instance, Harders (1987) and Roginko and LaMourie (1992).
17. See, for instance, Koivurova (2010).
18. See, for instance, Stokke (2006).
19. See, for instance, Kim and Blank (2011) and Blunden (2009, 2012).
20. See, for instance Joenniemi (1989), Heininen and Nicol (2007), Keskitalo (2007) and Wilson (2007).

21. See, for instance, Neumann (1994), Hønneland (1998), Medvedev (2001), Aalto et al. (2003) and Browning (2003).
22. See, for instance, Hønneland (1998) and Browning (2003).
23. See, for instance, Ebinger and Zambetakis (2009), Dodds (2010) and Brosnan et al. (2011).
24. An example is Rothwell (2008).
25. Examples include Stokke (2006), Hoel (2009) and Young (2011).
26. See, for instance, Pedersen (2012).
27. See, for instance, Tsygankov (2013).
28. As noted by Müller (2008), it is particularly in connection with Russian studies that IR scholars have been eager to embrace identity as a fruitful concept: 'Russia's inconsistent foreign policy and the imputed "identity crisis" after the collapse of the Soviet Union almost invited the application of identity research. Societal dislocation in post-Soviet Russia has opened an identificatory gap which needs to be filled by new imaginations of Russia's role and place in international politics and by a new sense of belonging – in short, by a new identity (p. 4).' Neumann's (1996) study of the role played by Europe in the constitution of Russian identity is a classic in modern IR study of identity. This is discussed further in Chapter 1.
29. My former student Torstein Vik Århus collected the media material through the search engine *Meltwater News* and the websites of selected national and regional media. Regional media in north-west Russia included the regional editions of *Argumenty i fakty*, the digital news agencies *Nord-News*, *Murmanskie Biznes-Novosti* and the regional radio and TV station *GTRK Murman*. At national level, the newspapers *Izvestia*, *Kommersant*, *Moskovski Komsomolets*, *Nezavisimaya Gazeta*, *Novaya Gazeta* and *Rossiyskaya Gazeta*, as well as the news agencies *Lenta.ru*, *Gazeta.ru*, *Regnum.ru* and *Vzglyad*, were chosen. This covers a mix of official, business, independent and openly critical media. The systematic search included the words 'Arctic' and 'Norway' (as much of Russian Arctic politics has been directed at this country; cf. Chapters 3, 4 and 5) and covered the period 2005–10. More occasional searches were made from 2011 to 2014.

Chapter 1   Russian Identity between North and West

1. This chapter builds on Hønneland (2010, Chapter 1) and Hønneland (2014, Chapter 4).
2. Byzantium was the city's name for only a few years in the 330s after which it was called Constantinople. It remained the capital of the Eastern Roman Empire, also called Byzantium.
3. Neumann (1996: 1) notes: 'Debate about Europe is a traditional staple of Russian intellectual life. [...] Indeed, the idea of Europe is the main "Other"

in relation to which the idea of Russia is defined. [...] Russians, when they set out to discuss Europe, also discuss themselves.'
4. BBC interview, 17 December 1984; see www.margaretthatcher.org
5. See, for instance, 'Zhirinovsky Admits Jewish Roots', *BBC News*, 19 July 2001; http://news.bbc.co.uk/2/hi/europe/1446759.stm.
6. See Cohen (2000) for a discussion of the term 'cold peace' in post-Soviet Russian politics.
7. See, for example, Mankoff (2012).
8. 'Vse dorogi veli v Krym', *Kommersant*, 19 March 2014.
9. Old Believers were religious dissidents who refused to accept the liturgical reforms introduced by Patriarch Nikon in the mid-seventeenth century. Numbering in their millions, they were oppressed and at times persecuted, until 1905 when Tsar Nicholas II introduced an act of religious freedom in Russia.
10. A few references (in brackets) to specific authors and literary concepts have been removed from this citation.
11. This echoes the more general nineteenth-century philosophical and spiritual romanticizing of the 'Arctic sublime', which presented 'an Arctic at once beautiful and terrifying, awesome and exotic, a world apart, a romantic, last frontier offering compelling opportunities and exhilarating risks' (Osherenko and Young 1989: 5).
12. The Great Patriotic War is the Russian name for that part of World War II which involved the Soviet Union (1941–5).
13. Speaking of empirical orientation, Kelly (2004: 150) takes an amusing pot-shot at the romantic view of kitchen table talk in Russia, presumably relished by Western ethnologists and anthropologists: 'Pubs may well be reckoned typically British, but few, on reflection, would argue seriously that a visit to a pub gives access to the essence of British identity, or indeed that putting on lederhosen and going for a walk in the Bavarian Alps will make you understand the rise of the Third Reich. But books and articles suggesting that a few hours at a Russian kitchen table or inside a Russian bath-house will let you comprehend the innermost recesses of the Russian mind seem far more respectable.' The cover of Ries's (1997) book about Russian talk (see below) wittily shows tea being poured from a teapot.
14. Boym (1994) tells a story about the Russian critic Mikhail Epstein who joined a march in the US against the first Gulf War. He was astounded to see the protesters after the rally – still beating drums and shouting slogans and insults about President Bush – stop at a red light even when there were no cars at the crossing! 'For an American, the protest and the stopping at the red light were both part of the democratic ritual; in fact both his protest and his everyday behaviour were lawful. For a Russian accustomed to routine violations of everyday prohibitions and cynical about the laws because they were part and parcel of the official order, this combination of simultaneously protesting and observing the rules is nearly inconceivable' (p. 289).

15. Explaining this approach in more detail: 'The existential question that inspires my own work is the same question I heard a thousand times in Moscow: Why is Russian experience so full of suffering and misfortune? Taking one of many conceivable approaches to grappling with that profound (and probably unanswerable) question, this book examines the possibility that the regular posing of such key rhetorical questions helps sustain the kinds of social and cultural institutions which perpetuate that "suffering". This, then, is an interpretation of cultural texts that keeps one eye on other things: social structures, power relations, models of resistance and reproduction, the difficulties of democratization, and the paradoxes of and potential for societal transformation' (Ries 1997: 5).

Chapter 2   The Rush for the North Pole

1. Interview in Moscow, December 2000; referred in Blakkisrud and Hønneland (2006b: 193–4). This section builds on that chapter.
2. For a thorough discussion of the continental shelf regime, see Jensen (2013).
3. See, for example, the *Guardian*, 2 August 2007.
4. See, for instance, www.nrk.no, 17 May 2011.
5. See, for instance, Rothwell (2008).
6. For an overview of EU Arctic politics, see Wegge (2012).
7. For a discussion of the Russian Arctic strategy in view of the other Arctic states' strategies, see Åtland (2014).
8. See Hønneland (2012).
9. The Arctic is also highlighted in political declarations such as the 2008 Foreign Policy Concept and the 2009 National Security Strategy. A common theme is the protection of Russian national interest, in the Arctic as elsewhere.
10. 'Arkticheskie territorii imeyut strategicheskoe znachenie dlya Rossii', *Rossiyskaya Gazeta*, 30 March 2009. Cited from Laruelle (2014: 10).
11. 'Shelf vzyat! V Moskvu: Uchastniki rossiyskoy arkticheskoy ekspeditsii vernulis s pobedoy', *Rossiyskaya Gazeta*, 8 August 2007.
12. 'Arkticheskie territorii imeyut strategicheskoe znachenie dlya Rossii', *Rossiyskaya Gazeta*, 30 March 2009. Cited from Laruelle (2014: 10).
13. Ibid., p. 11.
14. Cited from Blank (2011: 16).
15. Cited from Main (2011: 10).
16. 'Vozrodit rossiyski sever: Atomny ledokolny flot est tolko u nashey strany', *Kommersant*, 11 February 2011.
17. '"Bely medved" vyshel na okhotu: Kanada nachala voennye uchenia v Arktike', *Rossiyskaya Gazeta*, 18 August 2009.
18. 'Neft na dvoikh', *Vzglyad*, 4 February 2010.
19. 'Rossiya i Norvegiya podpishut soglashenie o razdele arkticheskogo dna', *Vzglyad*, 15 September 2010.

20. 'Na shirotnuyu nogu: Glava MID Rossii uznal plany Kanady i Ukrainy', *Rossiyskaya Gazeta*, 17 September 2010.
21. 'Udar po khrebru Lomonosova: Glava MID Kanady vyskazal v Moskve svoi vzglyady na Arktiku', *Rossiyskaya Gazeta*, 16 September 2010.
22. 'Bez boevykh pingvinov: Rossiya sozdaet arkticheskuyu gruppu voysk bez militarizatsii regiona', *Rossiyskaya Gazeta*, 30 September 2009.
23. For the record, there has been no discussion of 'changing Svalbard's demilitarized status' in Norway; to do so would infringe international law as the 1920 Svalbard Treaty (see Chapter 3), which gives Norway sovereignty over Svalbard, stipulates that no military bases can be installed on the archipelago and that it may not be used for military purposes. Nor is there in Norway 'a new policy' of using the national armed forces in the Arctic. Debate has centred on the need not to reduce, and possibly increase, the Coast Guard's presence in the Barents Sea. The Coast Guard is a branch of the Norwegian Navy, though its tasks are mainly civilian. Its instructions come from the Ministry of Justice and the Ministry of Industry and Fisheries. And its presence in the Barents Sea (which isn't actually in the High Arctic either) is not 'new'.
24. 'Kholodnoe NATO: Alyans prinyal reshenie o "vtorzhenii" v Arktiku', *Rossiyskaya Gazeta*, 16 January 2009.
25. 'Novoe osvoenie Arktiki', *Rossiyskaya Gazeta*, 12 February 2009.
26. 'Razdel shkury belogo medveda: Strany Arkticheskogo basseyna sobirayutsya "zabyvat kolyshki" na rossiyskikh mestorozhdeniyakh', *Rossiyskaya Gazeta*, 7 August 2007.
27. 'Goryachaya Arktika: Za chetvert mirovykh zapasov nefti i gaza Rossii predstoit srazitsya s SShA, Daniey i Kanadoy', *Rossiyskaya Gazeta*, 10 October 2008.
28. 'Po skolskomu ldu: Kanada rasshiraet predely svoey yurisdiktsii v Arktike', *Rossiyskaya Gazeta*, 29 September 2008.
29. 'Ledovy boy nomer dva: Arktika stanovitsya arenoy takticheskikh srazheniy Rossii i Kanady', *Rossiyskaya Gazeta*, 20 May 2008.
30. 'Artur Chilingarov razrabotal proekt o Severnom Morskom Puti', *Kommersant*, 12 February 2009.
31. 'Rossiyu zatknuli za polyus', *Kommersant*, 8 August 2009.
32. 'Severny Polyus prevrashaetsya v goryachuyu tochku', *Kommesant*, 27 March 2009.
33. 'Bezkhrebetnye: Kanada i SShA vystupili s rezkimi zayavleniyami po povodu rossiyskikh pretensiy na Arktiku', *Rossiyskaya Gazeta*, 4 August 2007.
34. 'Rossiyu zatknuli za polyus', *Kommersant*, 8 August 2009.
35. [No title], *Rossiyskaya Gazeta*, 29 May 2009.
36. 'Udar nizhe polyusa', *Kommersant*, 13 August 2007.
37. 'Arkticheski peredel: Napoleon nazyval Rossiyu "imperiey Severa"', *Rossiyskaya Gazeta*, 26 September 2005.
38. 'Severnoe siyanie', *Kommersant/Ogonyok*, 27 September 2010.

Notes to Pages 58–64

39. 'Vozrodit rossiyski sever: Atomny ledokolny flot est tolko u nashey strany', *Argumenty i fakty*, 11 February 2011.
40. 'Severnoe siyanie', *Kommersant/Ogonyok*, 27 September 2010.
41. Reference is probably made here to the elaborate system of transportation of supplies to the Russian North through the Northern Sea Route in Soviet times, the *severny zavoz*, organized by the State Committee for the North (*Goskomsever*).
42. 'Sevmorput – eto samoe nastoyashchee ministerstvo', *Kommersant/Ogonyok*, 27 September 2010.
43. 'Severnoe siyanie', *Kommersant/Ogonyok*, 27 September 2010.
44. 'Vozrodit rossiyski sever: Atomny ledokolny flot est tolko u nashey strany', *Argumenty i fakty*, 11 February 2011.
45. 'Snezhny chelovek: Artur Chilingarov – o vkuse studnya iz stoyarnogo kleya, pro smertelnye riski vo ldakh i glubinkakh, a takzhe o tom, zachem geroyam inogda vydayut pistolety', *Rossiyskaya Gazeta*, 17 September 2010.
46. 'Shelf vzyat! V Moskvu: Uchastniki rossiyskoy arkticheskoy ekspeditsii vernulis s pobedoy', *Rossiyskaya Gazeta*, 8 August 2007.
47. 'Rossiyski flag snova v Arktike', *Argumenty i fakty*, 8 October 2008.
48. '"Bely medved" vyshel na okhotu: Kanada nachala voennye uchenia v Arktike', *Rossiyskaya Gazeta*, 18 August 2009.
49. Summing up the narratives in this section (and in the concluding sections of the subsequent chapters), I present them in truncated form, defined mostly by just a couple of words. As mentioned in the Introduction, I understand a narrative as a stretch of talk about specific events. When I refer to the major narrative of this chapter as 'Russia vs the West', it therefore includes the stories laid out in the preceding sections, for instance about how the other Arctic states are behaving and that behaviour is perceived in Russia.
50. For the rest of this section, and in the concluding sections of the following chapters, I do not repeat the reference for newspaper articles that have already been cited above, only citations by other authors.
51. Admittedly, there are general calls for 'action' ('before it's too late'), but most often not specified as military action. See, e.g., 'Artur Chilingarov razrabotal proekt o Severnom Morskom Puti', *Kommersant*, 12 February 2009.
52. Laruelle (2014: 40); see also Chapter 1.
53. Hellberg-Hirn (1999: 54); see also Chapter 1.
54. Laruelle (2014: 40); see also Chapter 1.
55. Boele (1996: 252) referring to the eighteenth/nineteenth-century writer Maksim Nevzorov.
56. Ibid.
57. Griffiths (1990: 53) referring to the 'countryside writer' Valentin Rasputin; see also Chapter 1.
58. Laruelle (2014: 39); see presentation of Russia's 'geographical meta-narratives' above.
59. Widdis (2004: 33, 39) paraphrased; see Chapter 1 for the full quotation.

60. Hellberg-Hirn (1999: 56); see also Chapter 1.
61. Main (2011: 10) paraphrased; see above for the full quotation. All italics in this paragraph are mine.
62. Slezkine (1993: 5); edited for UK spelling. See Chapter 1 for the full quotation.
63. I use the term 'master narrative' to indicate a narrative that dominates the debate. This is not to be confused with 'meta-narratives' (Somers 1994), a category that reflects the *contents* of the narrative ('epic dramas'), not the frequency of its occurrence.

Chapter 3   Delimitation of the Barents Sea

1. See for example, 'Kak Putinu vernut Barentsevo more?' *Tikhookeanski Vestnik*, 13 February 2013. The empirical overview in this chapter draws on Hønneland (2014), Chapters 1–3.
2. Strictly speaking, before the Third UN Conference on the Law of the Sea, the rules were unclear and state practice regarding territorial and other functional (limited) zones varied. The Second Conference on the Law of the Sea, held in 1960, attempted to reach a compromise on territorial and functional zones of six nautical miles each, but failed. In the years that followed, several states created (functional) fishing zones beyond their territorial waters, though of varying breadth. Today, states are entitled to territorial waters extending 12 nautical miles from the coast.
3. The Grey Zone agreement was in force one year at a time and renewed annually until the delimitation treaty came into effect in 2011, making the Grey Zone agreement redundant. Contrary to popular belief, the Grey Zone agreement worked perfectly from start to stop.
4. www.nrk.no, 27 April 2010.
5. For a detailed examination, see Jensen (2011).
6. For a review of Russian policy on Svalbard after World War II, see J.H. Jørgensen (2010).
7. This situation continues to this day; see Pedersen (2008, 2009).
8. The logic of the argument is not entirely clear. One could say that Norway practices equal treatment as long as Norwegian *and* foreign vessels are arrested in the zone. The kernel of the argument is rather that other governments have no power to influence the regulations or fishing quotas in the area.
9. Norwegian enforcement in the Svalbard zone is extensively discussed in Hønneland (2012).
10. *Takogo kak Putin*, Poyushchie vmeste (pop group), 2002.
11. 'Postepenno nas vydavyat ottuda', *Vzglyad*, 27 October 2010.
12. 'Vyacheslav Zilanov: – Rossiya budet vynuzhdena vesti rybolovstvo, kak eto delalos v 50-60-gody proshlogo veka', *Nord-News*, 23 November 2010.
13. The adjective *promyslovy* occurs quite frequently in Russian fisheries terminology. Strictly speaking it means 'catch' where we in English would say 'fishery'.

NOTES TO PAGES 85-94

14. 'Rossiya i Norvegiya dogovorilis o razgranichenii morskikh prostranstv', *Kommersant*, 27 April 2010.
15. 'More po-polam: Rossiya i Norvegiya dogovorilis o demarkatsii granits', *Rossiyskaya Gazeta*, 28 April 2010.
16. 'Segodnya Norvegiya poluchit ot Rossii chast Barentseva morya', *Regnum*, 15 September 2010.
17. 'Murmanski proryv: Glavy Norvegii i Rossii reshili problemu, desyatiletiya oslozhnyavshuyu otnosheniya', *Argumenty i fakty*, 22 September 2010.
18. 'Dogovor o delimitatsii v Barentsevom more pozvolit Norvegii nas vyzhit: rossiyskie rybaki', *Regnum*, 28 October 2010. *Vysoki stroyny blondin* is translated rather broadly as 'tall, strapping blonds' by Århus (2012). *Blondin* is the masculine form of the noun derived from the adjective 'blond' (the feminine form is *blondinka*). While his variant is flamboyant – I considered using it myself – I ended up with a more literal translation.
19. 'Barentsevomorski proryv Lavrova-Stere – klon beringomorskogo proryva Beykera-Shevardnadze', *Nord-News*, 29 September 2010.
20. Around the turn of the millennium, Russian fishing vessels resumed the old Soviet practice of delivering their catches to transport ships at sea. Instead of going to Murmansk with the fish, however, these transport vessels now headed for other European countries: Denmark, the UK, the Netherlands, Spain and Portugal. Norway took the initiative to assess the possibility of overfishing, but the Russians were unwilling. Thereupon Norway took unilateral measures to calculate overfishing in the Barents Sea, and presented figures that indicated Russian overfishing from 2002, rising to nearly 75 per cent of the total Russian quota in 2005, gradually declining to zero in 2009. The Russian side never accepted these figures, claiming they were deficient at best, and an expression of anti-Russian sentiments at worst. The International Council for the Exploration of the Sea (ICES), however, used them in their estimates of total catches in the Barents Sea during the 2000s, thereby providing these figure with some level of approval. For details see Hønneland (2012: 73–6).
21. 'Podpisanie Dogovora o razgranichenii morskikh prostranstv v Barentsevom more i Severnom Ledovitom okeane prezhdevremennoe i pospeshnoe', *Nord-News*, 10 September 2010.
22. 'Pritormozit ratifikatsiyu dogovora po razgranicheniyu morskikh prostranstv', *Nord-News*, 18 October 2010.
23. 'Eto nash s Norvegiey perspektivny ogorod', *Vzgljad*, 27 April 2010.
24. 'Vyacheslav Zilanov: – Rossiya budet vynuzhdena vesti rybolovstvo, kak eto delalos v 50-60-gody proshlogo veka', *Nord-News*, 23 November 2010.
25. 'Sosedski mir luchshe konfrontatsiy: V Moskve ponimayut trevogi rybakov i gotovy pomogat', *Murmanski Vestnik*, 18 November 2010.
26. *BarentsObserver*, 5 March 2009. Other reasons suggested for Yevdokimov's removal were economic circumstances and the fact that he had supported a mayor candidate in Murmansk city who did not belong to the

presidential party United Russia. Of course, different factors can have played together here.
27. See Hønneland (2012).
28. When Zilanov talks about how much fish the Russians are 'losing', he is talking about everything caught on the western side of the new delimitation line – including in the Norwegian economic zone and the Svalbard zone – not just the part of the old, disputed area which became Norwegian with the signing of the treaty.
29. Cf. also President Medvedev's cheerful remark that in Russia conspiracy traditions are deep-rooted and well-practised.

Chapter 4   Management of Marine Resources

1. This chapter builds on Hønneland (2014), which in turn draws on Hønneland (2003, 2012).
2. For a general appreciation of the Commission's work, see Hønneland (2012).
3. *Protokoll for den 28. sesjon i Den blandete norsk-russiske fiskerikommisjon*, Oslo: Ministry of Fisheries, 1999, Art. 5.1.
4. There have been no signs in official statements, in the press or in my numerous interviews with actors within the Russian fisheries sector of divergent opinions within the Russian delegation to the Joint Fisheries Commission. As far as the Russian population at large is concerned, some people may well be sympathetic to the Norwegian position, but I have been unable to find representatives of this view during my stays in Russia or in written material.
5. *Rybnaya stolitsa*, 15 November 1999.
6. Interview with Russian bureaucrat, Murmansk, February 2000.
7. *Rybatskie novosti*, No. 3–4, 2001.
8. *Rybny biznes*, November 2000.
9. *Rybatskie novosti*, No. 3–4, 2001.
10. Interview with inhabitant of Murmansk, April 2001.
11. *Fiskeribladet*, 14 December 1999.
12. *Rybny biznes*, November 2000.
13. Vice Governor of Murmansk oblast to *Murmanski vestnik*, November 2000.
14. www.intrafish.com, 2 November 2001.
15. I have elsewhere argued, though, that the management of the fisheries by the Norwegians in the Svalbard zone has been relatively successful despite the unclear jurisdictional status of this ocean area (Hønneland 2012; 2014).
16. This can be explained by the fact that Norway allocates approximately seventy-five per cent of its cod quota in the Barents Sea to coastal vessels operating closer to the Norwegian mainland while the Russian fleet consists almost exclusively of ocean-going trawlers.
17. This happened for the first time in 1993, when Icelandic trawlers and Faroese vessels under flags of convenience started fishing here. Warning shots were

fired at the ships by the Norwegian Coast Guard, and the fishing vessels left the zone. The following year, an Icelandic fishing vessel was arrested for fishing in the Svalbard zone without a Barents Sea quota.

18. *Fiskeribladet*, 28 September 2001.
19. See, for example, *Rybnaya stolitsa*, no. 24, 2001. Russian reactions to these events are discussed in detail in Hønneland (2003).
20. *Murmanski vestnik*, 18 September 1999.
21. When this was written, the Svalbard Treaty was already eighty years old.
22. *Rybnaya stolitsa*, No. 39, 2000.
23. *Fiskeribladet*, 17 October 2000.
24. Jørgensen (2003). All interview excerpts are from Chapter 4, pp. 36–46 of this report. Original references are given for excerpts from newspapers and journals, but not for the author's personal interviews.
25. *Voennaya mysl*, No. 6, pp. 8–10, 2000.
26. 'Shpitsbergen – eto geopolitika! Vsem obernetsya dlya Rossii poterya strategicheskogo severnogo forposta', *Literaturnaya Gazeta*, 15 October 1997.
27. See Jakobsen and Ozhigin (2011) for an overview of the Norwegian–Russian fisheries research cooperation.
28. See Aasjord and Hønneland (2008). All interview extracts are taken from this report, based on interviews with VNIRO scientists in Moscow in December 2007 and PINRO scientists in Murmansk in February 2008. For a shortened version in English, see Hønneland (2012).
29. *On {the} Necessity of Improvement of the Russian–Norwegian Management Strategy for Cod in the Fisheries in the Barents Sea*, Workshop for Discussion of the Joint Management of the Barents Sea Cod Stock, Nor-Fishing 2006, Moscow: VNIRO Publishing, 2006, p. 4 (emphasis added).
30. Interview in Moscow, December 2007.
31. Ibid.
32. PINRO scientists, in turn, described their colleagues at VNIRO as rank amateurs, incompetent in quantitative analysis: 'Until the authors begin to add maximum values of biomass found for different "synoptic periods" [...], it seems as if one can at least observe a simple logic in their reasoning. [...] But when one comes to the addition of the different maximum biomasses emerging from different time periods, this reminds too much of a pupil's attempts to fit the response to the standard answers in the back of the exercise book. [...] One is amazed at the authors' lack of logic or sophisticated reasoning' (Berenboym et al. 2007: 25–6).
33. In terms of jurisdiction, the Loophole is in international waters, although Norway and Russia both claim – doubtless with some basis in the Law of the Sea – to be in charge of managing the fish stocks throughout their range in the Barents Sea. Most of the time there is little fish in the Loophole and the cost of transportation is huge anyway – it takes about two days to get there from the mainland. Icelandic vessels began fishing in the Loophole in

1992, amid widespread condemnation from the two coastal states, Norway and Russia. The conflict was not resolved until 1999 when Iceland was given a fishing quota in the Barents Sea in exchange for Norwegian and Russian quotas in the Icelandic zone.
34. 'Uchastie Norvegii gonit Rossiyu iz Arktiki', utro.ru, 1 November 2005.
35. *Kommersant*, 21 April 2007.
36. 'Rossiya poymala rossiyskikh brakonerov', *Vzglyad*, 28 January 2008.
37. 'Makoedov: Norvezhskie i rossiyskie rybaki: siamskie bliznetsy', *Regnum*, 28 October 2005.
38. 'Vedro na mashte', *Novaya Gazeta*, 20 October 2005.
39. The literal translation of the final sentence in this quotation is: 'The Norwegians are so well-mannered they observe the etiquette'. I assume the meaning is the same as the, in this context, idiomatically more correct expression 'comply with the law'.
40. 'Ne neftyu edinoy', *Nezavisimaya Gazeta*, 14 August 2007.
41. 'Potomki vikingov na rossiyskom shelfe', *Rossiyskaya Gazeta*, 15 August 2006.
42. I discuss that at some length in Hønneland (2003).

Chapter 5 Region Building, Identity Formation

1. This introduction and the subsequent section build on Hønneland (2014, Chapter 5), the following section on Hønneland (2010, Chapter 4).
2. For a wider discussion of the project, see Stokke and Tunander (1994), Hønneland (2003) and Stokke and Hønneland (2007).
3. For a discussion of region building in the Arctic more widely, see Keskitalo (2003).
4. For a theoretically informed study of early region building in the European Arctic, see Neumann (1994).
5. See Stokke and Tunander (1994) and Hønneland (2003).
6. Even though some claim this is not true, they draw from the same pool of narrative resources, questioning the established truths about northerners.
7. The usual Russian word for Norwegian is *norvezhets*. *Norg* (plural *norgi*) and *nord* (plural *nordy*) are slang for Norwegians, slightly derogatory but very common in north-west Russia in recent years. While in my interviews I explicitly asked people's opinions about Scandinavians, most reference was indeed to Norwegians, as few had experience with or opinions about Finns, nor Swedes. In the rest of this chapter, I use Norwegians/Norgs and Scandinavians intermittently.
8. In my experience, 'boring' is arguably how most north-west Russians think about life in the Nordic countries. I have heard it said countless times, by friends, taxi drivers, newspaper articles and lectures (on how the Russian diaspora in Norway perceive life there). It also looms large in my interviews; cf., e.g. the following quote (female, late thirties): 'We've heard it's quiet,

Notes to Pages 133–46 191

clean but, you know, a bit boring perhaps [*skuchnovato*]. Yeah, that's what they say, that Norway's boring [*skuchno*]'.

9. The Russians' liberal attitude to compliance with the law is key to their self-perception, according to Boym (1994: 289). The Russian inclination to violate everyday regulations whenever they have the opportunity is infamous. For instance, many Russians don't attach their safety belts when driving because it would be doing what the authorities tell them to do. To avoid fines, however, they hold the seat belts in place, but without fastening them.

10. Line from the late 1990s international hit *Barbie Girl* by the Scandinavian (i.e. Danish–Norwegian) pop group Aqua.

11. One of the interviewees (female, mid-forties) described her shock when the parents of the bride at a Norwegian wedding had to take time out to rest between the ceremony and reception.

12. Scandinavians, one of my interviewees (male, around forty) says, find no pleasure in picking and eating wild mushrooms. They prefer to stuff themselves (*davitsya*, indicating lack of pleasure) with mushrooms bought in the shop. Russians tend to have a low opinion of the Norwegian kitchen, in my experience. Those dry open sandwiches can't be compared with the vast riches of the Russian table.

13. This formulation was used by one of my interviewees (female, late thirties) when she reported what she had heard about Norwegian schools.

14. Many interviewees – especially female – lamented Norwegian women's lack of femininity.

15. Hellberg-Hirn (1999: 56). A poignant description of the Russian perception of soul is given by one of Ries's (1997: 30) interviewees, a Russian philosopher, 'The Russian people think they have soul and they doubt that anyone else has. Russians have *dusha* [soul] because they are moral. Being moral – it is not just to be kind, generous, it is basically some kind of connection between individual and community and nature.'

16. The expression and gesture are supposed to prevent bad luck from ensuing after commenting on a spate of good (or at least neutral) luck.

17. See Nielsen (1994) for an overview.

18. 'Return of the Pomors', *BarentsObserver*, 27 September 2012. The rest of the paragraph also builds on this article.

19. 'No Charge for High Treason', *BarentsObserver*, 21 November 2012.

20. 'Zachem "norvezhsko-pomorskoe vozrozhdenie" russkim detyam?', *Regnum*, 3 December 2012.

21. '"Pomorskaya isteria": kogda v Russkoy Arktike Norvegia budet "vesti peregovory s pomorami", a ne s Rossiey?', *Regnum*, 3 December 2012. Note that the adjective 'russki' is used instead of the more common, in this context, 'rossiyski'. The former refers to the Russian nation, the latter to the Russian state, the Russian Federation.

22. 'Kak i zachem norvezhtsy napisali dlya russkikh detey "pomorskie skazki"?' *Regnum*, 3 December 2012.

23. 'Ivan Moseev Found Guilty', *BarentsObserver*, 1 March 2013.
24. 'Pomor Ivan Moseev Turns to European Court of Human Rights', *BarentsObserver*, 26 November 2013.

Chapter 6   Arctic Talk, Russian Policy

1. I place this event in parentheses because it was not, as I have argued above, primarily, if at all, intended as a foreign policy act, as it was perceived by many abroad.
2. This happened in the aftermath of the so-called August crisis in 1998; see Hønneland (2003, 2014).
3. See, for instance, Moe et al. (2011).
4. [No title], *Rossiyskaya Gazeta*, 29 May 2009.

BIBLIOGRAPHY

Aalto, P., S. Dalby and V. Harle (2003). 'The Critical Geopolitics of Northern Europe: Identity Politics Unlimited', *Geopolitics* 8: 1–19.
Aasjord, B. and G. Hønneland (2008). 'Hvem kan telle "den fisk under vann"? Kunnskapsstrid i russisk havforskning', *Nordisk Østforum* 22: 289–312.
Agranat, G.A. (1998). 'The Russian North at a Dangerous Crossroads', *Polar Geography* 22: 268–82.
Anderson, A. (2009). *After the Ice: Life, Death and Politics in the New Arctic* (London, Virgin Books).
Anderson, B. (1983). *Imagined Communities: Reflections on the Origin and Spread of Nationalism* (London, Verso).
Århus, T.V. (2012). *Maritim mistru og petroleumspartnarskap: Ein diskursanalyse av russiske reaksjonar på norsk nordområdepolitikk*, MA thesis (Oslo, Department of European and American Studies – Russian Studies, University of Oslo).
Arutiunova, E. (2008). 'Russian Identity as Perceived by College Students in Moscow', *Russian Education and Society* 50: 53–70.
Åtland, K. (2014). 'Interstate Relations in the Arctic: An Emerging Security Dilemma?', *Comparative Strategy* 33: 145–66.
Benwell, B. and E. Stokoe (2006). *Discourse and Identity* (Edinburgh, Edinburgh University Press).
Berenboym, B.I., V.A. Borovkov, V.I. Vinnichenko, E.N. Gavrilov, K.V. Drevetnyak, Yu.A. Kovalev, Yu.M. Lepesevich, E.A. Shamray and M.S. Shevelev (2007). 'Chto takoe sinopticheski monitoring treski v Barentsevom more?' *Rybnye resursy* 4: 24–29.
Berenskoetter, F. (2007). 'Friends, There Are No Friends? An Intimate Reframing of the International', *Millennium – Journal of International Studies* 35: 647–76.
Blakkisrud, H. and G. Hønneland (2006a). 'The Russian North – An Introduction' in H. Blakkisrud and G. Hønneland (eds), *Tackling Space: Federal Politics and the Russian North* (Lanham, MD, University Press of America), pp. 1–24.

——— (2006b). 'The Burden and Blessing of Space' in H. Blakkisrud and G. Hønneland (eds), *Tackling Space: Federal Politics and the Russian North* (Lanham, MD, University Press of America), pp. 193–203.
Blank, S.J. (ed) (2011). 'Russia in the Arctic', *Strategic Studies Institute Monographs* (Carlisle, PA, Strategic Studies Institute).
Blunden, M. (2009). 'The New Problem of Arctic Stability', *Survival* 51: 121–41.
——— (2012). 'Geopolitics and the Northern Sea Route', *International Affairs* 88: 115–29.
Boele, O. (1996). *The North in Russian Romantic Literature* (Amsterdam, Rodopi).
Borgerson, S.S. (2008). 'Arctic Meltdown: The Economic and Security Implications of Global Warming', *Foreign Affairs* 87: 63–77.
Boym, S. (1994). *Common Places: Mythologies of Everyday Life in Russia* (Cambridge, MA, Harvard University Press).
Brosnan, I.G., T.M. Leschine and E.L. Miles (2011). 'Cooperation or Conflict in a Changing Arctic', *Ocean Development and International Law* 42: 173–210.
Browning, C.S. (2003). 'The Region-Building Approach Revisited: The Continued Othering of Russia in Discourses of Region-Building in the European North', *Geopolitics* 8: 45–71.
——— (2008). *Constructivism, Narrative and Foreign Policy Analysis: A Case Study of Finland* (Bern, Peter Lang).
Brunstad, B., E. Magnus, P. Swanson, G. Hønneland and I. Øverland (2004). *Big Oil Playground, Russian Bear Preserve or European Periphery? The Russian Barents Sea Region towards 2015* (Delft, Eburon).
Cameron, D. (2001). *Working with Spoken Discourse* (Thousand Oaks, CA, SAGE Publications).
Campbell, D. (1998). *Writing Security: United States Foreign Policy and the Politics of Identity*, revised edition (Manchester, Manchester University Press).
Caron, D.D. (1993). 'Toward an Arctic Environmental Regime', *Ocean Development and International Law* 24: 377–92.
Carr, D. (1986). *Time, Narrative, and History* (Bloomington, IN, Indiana University Press).
Churchill, W.S. (1948). *The Gathering Storm* (London, Cassell).
Cohen, S.F. (2000). *Failed Crusade: America and the Tragedy of Post-Communist Russia* (New York, W.W. Norton and Company).
Craciun, A. (2009). 'The Scramble for the Arctic', *Interventions: International Journal of Postcolonial Studies* 11: 103–14.
Czarniawska, B. (2004). *Narratives in Social Science Research* (London, SAGE Publications).
De Fina, A., D. Schiffrin and M. Bamberg (2006). 'Introduction' in A. De Fina, D. Schiffrin and M. Bamberg (eds), *Discourse and Identity* (Cambridge, Cambridge University Press), pp. 1–23.
Delehanty, W.K. and B.J. Steele (2009). 'Engaging the Narrative in Ontological (In)security Theory: Insights from Feminist IR', *Cambridge Review of International Affairs* 22: 523–40.
Diment, G. (1993). 'Introduction: Siberia as Literature' in G. Diment and Y. Slezkine (eds), *Between Heaven and Hell: The Myth of Siberia in Russian Culture* (New York, St. Martin's Press), pp. 7–10.

Bibliography

Diment, G. and Y. Slezkine (eds) (1993). *Between Heaven and Hell: The Myth of Siberia in Russian Culture* (New York, St. Martin's Press).

Dodds, K. (2010). 'Flag Planting and Finger Pointing: The Law of the Sea, the Arctic and the Political Geographies of the Outer Continental Shelf', *Political Geography* 29: 63–73.

Ebinger, C.K. and E. Zambetakis (2009). 'The Geopolitics of Arctic Melt', *International Affairs* 85: 1215–32.

Franklin, S. and E. Widdis (eds) (2004). *National Identity in Russian Culture: An Introduction* (Cambridge, Cambridge University Press).

Gergen, K. (2001). 'Self-Narration in Social Life' in M. Wetherell, S. Taylor and S. J. Yates (eds), *Discourse Theory and Practice: A Reader* (Thousand Oaks, CA, SAGE Publications), pp. 247–60.

Gibson, J.R. (1993). 'Paradoxical Perceptions of Siberia: Patrician and Plebeian Images up to the Mid-1880s' in G. Diment and Y. Slezkine (eds), *Between Heaven and Hell: The Myth of Siberia in Russian Culture* (New York, St. Martin's Press), pp. 67–93.

Goff, P.M. and K.C. Dunn (2004a). 'Introduction: In Defence of Identity' in P.M. Goff and K.C. Dunn (eds), *Identity and Global Politics: Empirical and Theoretical Elaborations* (New York, Palgrave Macmillan), pp. 1–8.

——— (eds) (2004b). *Identity and Global Politics: Empirical and Theoretical Elaborations* (New York, Palgrave Macmillan).

——— (2004c). 'Conclusion: Revisiting the Four Dimensions of Identity' in P.M. Goff and K.C. Dunn (eds), *Identity and Global Politics: Empirical and Theoretical Elaborations* (New York, Palgrave Macmillan), pp. 237–47.

Griffiths, F. (1990). *Arctic and North in the Russian Identity* (Toronto, Centre for Russian and East European Studies, University of Toronto).

Gubrium, J.F. and J.A. Holstein (2009). *Analyzing Narrative Reality* (Thousand Oaks, CA, SAGE Publications).

Harders, J.E. (1987). 'In Quest of an Arctic Legal Regime: Marine Regionalism – A Concept of International Law Evaluated', *Marine Policy* 11: 285–98.

Heininen, L. and H.N. Nicol (2007). 'The Importance of Northern Dimension Foreign Policies in the Geopolitics of the Circumpolar North', *Geopolitics* 12: 133–65.

Hellberg-Hirn, E. (1998). *Soil and Soul: The Symbolic World of Russianness* (Aldershot, Ashgate).

——— (1999). 'Ambivalent Space: Expressions of Russian Identity' in J. Smith (ed), *Beyond the Limits: The Concept of Space in Russian History and Culture* (Helsinki, Finnish Historical Society), pp. 49–69.

Hoel, A.H. (2009). 'Do We Need a New Legal Regime for the Arctic Ocean?', *The International Journal of Maritime and Coastal Law* 24: 443–56.

Hønneland, G. (1998). 'Identity Formation in the Barents Euro–Arctic Region', *Cooperation and Conflict* 33: 277–97.

——— (2003). *Russia and the West: Environmental Cooperation and Conflict* (London, Routledge).

——— (2004). *Russian Fisheries Management: The Precautionary Approach in Theory and Practice* (Leiden, Martinus Nijhoff/Brill).

——— (2010). *Borderland Russians: Identity, Narrative and International Relations* (Basingstoke, Palgrave Macmillan).

——— (2012). *Making Fishery Agreements Work: Post-Agreement Bargaining in the Barents Sea* (Cheltenham, Edward Elgar).

——— (2014). *Arctic Politics, the Law of the Sea and Russian Identity: The 2010 Barents Sea Delimitation Agreement in Russian Public Debate* (Basingstoke, Palgrave Macmillan).

Howard, R. (2009). *The Arctic Goldrush: The New Race for Tomorrow's Natural Resources* (London and New York, Continuum).

Jakobsen, T. and V.K. Ozhigin (eds) (2011). *The Barents Sea: Ecosystem, Resources, Management. Half a Century of Russian–Norwegian Cooperation* (Trondheim, Tapir).

Jensen, Ø. (2011). 'The Barents Sea: The Treaty between Norway and the Russian Federation concerning Maritime Delimitation and Cooperation in the Barents Sea and the Arctic Ocean', *International Journal of Marine and Coastal Law* 26: 151–68.

——— (2013). *The Commission on the Limits of the Continental Shelf: Law and Legitimacy*, PhD thesis (Oslo, Faculty of Law, University of Oslo).

Joenniemi, P. (1989). 'Competing Images of the Arctic: A Policy Perspective', *Current Research on Peace and Violence* 12: 111–22.

Jørgensen, A.-K. (2009). 'Recent Developments in the Russian Fisheries Sector' in E. Wilson Rowe (ed), *Russia and the North* (Ottawa, University of Ottawa Press), pp. 87–106.

Jørgensen, J.H. (2003). *Svalbard og Fiskevernsonen: Russiske persepsjoner etter den kalde krigen*, FNI Report 13/2003 (Lysaker, Fridtjof Nansen Institute).

——— (2010). *Russisk svalbardpolitikk: Svalbard sett fra den andre siden* (Trondheim, Tapir).

Jørgensen, K.E. (2010). *International Relations Theory: A New Introduction* (Basingstoke, Palgrave Macmillan).

Kelly, C. (2004). '*Byt*: Identity and Everyday Life' in S. Franklin and E. Widdis (eds), *National Identity in Russian Culture: An Introduction* (Cambridge, Cambridge University Press), pp. 149–67.

Keskitalo, C. (2003). *Negotiating the Arctic: The Construction of an International Region* (London, Routledge).

——— (2007). 'International Region-Building: Development of the Arctic as an International Region', *Cooperation and Conflict* 42: 187–205.

Kim, Y. and S. Blank (2011). 'The Arctic: A New Issue on Asia's Security Agenda', *The Korean Journal of Defense Analysis* 23: 303–20.

Koivurova, T. (2010). 'Limits and Possibilities of the Arctic Council in a Rapidly Changing Scene of Arctic Governance', *Polar Record* 46: 146–56.

Lapid, Y. (1996). 'Culture's Ship: Returns and Departures in International Relations Theory' in Y. Lapid and F. Kratochwil (eds), *The Return of Culture and Identity in IR Theory* (Boulder, CO, Lynne Rienner Publishers), pp. 3–20.

Laruelle, M. (2014). *Russia's Arctic Strategies and the Future of the Far North* (Armonk, NY, M.E. Sharpe).

Main, S.J. (2011). 'If Spring Comes Tomorrow... Russia and the Arctic', *Russian Series* (Swindon, Defence Academy of the United Kingdom).

Mankoff, J. (2012). *Russian Foreign Policy: The Return of Great Power Politics* (Lanham, MD, Rowman & Littlefield).

McCannon, J. (1998). *Red Arctic: Polar Exploration and the Myth of the North in the Soviet Union 1932–1939* (New York, Oxford University Press).

BIBLIOGRAPHY

Medvedev. S. (1999). 'A General Theory of Russian Space: A Gay Science and a Rigorous Science' in J. Smith (ed), *Beyond the Limits: The Concept of Space in Russian History and Culture* (Helsinki, Finnish Historical Society), pp. 15–48.

―――― (2001). '[the_blank_space] Glenn Gould, Finland, Russia and the North', *International Politics* 38: 91–102.

―――― and I. Neumann (2012). 'Identity Issues in EU–Russian Relations' in R. Krumm, S. Medvedev and H.-H. Schröder (eds), *Constructing Identities in Europe: German and Russian Perspectives* (Berlin, Nomos), pp. 9–29.

Moe, A., D. Fjærtoft and I. Øverland (2011). 'Space and Timing: Why was the Barents Sea Delimitation Dispute Resolved in 2010?' *Polar Geography* 34: 145–62.

Müller, M. (2008). 'Situating Identities: Enacting and Studying Europe at a Russian Elite University', *Millennium: Journal of International Studies* 37: 3–25.

Nau, H.R. (2002). *At Home Abroad: Identity and Power in American Foreign Policy* (Ithaca, NY, Cornell University Press).

Neumann, I.B. (1994). 'A Region-Building Approach to Northern Europe', *International Studies* 20: 53–74.

―――― (1996). *Russia and the Idea of Europe: A Study in Identity and International Relations* (London, Routledge).

―――― (2008). 'Discourse Analysis' in A. Klotz and D. Prakash (eds) *Methods in International Relations: A Pluralist Guide* (Basingstoke, Palgrave Macmillan), pp. 61–77.

Nielsen, J.P. (1994). 'The Barents Region in Historical Perspective' in O.S. Stokke and O. Tunander (eds), *The Barents Region: Cooperation in Arctic Europe* (London, SAGE Publications), pp. 87–100.

Nishimura, K. (2011). 'Worlds of Our Remembering: The Agent–Structure Problem as the Search for Identity', *Cooperation and Conflict* 46: 96–112.

Osherenko, G. and O.R. Young (1989). *The Age of the Arctic: Hot Conflicts and Cold Realities* (Cambridge, Cambridge University Press).

Paasi, A. (2003). 'Region and Place: Regional Identity in Question', *Progress in Human Geography* 27: 475–85.

Pedersen, T. (2008). 'The Constrained Politics of the Svalbard Offshore Area', *Marine Policy* 32: 913–19.

―――― (2009). 'Norway's Rule on Svalbard: Tightening the Grip on the Arctic Islands', *Polar Record* 45: 147–52.

―――― (2012). 'Debates over the Role of the Arctic Council', *Ocean Development and International Law* 43: 146–56.

Petersson, B. (2001). *National Self-Images and Regional Identities in Russia* (Aldershot, Ashgate).

Ries, N. (1997). *Russian Talk: Culture and Conversation during Perestroika* (Ithaca, NY, Cornell University Press).

Ringmar, E. (1996). *Identity, Interest and Action: A Cultural Explanation of Sweden's Intervention in the Thirty Years War* (Cambridge, Cambridge University Press).

―――― (2002). 'The Recognition Game: Soviet Russia against the West', *Cooperation and Conflict* 37: 115–36.

―――― (2006). 'Inter-Textual Relations: The Quarrel over the Iraq War as Conflict between Narrative Types', *Cooperation and Conflict* 41: 403–21.

Roginko, A.Yu. and M.J. LaMourie (1992). 'Emerging Marine Environmental Protection Strategies for the Arctic', *Marine Policy* 16: 259–76.
Rothwell, D. (2008). 'The Arctic in International Affairs: Time for a New Regime?', *Brown Journal of World Affairs* 15: 241–53.
Sale, R. and E. Potapov (2010). *The Scramble for the Arctic: Ownership, Exploitation and Conflict in the Far North* (London, Frances Lincoln).
Scrivener, D. (1999). 'Arctic Cooperation in Transition', *Polar Record* 35: 51–8.
Slezkine, Y. (1993). 'Introduction: Siberia as History' in G. Diment and Y. Slezkine (eds), *Between Heaven and Hell: The Myth of Siberia in Russian Culture* (New York, St. Martin's Press), pp. 1–6.
Smith, J. (1999). 'Introduction' in J. Smith (ed), *Beyond the Limits: The Concept of Space in Russian History and Culture* (Helsinki, Finnish Historical Society), pp. 7–14.
Somers, M.R. (1994). 'The Narrative Constitution of Identity: A Relational and Network Approach', *Theory and Society* 23: 605–49.
Stokke, O.S. (1990). 'The Northern Environment: Is Cooperation Coming?', *Annals of the American Academy of Political and Social Science* 512: 58–68.
——— (2006). 'A Legal Regime for the Arctic? Interplay with the Law of the Sea Convention', *Marine Policy* 31: 402–8.
——— (2011). 'Environmental Security in the Arctic: The Case for Multilevel Governance', *International Journal* 66: 835–48.
——— and G. Hønneland (eds) (2007). *International Cooperation and Arctic Governance: Regime Effectiveness and Northern Region Building* (London, Routledge).
——— and O. Tunander (eds) (1994). *The Barents Region: Cooperation in Arctic Europe* (London, SAGE Publications).
Tajfel, H. (1982). *Social Identity and Intergroup Relations* (Cambridge, Cambridge University Press).
Tsygankov, A.P. (2013). *Russia's Foreign Policy: Change and Continuity in National Identity* (Lanham, MD, Rowman & Littlefield).
Waage, P.N. (1990). *Russland er et annet sted: En kulturhistorisk bruksanvisning* (Oslo, Aventura).
Wegge, N. (2012). 'The EU and the Arctic: European Foreign Policy in the Making', *Arctic Review on Law and Politics* 3: 6–29.
Wendt, A. (1992). 'Anarchy is What States Make of It: The Social Construction of Power Politics', *International Organization* 46: 391–425.
White, A. (2004). *Small-Town Russia: Postcommunist Livelihoods and Identities* (London, RoutledgeCurzon).
Widdis, E. (2004). 'Russia as Space' in S. Franklin and E. Widdis (eds), *National Identity in Russian Culture: An Introduction* (Cambridge, Cambridge University Press), pp. 30–49.
Wilson, E. (2007). 'Arctic Unity, Artic Difference: Mapping the Reach of Northern Discourses', *Polar Record* 43: 125–33.
Wæver, O. (1998). 'Insecurity, Security and Asecurity in the West European Non-war Community' in E. Adleer and M. Barnett (eds), *Security Communities* (Cambridge, Cambridge University Press), pp. 69–118.
Young, O.R. (1985). 'The Age of the Arctic', *Foreign Policy* 61: 160–79.
——— (1994). *International Governance: Protecting the Environment in a Stateless Society* (Ithaca, NY, Cornell University Press).

―――― (1999). *Arctic Politics: Conflict and Cooperation in the Circumpolar North* (Hanover, NH, Dartmouth College Press).

―――― (2002). 'Can the Arctic Council and the Northern Forum Find Common Ground?', *Polar Record* 38: 289–96.

―――― (2005). 'Governing the Arctic: From Cold War Theater to Mosaic of Cooperation', *Global Governance* 11: 9–15.

―――― (2011). 'If an Arctic Treaty is not the Solution, What is the Alternative?', *Polar Record* 47: 327–34.

Zellen, B.S. (2009). *Arctic Doom, Arctic Boom: The Geopolitics of Climate Change in the Arctic* (Santa Barbara, CA, Praeger).

Zysk, K. (2015). 'Russia Turns North, Again: Interests, Policies and the Search for Coherence' in L.C. Jensen and G. Hønneland (eds), *Handbook on the Politics of the Arctic* (Cheltenham, Edward Elgar), pp. 437–61.

INDEX

Abkhazia, 58, 63
Abramovich, Roman, 60, 62
Alaska, 46
Alexander II, Tsar, 26
Antarctic Treaty, 18
anti-Semitism, 29–30
Arctic, the, 14–15, 16–17, 153–8
   and Canada, 50–2
   and jurisdiction, 18–19, 46–7
   and NATO, 52–3
   and Russia, 1–2, 35–6, 47–50,
     58–65, 68–9, 176–7
   and Soviet Union, 34–5
Arctic Council, 15, 16, 17, 154–5
Arctic Environmental Protection
   Strategy (AEPS), 14–15, 154
Arctic Ocean, 19, 75, 161–2
Arkhangelsk, 144, 145, 149, 161
'Arktika-2007' expedition, 54–5,
   65, 176
Arktikugol, 115
Asia, 16, 28, 155
Atlanticism, 27–8

Barents Euro-Arctic Region (BEAR),
   14, 15, 27, 28, 127–9, 143, 154
   and motive, 160–1
Barents Sea, 22, 82–7, 105, 162
   and delimitation, 71, 72, 73–6,
     80–1, 87–97, 100–1, 158–9,
     164–6, 173
Barentz, Willem, 77
Bering Sea, 53, 87, 90
Bolsheviks, 78
Bosnian War, 28
Brezhnev, Leonid, 27
byt (everyday life), 39, 41
Byzantium, 24

Canada, 1, 14–15, 22, 46, 175
   and the Arctic, 48, 50–2, 53, 57,
     67–8, 162–3
   and continental shelf, 47, 156
   and fishing, 90
Cannon, Lawrence, 51–2
Catherine the Great, 25
Central Asia, 8
Chernigov (trawler), 113, 114
Chilingarov, Artur, 49, 54, 55, 58,
   65, 69
China, 16, 18, 29, 61, 155
Chukotka, 53, 56, 59, 60–2, 63, 64
Churchill, Winston, 2, 23
Civilizationism, 28, 29, 31
climate change, 1, 153
coal, 77, 79, 115, 168

cod, 79, 89, 95, 118–19
  and quotas, 103–4, 105–6, 107–8, 109–10, 167
Cold War, 2, 8, 14, 27, 123
Commission on the Limits of the Continental Shelf, 44–5, 46, 47, 53, 155–6
Committee on Natural Resources Use and Agricultural Sector, 90, 92, 93
Committee on the Problems of the North, 43
Committee for Socio-economic Development of the North, 43–4
conceptual narrative, 5
constructivism, 17, 18, 174
Continental Shelf Convention, 15, 96, 72–3, 157–8
continental shelves, 44–5, 46, 47, 72–3, 155–8
Crimea, 19, 31, 171
Crimean War, 26

Decembrist Uprising, 25
Denmark, 1, 15, 46, 47, 52, 156

Eastern Europe, 8
economic zones, 44, 72, 155–6
Elektron (trawler), 119, 120
environment, the, 14, 15, 48, 140–2, 154
  and cooperation, 17
  and Law of the Sea, 18
  and Svalbard, 114–16, 124
ethnic hatred, 145, 149, 161
Eurasianism, 28–9, 31
European Union (EU), 8, 12
  and Northern Dimension, 14, 15, 129

Federal Russian Fisheries Agency, 83, 120–1
Finland, 14, 15, 35
Finnmark, 73

fish stocks, 71–2, 77, 89, 106–12, 118–19; *see also* cod
fisheries, 76, 83–91, 94–5, 117–18
  and protection zones, 79–80, 81, 112–13, 114, 116
  and quotas, 105–8
Fishing Industry Union of the North, 86, 90, 91, 112, 120
foreign policy, 152–3, 172, 174
  and identity, 9–12, 13–14
  and Russia, 19–20, 27–9, 30–1

gas, 1, 46, 122–3, 171
Gazprom, 123
Genghis Khan, 24
gentlemen's agreements, 80, 113, 116, 124, 160
geopolitics, 17, 63
Georgia, 58, 63
glasnost, 27
global warming, 18, 153
Gogol, Nikolai, 66
Gorbachev, Mikhail, 11, 27, 28, 75
Great Patriotic War, 37
Greenland, 1, 46, 47
Greenpeace, 119
Grey Zone, 73–4, 91

haddock, 106, 108
Harald V, King of Norway, 94
Harper, Stephen, 50, 51
hydrocarbons, 158, 171

ice cap, 15–16
Iceland, 15
identity, 2–3, 4, 7–9, 151–3, 171–2
  and foreign policy, 9–12, 13–14, 20
  and Russia, 64–5, 66–7, 68
India, 29
indigenous peoples, 15, 19, 145, 154
infrastructure, 14, 48, 161
institutionalism, 17
intelligence, 52, 163

INDEX

International Council for the Exploration of the Sea (ICES), 103, 104, 106–10, 117–19, 124, 167, 173
International Court of Justice, 81
International Seabed Authority (ISA), 45
internationalism, 26, 30
Iraq War, 13
Ivan the Terrible, 24
Ivanov, Andrei, 90, 92

Japan, 16, 155
Jarlsberg, Count Wedel, 78
Joint Norwegian–Russian Fisheries Commission, 76, 103–4, 106, 107, 112, 158, 173
Jørgensen, Jørgen Holten, 115

Kasatkin, Vitali, 91
Khrushchev, Nikita, 26–7, 39
Kola Peninsula, 73, 105, 131–2
Kozyrev, Andrei, 27, 28, 143
Kraini, Andrei, 120–1

Lavrov, Sergei, 76, 89, 120, 158
Law of the Sea, 15, 17, 18–19, 44, 46–7
  and Barents Sea, 71, 72, 73, 173
  and Svalbard, 79
  and Third Conference, 72
  see also UN Convention of the Law of the Sea (UNCLOS)
Lenin, Vladimir, 34
Lepesevich, Yuri, 90
Liberal Democratic Party (LDPR), 29–30
litanies, 40
Lomonosov Ridge, 51, 52
longline fishing, 90
Loophole, 119

MacKay, Peter, 46
marine resources, 22; see also fish stocks; fisheries

Maritime Boundary Agreement, 87, 90
master narrative, 5, 64–5
median line principle, 72–3, 75, 88, 158
Medvedev, Dmitri, 31, 37, 49, 65, 94, 129
  and Barents Sea, 75–6, 81–2, 85, 89, 97, 158, 164
military forces, 48, 51, 52, 53–4, 62–3
mining, 115
Mongols, 24
Moscow State Institute of International Relations (MGIMO), 38
Moseev, Ivan, 145, 146, 147, 149
Murmansk, 105, 166–7
Murmansk Regional Duma, 90, 92, 98, 99

Nansen Basin, 47
Napoleon Bonaparte, 25, 33
narrative, 3–8, 9–10, 13, 151–3, 174–5
  and Russia, 21, 40–1, 64–5, 66–7, 68–9, 98–101
nationalism, 30
NATO, 1–2, 19, 22, 28, 51, 62
  and Arctic Five, 163
  and control, 69
  and Russia, 52–3, 113, 123, 175–6
NGOs, 46, 52, 163
Nicholas I, Tsar, 25
Nikitin, Vasili, 86–7, 90–1, 166
Nikora, Evgeni, 92
North East Atlantic Fisheries Commission (NEAFC), 105, 108, 173
North Pole, 1, 47, 54–5, 58, 63, 156
  and Russian flag, 15, 16, 45–6, 65–6, 154
Northern Fleet, 73, 158
Northern Sea Route, 48, 52

Norway, 1, 14, 15, 46, 123–6
  and Barents Sea, 71, 73–6, 82–93, 94–7, 164–6
  and cod, 103–4
  and continental shelf, 47, 156
  and fishing, 105–14, 120–2, 167–8
  and High North, 48, 149
  and oil/gas, 122–3
  and Russia, 22, 52, 53, 98–9, 130–1, 146
  and Svalbard, 78, 79–81, 114–17, 119–20, 159–60
  and trade, 143–4
  see also Scandinavians
Norwegian Coast Guard, 80, 86, 91
  and arrests, 112–13, 114, 119–20, 159–60
Norwegian Institute of Marine Research, 117
nuclear security, 140–1, 143

October Revolution, 26, 78
oil, 1, 46, 171, 122–3
oligarchs, 28
ontological narrative, 4–5
Orthodox Church, 24, 29, 39
othering, 12–13, 21, 67–8, 169, 175
  and Russia, 24–5, 38, 96–7, 98

Paris Peace Conference, 78
Patrushev, Nikolai, 48–9, 53
perestroika, 27
Peter the Great, 25, 37
petroleum, 16, 18
Polar Research Institute of Marine Fisheries and Oceanography (PINRO), 90, 117
politics, 29–30, 98–101; *see also* foreign policy
pollution, 15
Pomor Fairy-Tales, 145–6, 161, 169
Pomor region, 128, 143–7, 149, 161, 175–6
post-positivism, 9

Primakov, Yevgeni, 28–9
privatization, 28
propaganda, 10, 69
public narrative, 5
Putin, Vladimir, 19, 30–1, 49, 50, 122–3, 175
  and Barents Sea, 71, 80, 81–2, 88, 97

Rasputin, Valentin, 34
realism, 17, 174
recognition, 10–11
region building, 17, 128–31, 154
Romanticism, 25, 26, 32
Russia, 14, 46, 54–7, 166–7
  and the Arctic, 1–2, 21–2, 47–50, 52–4, 58–65, 68–9, 155–7, 161–4, 169–73, 176–7
  and Barents Sea, 75–6, 81–7, 88–93, 94–7, 164–6
  and Canada, 51
  and cod, 103–4
  and fishing, 107–14, 120–2, 167–8
  and foreign policy, 19–20, 27–9, 30–1
  and identity, 11, 23, 36–41, 66–7, 68, 123–6
  and the North, 32–4, 35–6, 131–43, 146, 147–9, 161
  and North Pole flag, 15, 16, 45–6, 65–6, 154
  and politics, 29–30, 98–101
  and region building, 129–31
  and Svalbard, 78, 80, 115–17, 159–60
  and trade, 143–4
  and the West, 24–7, 175–6
  see also Soviet Union
Russian Federal Research Institute of Fisheries and Oceanography (VNIRO), 117–19
Russian Geographical Society, 49
Russia's Choice, 30

INDEX

Saburov, Igor, 90, 92, 93
Scandinavians, 131–43, 147–8, 161, 176
science, 15, 17, 48, 154
sea routes, 1, 48
seabed, the, 45
search and rescue, 16
sector line principle, 73, 75, 87, 95, 158
security, 50
Shevardnadze, Eduard, 87
Shtokman field, 66, 91
Siberia, 31–4, 37
Singapore, 16, 155
Slavophilism, 26
Sochi Olympics, 66
social identity theory, 3
socialism, 26
Solzhenitsyn, Aleksandr, 29, 33
South Korea, 16, 155
Soviet Union, 2, 11, 15, 39, 66
   and the Arctic, 34–5, 157–8
   and Barents Sea, 72, 73–5, 96
   and Bering Sea, 87, 90
   and collapse, 14, 172
   and Europe, 26–7
   and fishing, 105–6
   and the North, 33, 43
   and Svalbard, 78–9, 80
Spitsbergen, 77–8
Stalin, Joseph, 26, 34
Statism, 28, 30–1
Stepakhno, Gennadi, 112, 120
Stoltenberg, Jens, 149, 158
Stoltenberg, Thorvald, 27, 28, 160–1
   and Barents Sea, 75, 76, 85
   and Pomor region, 143, 144–5, 149
Støre, Jonas Gahr, 75, 76, 158
story-telling, 6–7, 40–1, 151–3
Svalbard, 47, 52, 71, 77–81, 159–60
   and the environment, 114–16, 124
   and fishing, 83–4, 88–9, 95, 112–13, 114
Sweden, 11, 15

Thatcher, Margaret, 27
Timofeevich, Ermak, 31
total allowable catch (TAC), 106, 107, 108, 109, 119
trade, 143–4, 154
transport, 48
'trawler terrorism', 119–20
Treaty on the Maritime Delimitation and Cooperation in the Barents Sea and Arctic Ocean, 76, 158–9
Tyuchev, Fyodor, 23

Ukraine, 31, 171
UN Convention of the Law of the Sea (UNCLOS), 44, 45, 46, 47, 155
UN Third Conference on the Law of the Sea, 72
United Kingdom (UK), 105
United Nations (UN), 18
United States of America (USA), 1, 11, 12, 15, 46
   and the Arctic, 48, 156
   and Bering Sea, 87, 90
   and Law of the Sea, 45, 47
   and Norway, 120
   and Russia, 52, 53

Vardø, 144

Westernism, 26–8, 29, 30, 31, 38
winter, 32–3

Yeltsin, Boris, 27, 28, 44, 88
Yevdokimov, Yuri, 91–2, 94, 98, 116–17, 165, 167
Young, Oran R., 14

Zhirinovsky, Vladimir, 29–30
Zilanov, Vyacheslav, 82–5, 86, 87–9, 92, 94–7, 100, 166
   and Norway, 114